Meta Story

WHAT MARVEL & THE MESSIAH CAN TEACH US ABOUT GREAT STORYTELLING

SEAN GAFFNEY

Gaffney Inkwell
NICHOLASVILLE, KENTUCKY

Gaffney Inkwell
Nicholasville, Kentucky 40356
www.GaffneyInkwell.com

Illustrations © 2025 Bryan Ballinger www.Breadwig.com

Book layout © 2015 BookDesignTemplates.com
Book cover design by 100covers.com
Cover artwork created by Sarah Hogencamp & Bryan Ballinger

Ordering Information: Special discounts are available on quantity purchases by educational institutions, corporations, associations, and others. For details, contact www.GaffneyInkwell.com.

Meta Story: What Marvel & the Messiah Can Teach Us About Great Storytelling / Sean Gaffney —1st ed.

Library of Congress Control Number: 2025904356
ISBN (paperback): 979-8-9922664-0-5
ISBN (digital): 979-8-9922664-1-2

Contents

Dedication

For Howard, who mentored me

~

And for Dad, who gave me my image

All Jesus did that day was tell stories—a long storytelling afternoon. His storytelling fulfilled the prophecy:

> *I will open my mouth and tell stories;*
>
> *I will bring out into the open*
>
> *things hidden since the world's first day.*

—Matthew 13:34-35, The Message

FOREWORD

I once led a workshop at a film festival called "Story Doesn't Matter."

The title was designed to get people into the room, but I feel like I made a pretty good case. Now, keep in mind, at that point in my life I had been a writer and producer on at least 200 episodes of television, on my way to the current "more than 350." I had taken part in coming up with ideas and scenes and structure for at least 500 different storylines — main stories and lesser "B" stories and runners, along with season-long arcs and various kinds of character development on shows like *Buffy the Vampire Slayer, That 70s Show, and The Adventures of Pete & Pete.*

So, did I really believe that story didn't matter?

Yes, I think I did. But mostly because a lot of people don't understand what they mean when they talk about "story," which is why I'm glad Sean Gaffney has written a book that so clearly defines what it is. Because you have to fully understand what story is, what it does, how it works, what makes it good, why it fails, and how to get from the beginning of a story to the end of it in a way that makes others want to keep reading, watching, streaming — *experiencing* it. Because the only time story doesn't matter is when it's working so well that you don't even notice that it's there.

It's sort of like what they say about jazz music. "You need to know all of the rules before you can break them." And *Meta Story* is the kind of book that has figured out the rules and then presents them in a way so you can turn your own stories into jazz.

Sean Gaffney (he's one of the best writing teachers I know, and I've suffered through a load of them) has taken everything he knows about story and put it into this book — which is as well-structured and compelling as the stories he is going to tell you are so good. He's the kind of guy who, after a movie or a play or a TV show, wants to talk about why what he just saw was good or not — not just why, but also *how*. So don't go see a movie with him unless you have time afterwards to discuss the inner workings of the plot. Or, if you can't go see movies with him, just read this book, instead. Even if you're not a writer (maybe you're simply a fan of Marvel movies or have something between appreciation and/or adoration for the Messiah), you'll find truths to admire here. Think of this book as a side-commentary to some of the best movies, TV shows, and plays ever written.

At that film festival (which did attract a lot of people into the room, so I learned that workshop titles matter) I was asked, "So, if story doesn't matter, what does?"

"Execution" was the word that first came out of my mouth. "How good the writing is." (I was talking to screenwriters, but the advice applies to novelists and playwrights and filmmakers alike.) "If page one makes you want to read page two, and page two makes you want to read page three, that's what makes for a story that is well-told."

In reality I was saying that story matters a whole lot. But only if it's told well. Only when it makes you want to know what happens next. And only when you barely notice it's there. So when things happen, you're thinking, "Of course, that's exactly what *should* have happened!" In surprising, effective, and satisfying ways.

This is the kind of book that will help you write stories that make people wonder what is going to happen next. It's also surprising, effective, and satisfying. Which makes it a book that only "matters" if you decide not to read it. Because if you choose not to, you won't fully understand why story matters so much — and the kinds of things to think about before you write, read, and experience stories in any way. But putting "This book doesn't matter" on the cover is probably not the best way to sell books. What *could* have been there is "*Meta Story* is a book where page one makes you want to read page two, and page two makes you want to read page three..."

That is, simply, what matters the most.

— **DEAN BATALI**
TELEVISION WRITER & SHOWRUNNER

PREFACE

"Daddy, tell me a story." "Grandma, please read it again." Most adults, at one time or another, have heard such pleas across the generations. These requests evidence that learning and growing are, as Sean Gaffney asserts, hard-wired by our Creator into human understanding and maturation.

As an educator, leadership consultant, public speaker, and a Christian values communicator, I find that stories are the primary way abstract ideas of theory and theology are best understood, relayed, and appropriated. A lifetime of studying and applying effective communication strategies has validated the efficacy of well-constructed and presented stories for learning, living, and serving with both joy and purpose. Gaffney's *Meta Story* has opened new understandings of process and practice in my calling to communicate "stained glass" values in "plain glass" terms to a generation whose primary frames of reference are rooted in contemporary media contexts.

We marvel at the continued popularity of Aesop's Fables, Shakespeare's plays, opera, musical theater, and children's classics like *The Cat in the Hat*. Also, business resources such as the Harvard case studies, contemporary social engagement platforms like Netflix, TikTok and a multitude of other modalities, validate that there is something about masterful storytelling that grabs the heart and helps the mind grasp life-long lessons that shape values, establish convictions, and form behaviors. I find that in organizational consulting and leadership coaching, as well as in formal university teaching and spiritual counseling, the power of story is my best tool for helping audiences experience the "Ah-Ha" moments of discovery, embrace the joy and pathos of the human condition, and understand immutable truths that undergird our reason for being.

Sean Gaffney is a master storyteller from whom I am learning how to better communicate in these days when so much noise distracts us from the essential truths needed to navigate our current challenges and opportunities. His writing draws from historical and contemporary genres. It is engaging, focused, and seasoned with laugh-out-loud humor. His in-depth understanding of communication theory is buttressed with a breadth of real-world experiences in theater, film, television, script writing/consulting, teaching, and publishing. He draws from all of these to assist the intentional communicator in understanding not only the how but also the why of stories for times like these.

As a Christian, I particularly am intrigued with Sean's understanding of biblical narrative, helping those of us who look to the Scriptures for universal principles and practices that resonate with the realities of life and serving. The Old Testament is filled with the accounts of success and failure that informed the people of that day, and us in this day, about God's ultimate plans for His human creation. Story was the means of elucidating the truths represented by the Ebenezer "hither to has the Lord helped us" stone markers erected as remembrances along the pilgrimage pathways. The stories behind many Hebrew religious liturgies and traditions, such as the weekly Shabbat meal affirmations and festivals such as the Passover remembrance, are still used today by Jewish fathers in their rabbinical roles for their families.

Jesus' parables serve as overtures to the deeper truths of living and learning that the Apostles amplify in their letters to believers and churches of their day and ours. Gaffney's biblical insights have helped craft my understanding of both the orthodoxy and orthopraxy, the theology and contemporary applications, needed in communicating, as an "evangel," Christ's messages of forgiveness, reconciliation, hope, and restoration.

Many will find *Meta Story* an entertaining resource as they travel the yellow brick roads of imaginative reading, viewing, and listening. Also, it will serve as an engaging primer for those beginning their journey as creative authors and multi-media communicators. And its depth of research into theoretical and theological essentials of purposeful, effective narrative will make it a must-have textbook for those equipping a new generation of authors, filmmakers, and media entrepreneurs called to respond, even more creatively, to the universal invitation — "please tell me a story."

— DAVID GYERTSON, PH.D.
FORMER PRESIDENT OF REGENT, TAYLOR AND ASBURY UNIVERSITIES

PART ONE

The Eternal Story

Chapter One

Art and Faith

While in graduate school at Columbia University, I had the great fortune to be mentored by Howard Stein. Playwright Oliver Mayer describes Howard this way:

He knew more about plays than anyone I've ever met to this day, but he was anything but didactic: Rather, he was playful, curious and incredibly trusting of our voices as young playwrights. His style was passionate, rabbinical, and funnier than you'd have ever thought. He loved to teach... I hear his voice in my head often...[1]

I, too, hear Howard's voice in my head as I teach and write. It is unlikely that I would be a professional writer or professor today if my life hadn't intersected with Howard's life.

The surprise in that is I was not a playwriting student under Howard — I was studying producing. I was also the theater department administrative assistant, and Howard's personal assistant — probably the best day job of my life. My job included typing up Howard's articles, being a test audience for his talks/presentations, and spending lots of time listening to Howard give discourses on whatever topics held his interest at the time.

There were two gifts that Howard gave me that transformed my life. The first was an independent study in play analysis. Every week, he gave me five plays to read — and on Friday we would sit and discuss them. Then five more, then five more... Until he was convinced that I

---

1. Columbia University School of the Arts Alumni Newsletter, May 2020

understood what made a great story great, and what could make a good story better.

The second was a shift in my approach to art. One day, Howard called me into his office and sat me down. He stared curiously at me from across his desk and asked me if I was a Christian.

I knew this question was coming and dreaded it. I had become active with Intervarsity Christian Fellowship, and my faith was moving from the Lone Ranger style to a public stance. The problem, in my mind, was that the theater department was no friend to faith. (I say, "in my mind," because as life was to teach me over and over, places that embrace the arts tend to be much less judgmental than the Church.) Anti-Christian comments were heard on a regular basis; and Howard himself, though not one to bash, was clearly not a Christian.

What would happen to our relationship when he found out I was one?

I quietly answered his question. "Yes, I guess."

Howard became quite animated.

"No, no," he said. "You don't understand. I'm asking, do you really believe that stuff?"

I became slightly bolder.

"Yes. Yes, I do."

Howard just about came over his desk at me.

"Sean, you have to understand," he said, trying to drive his point into me. "Faith and art do the same thing. They ask the same questions. Who are we? Where do we come from? Where are we going to?"

He continued, "I believe there is no great theater being made in America today because we have separated our faith and our art. It is your responsibility, as an artist with faith, to combine your faith and your craft."

"Who are we?"

"Where do we come from?"

"Where are we going to?"

Please do not get Howard or me wrong here. Howard was not saying that I needed to make religious works. He knew that in art there should be no such separation.

And he wasn't trying to get me to work in the ghetto of "Christian" theater. I doubt Howard was even aware of the Christian subculture; and why would he be? The Christian subculture had not been relevant outside of the church for a long, long time.

Instead, he was trying to get me to not shy away from the big questions, to grapple with humanity and Truth. His role model for me would be Eugene O'Neill, a playwright who would wrestle with the questions and themes born of his Catholic imagination even as he rejected the doctrines of the church.

Howard would point to the Greeks — Sophocles, Aeschylus, Euripides — working out their human dramas in the temples of the gods. And he would refer to a movement nearer his own time and heritage, the Yiddish theatre popular prior to World War II. This tradition within the Jewish immigration to America was the antithesis to the idea of using subculture to "escape" the wider world. More than just entertainment for an isolated community (and it was entertaining!), the Yiddish Theatre refined its art, taking the best of the wider world and viewing it through a unique cultural lens.

This arts community would go on to change the wider culture — whether introducing the works of Ibsen and Tolstoy to the American stage, or cultivating artists like Stella Adler and Lee Strasberg, who would build on their earlier theater exposure to shape a generation of Broadway and Hollywood actors.

Sholem Aleichem was a famous writer from this tradition — you may know his work as the stories that became *Fiddler on the Roof*.[2] *The Dybbuk*, by S. Ansky, spawned several translations, moving from theater to television, film, opera, ballet, and musical composition.

The humor refined on the Yiddish stages (known now as Jewish humor) is still prevalent today. Who knew?

Howard pushed me to think of theatre (and art) through a lens of eternal questions and larger Truths. He wanted art to touch the soul, the way plays touched and transformed him in his youth.

---

2. See Aleichem's story collection, *Tevye the Dairyman*.

He told stories of his father and brother collecting pennies in a jar. When the jar held enough coins to buy a ticket to a play, one of them would get on the train into New York and take in a show. He then returned to the waiting family to retell the story as best as he could, sharing the experience.

Howard wanted plays that fed our thirsts as much as those childhood plays did. He did not want discussions of humanity to be left to philosophers, theologians, or historians.

He wanted his artists to be our world's philosophers, theologians, and historians. To ask the questions that mattered through our comedies, farces, tragedies, and kitchen sink dramas. To ground our silly entertainments in cosmic scope; to expand our serious entertainments with the humility of the seeker.

To make our audiences ponder:

Who are we?

Where did we come from?

Where are we going to?

CHAPTER TWO

The Big Idea

*Story is what makes us human, not just metaphorically but literally.
Recent breakthroughs in neuroscience reveal that our brain
is hardwired to respond to story...*

—Lisa Cron, *Wired for Story*

The universal elements that our souls long for when we hear "Once upon a time..." are more than flights of escape; they are nuanced elements that draw us to a home we don't yet know. They give us ears to hear — even when we don't quite understand all we hear.[3] The central thesis of this book is simple: God has hardwired in us how to tell and receive stories in the hopes that in understanding story, we might better understand Him.

Tim Keller says, "We need art so much because we are cut off from something, and art is our effort to try to get back to it, to try and get a hold of it."[4]

Each element of story tells us something about the Creator. The form we seek in all stories is the form of His story. The yearning for a payoff to the setups is the yearning of prophecy and promise. Our draw to reluctant heroes and protagonists who don't deserve their journey is really us acknowledging gratitude that we have a God who

---

3. Shades of Luke 8:9-10. It is all there for those with ears — and the willingness to engage the ears.

4. From *Navigating Hollywood*, "Timothy Keller, NY Times Bestselling Author & Speaker: Why Do We Need Artists", episode 20, July 11, 2023.

doesn't always give what is deserved. Finding function in supporting characters is a chance to find a way to be supporting players in our own communal bodies. Subtext is how the world really communicates; character as action and not words is how the world's people really behave. And on and on.

> *For a story to captivate a reader, it must continually meet his or her hardwired expectations. This is no doubt what prompted Jorge Luis Borges to note, "Art is fire plus algebra." ... Borges intuitively knew what cognitive psychology and neuroscience has since revealed: there is an implicit framework that must underlie a story in order for that passion, that fire, to ignite the reader's brain. Stories without it go unread; stories with it are capable of knocking the socks off someone who's barefoot.*[5]

There is a commonality in storytelling — basic precepts that echo repeatedly in the stories in which we engage. Whether the simple stories of our childhoods or the more grown-up tales of our adulthood, from "Little Red Riding Hood" to *The Lord of the Rings*, common threads unite them all.

This book is going to dive into those common, universal ideas — ways of presenting plot and character and theme, forms of how stories are told, pervasive tools in every storyteller's arsenal. While there are variations galore, the foundations of our tales are found in these classic ideas.

To be clear, we aren't simply talking about convenient forms that Hollywood has glommed on to; this shape goes back to the start of storytelling. It is found in the pre-historic myths and discussed by the ancient Greeks. It is a matter of physics more than choice. John Yorke (*Into the Woods: How Stories Work and Why We Tell Them*) tells us, "All stories are forged from the same template, writers simply don't have any choice as to the structure they use and, as I hope to show, the laws of physics, of logic and of form dictate they must all follow the very same path."

---

5. Lisa Cron, *Wired for Story*

If we can come to understand storytelling in light of the elements planted in our hearts, then we gain two wonderful gifts.

First, we start to see God in all the stories our world tells — secular and sacred. For God is everywhere — it is such a shame when we don't notice Him!

And perhaps more interesting, we start to see the Story in how God communicates with us. We start to understand better the theology — the God in Logos — that surrounds us in His Word, His history, His living Spirit. We have perhaps spent too long seeing God as an intellectual exercise, a puzzle to solve and then shelve. Perhaps through Story we can renew our vision.

This book will look at Story from macro to micro, predominantly through the scripted arts — film, television, and theater. I will isolate the universal elements of plot, character, dialogue, subtext, setups, images and more — and use enough examples from media to show a consistent pattern. And along the way, we will explore why these story patterns are the norm — the hardwiring from God — and the effect the elements have on our souls.

So, let's start that search for God in story, and for story in God.

CHAPTER THREE

Faith and Art

"We didn't need a writer. Jesus wrote this film!"

This was the brag by the producer in an interview after the opening of a film targeted to the Christian sub-culture. I happened to see that movie, and can say with confidence, Jesus did not write that movie.

First off, we know that Jesus was present at the laying of the foundations of the earth,[6] so it is a good bet that Jesus knew something about structure. This movie's writer did not.

---

6. Hebrews 1:10

More to the point, we have samples of Jesus' storytelling. It is highly unlikely that Jesus would have been that lazy, sloppy, and careless in his storytelling to have written that movie.

The notion that Jesus wrote the script is often code for, "Writing is hard work; and I didn't get into Christian art to have to work hard. So, we ignored that part in making our project."

There is an idea that seems prevalent in subculture art that God somehow wants us to be lazy in crafting our stories. I was once harangued for criticizing a play being done by a Christian organization. "The quality of the production is not important," went the argument. "God only cares about the message!"[7]

This argument is built on two fallacies: One, that the message is somehow disconnected from the craft. The truth is, if the vehicle for transporting the message is sloppy and careless, that is a clear sign that the deliverer of the message doesn't think the content has much value.

The second fallacy is that God does not care about the quality of art. To combat this, let's look at Bezalel.

---

7. I have been told that since God can use anything to get His word out, we shouldn't care about the "how." My unpopular response is, "Yes, God has proven he can even use a donkey to spread His Word. But that does not mean we should aspire to be donkeys."

When it came time for the tabernacle and the Ark of the Covenant to be built, God had some pretty strong (and specific) opinions about what art made in His name should be like.

After receiving the Ten Commandments and the discourse on the law (Exodus, chapter 20-24), God then described to Moses the plans for the place of worship and the box to contain the commandments (Exodus, chapters 25-31).

The first thing to note here is the amount of ink given to the topics. Five chapters given for the law, seven for art; an odd balance for a deity that doesn't care about quality of craft. Just saying.

In chapter 31, God tells Moses about the artist that He picked to run the creative project, Bezalel. He explains to his servant what makes Bezalel ready to be an artist for God. "Look, I have specifically chosen Bezalel son of Uri, grandson of Hur, of the tribe of Judah. I have filled him with the Spirit of God, giving him great wisdom, ability, and expertise in all kinds of crafts."[8]

The Expanded Bible puts verse 3 like this: "I have filled Bezalel with the Spirit [or spirit] of God and have given him the skill [wisdom], ability, and knowledge to do all kinds of work."

The Contemporary English Version throws in this wording: "Not only have I filled him with my Spirit, but I have given him wisdom and made him a skilled craftsman..."

Note that God Himself does not say, "Look, I filled him with my Spirit, and that's enough." Or "Hey, since my Spirit is involved, my artist doesn't need anything else." Or "The artist doesn't need to work, really, it's only the message that counts."

He instead says, "I expect something real from my artists, something difficult, something that takes skill and effort. This can't just be tossed off by anyone without thought. My artist needs more."

The Spirit of God ("inspiration" for those who quibble with the source), wisdom, skill, ability, knowledge, expertise. These are the qualities of God's artist.

---

8. Exodus 31:2-3, NLT

These are the qualities that need to be put into use in God's art. Scriptwriting is no exception.

Okay, but what about the writer who isn't working in religious art?

Truth is — there is no such thing. Madeleine L' Engle says, "There is nothing so secular that it cannot be sacred, and that is one of the deepest messages of the Incarnation."[9]

We have created a false dichotomy, a separation of work and faith that isn't supported by the Bible. "So whether you eat or drink, or whatever you do, do it all for the glory of God."[10]

The idea that we writers should bring all our intelligence, emotions, and skill to our craft, but should leave our spiritual selves at the door is a rather odd notion. We should bring all of who we are into our stories — including our eternal sparks.

Isn't that what inspiration is all about?

"Inspiration" comes from the Latin "to breathe into." It is tied to the same root as "spirit," and the figurative uses come straight from religion. Earliest English usages tie inspiration directly to divine or supernatural power.

How does it make sense to desire to use everything about a writer in creation, except for inspiration?

Then how does it make sense to separate faith from craft? Not as a message, not as a dictator of content, but rather as a resource for creation and creativity.

If one is a Christian, or Buddhist, or just plain Spiritual — if that person is not drawing on their spiritual side, they are robbing their craft of a valuable asset.

---

9. L'Engle, *Walking on Water: Reflections on Faith and Art*
10. 1 Corinthians 10:31, NLT

CHAPTER FOUR

Rules, Examples, and More

Teachers (like me) love to think in terms of "rules," such as "the rules of scriptwriting." And it is a mistake to think that way. Story doesn't have rules so much as guides; for formula kills creativity — while form releases creativity.[11]

In a recent class, I was discussing the event of the Catalyst. A student, diligently taking notes, raised her hand to ask, "And on what page should the Catalyst happen?"

It took me a second to come up with the right answer.

"How should I know? I haven't read your script yet."

Story theory is there to help the Story, not the other way around. As Jesus says about the rules of religion in Mark 2:6 (NLT), "The Sabbath was made to meet the needs of people, and not people to meet the requirements of the Sabbath."

To try and bend a story to a set of rules would be putting the cart before the horse, or the Sabbath before the people.

For the record, the Catalyst for *Dunkirk* happens on page 3; and the Catalyst for *Up* doesn't happen until the bottom of page 20. And both films are expertly structured.

---

11. Ellen Sandler in *The TV Writer's Workbook* puts it this way. "By rules, I don't mean formula — *formula* is what makes a writer a hack, and leads to predictable, dull scripts that nobody wants to read past page 8. However, there is *form* — quite a different thing."

Each story is different with different needs, and the guidelines are there to help channel and provide for those needs. So, a strict adherence to things like page count is a sign that some guru somewhere is missing the point. Or trying to make their lives easier, and more box-like.

For example, young writers are often told to never use flashbacks. This isn't because flashbacks are not highly useful and effective story-telling tools (*Lost*, *Casablanca*, *Knives Out*, *Death of a Salesman*, and on); rather it is because when used poorly, flashbacks become a crutch for the lazy writer. And painful for a teacher to read.

Rather than telling a student that they shouldn't use flashbacks (or any other number of such rules), we should be saying, "Don't use flash-backs poorly. And as you aren't ready to use them well, set them aside for now." Most ridiculous do's and don'ts are reflective of the level of the writer, and sadly of the teacher.

On the flip side, Story does have consistent guidelines, forms and structures that are universal and work. The forms are there to help the lost find their way — for those who forget to use the Sabbath to rest, restore, and re-create. (Ignoring the Sabbath is just as bad as abusing the purpose, yes? Ignoring the forms of story...)

Knowing what you are doing when you break a rule, however, can be quite powerful.

We will see this later when discussing the stories that break the rules well — each of them knowing the effect the break would have on the audience. *If Beale Street Could Talk* leaves the audience intentionally unsettled — and does so by breaking a specific story need.

So, "rules" are not rules but forms that work. Rules can be broken, but only if one understands them, and understands the effect of the break.

~

Does a writer need to know and understand the rules of Story in order to be a good writer?

Nope. History has proven this — many artists couldn't begin to explain what they do, and how they got there. Which is why being a great writer does not mean one would be a great teacher.

All good writers feel the craft in their bones; stories come out of their hearts and souls, more than out of their brains. Inspiration is a gift from the Spirit and cannot be intellectualized. My friend Peter Glus' grandmother was an amazing baker and never used measuring cups or spoons, or printed recipes for that matter. She felt her way through cakes. And her cakes were amazing.

So, if a writer can feel whether dialogue is working, whether a plot point is hitting at the right moment, if a character rings true — who cares if they know why it does so?

So why do story analysis at all?

Because there are so many bad stories, mediocre stories, and good but not great stories out there. Stories can usually be made better, and that is where analysis comes in.

The first thing that I tell my scriptwriting students is that my class will not help them write a great first draft.

But it will help them make that draft better. Understanding story can diagnose where a script can be improved and where a story might have gone off the rails. We must constantly switch between the artist — the vessel for inspiration — and the editor. David Trottier (*The Screenwriter's Bible*) says, "Write from the heart. Edit from the brain."

I believe that creativity and inspiration come from God; I also believe that creativity and inspiration can be guided. Not put into block forms, mind you, but guided.

The constant battle amongst writers is between those who are formulaic (they do not use enough creativity), and those who create beautiful, incoherent messes (lacking discipline). The key isn't deciding which side is the right one; the key is in finding the balance — the places in the process that are pure, uninhibited creation, and the places in the process that are about critical thinking.

Writing is rewriting — meaning that the work isn't done in the first draft (unless you are a super genius like Mozart; and if you are a super genius like Mozart, you aren't reading books like this one).

So, we work on our beautiful messes to give beautiful form and create beautiful final products.

A Word on Examples

Throughout this book I will draw on a wide variety of plays, television shows, and movies as my examples. I am making no attempt to limit myself to religious or church appropriate works — I pull them from everywhere.

This is because I see God everywhere. Any writer worth his salt exploring truth is going to end up with some Truth reflected in their work; so, I try not to ignore even suspect sources. If an example models a point I am trying to make well, I will use that point.

Please note, however, that just because God is in all things does not mean that all things are godly. Likewise, just because I point out that a movie does an expert job of illustrating theme (or any aspect of scriptwriting), does not mean that I am saying that the movie is a moral or godly film.

In my screenwriting class, each student must present a devotion at some point using something about God that they learned from a film. One student used the *Final Destination* horror franchise. The basic premise of each film is that a group of people have somehow avoided the death they were supposed to encounter, and so Death stalks them to collect their souls.

My student's initial point was how the movies confronted the universal truth — we all are destined to die. As much as we try to make ourselves immortal, or think of ourselves as everlasting, our time on earth has a limit. So far, the student was drawing good devotional themes from the material.

Then the student announced that therefore these movies were God-approved and "Christian." And that's where he missed the point. Yes, principles can be drawn from the films; however, that doesn't make the whole beneficial. The first movie made the point the student was trying to make; some of the follow-ups weren't trying to say anything at all. They were simply looking for gross-out ways to kill off their characters.

In other words, the movies went from saying something about mortality to glorifying death. Not a God-approved message.

I would suggest that *Game of Thrones* is a mostly well-made series with high production values and great acting. There are even parables within the series that are very insightful and constructive to a Christian worldview. And there are plenty of elements that are downright destructive to a healthy soul.

Are there good examples to draw from in the series? Yes. Would I recommend the series to fellow Christians? Nope. Hopefully one can see that this dichotomy is not a judgment, it's just the way of the world. Peter's sheet covered with food — who can tell God what he has called clean is unclean? Yet those same foods would cause another to stumble — and God would caution that person to avoid those foods (Romans 14).

I tell my students at the start of any class where we look at a variety of examples that we are all adults and need to treat the course as such. This is not to persuade them to explore R-rated content — exactly the opposite. We all should know where we stand with God — including in the content of what we consume, aware of how that content affects us. If a student is going to be hurt by (or in some cases tempted by) certain content, they need to let me know and find another example to look at. (Another reason I like to use a wide variety of examples.)

My wife does not deal well with visual violence; therefore, we avoid exposing her to images that will haunt her dreams. For this reason, she will never watch *The Passion of the Christ* — a wonderfully made, deeply devout movie. For me, it is sexual violence that gives me nightmares; even a PG-13 movie on the topic would wound me. Shows such as *Law & Order: SVU* or *Criminal Minds* are unhealthy for me. Which doesn't mean they would be unhealthy for someone else.

Let me give you a positive negative example: *Ted Lasso* is wonderfully done, and a truly honest look at what it would be like for someone to try and live in the world in a Christ-like manner. I'm hard pressed to think of many other examples that are nearly as profound — in and out of the religious market. At the same time, the show takes place in a literal locker room, accompanied by crude locker room humor.

Which means that it would not be good for many audiences. I won't lie and say that it is not a show worth contemplation (it most assuredly is); nor will I say it is a perfect show in understanding Gospel principles.

This is the power and limit of examples. Examples, like metaphors, are not meant to be complete. They are not meant to be full in any way.

"The kingdom of God is like a mustard seed" shows only one aspect of the kingdom of God. The critic of such a metaphor would point out that if one were to plant the Kingdom of God into the soil, a mustard tree would not pop out. Therefore, the Kingdom of God is *not* like a mustard seed.

Of course, that critic would be an idiot; Jesus did not intend to imply that a mustard tree would pop out. The kingdom is not like every aspect of the mustard seed. The metaphor is incomplete, and we all should understand the limitation.

The same is true of any Story that reflects an aspect of the kingdom — by definition, by design even, the reflection will be incomplete. Even in the most intentional of metaphors.

Dallas Jenkins[12] is doing an excellent job with *The Chosen*, telling the behind-the-scenes story of Jesus and His ministry. Despite the subject matter, Jenkins himself would agree that his series is not meant to replace our understanding of the Bible. It is there to supplement, to deepen, to widen.

"Did John say that line? Did he say it that way?" Such questions miss the point. Just as demanding if there really was an actual, historical man attacked on the way to Jericho, or a son spending his inheritance, or a widow knocking on the door of a judge. The stories are there to open our eyes, to get us to think anew, to allow understanding outside of the ruts we've dug in our minds.

The mistake comes when we ever look at any example and think of it as more than a tool to understanding. Stories, then, are made for humanity, not humanity for stories.

---

12. When I say Dallas Jenkins and *The Chosen*, what I really mean is the marvelous writing team of Dallas Jenkins, Ryan Swanson, and Tyler Thompson.

Spoilers

When I was in college, a friend of my girlfriend decided she didn't like me and needed to put me in my place. She asked, "Have you ever seen *Citizen Kane*?" I admitted that up to that point, I had not. So she said, "Rosebud is..."

And stated what Rosebud was. Which meant nothing to me, until a few years later when I finally watched the movie — and realized she had spoiled the final reveal.

Don't let this happen to you!

There are many, many spoilers ahead. In discussing various plays, movies and television shows I will be giving away endings, surprises, and basic plot elements.

Not sure how to avoid that in a book about stories using as many examples as I do.

So, if you want to avoid spoilers, you may want to get caught up.

I reference *Knives Out* quite a bit — and it is a murder mystery. I recommend watching it before diving too deep into the book. Other stories with twists that you may want to experience yourself include *1917*, *Avengers: Infinity War*, *Mare of Easttown*, and *I and You*. I give away all of *Hamilton*, but then again, the ending is given away in the opening song. So don't blame me, blame Lin-Manuel.

I also give away the endings of scripts that have been around a long time and refuse to feel too bad for spoiling the ending of *Macbeth* or *Hamlet*.[13]

You have been warned.

Capitalization and Call Outs

Note that throughout this book, I will be capitalizing words like Story and Need and the like.

---

13. Although you will notice I protected you on *Citizen Kane*. I'm that kind of guy.

I am doing this to separate out when I mean a specific story being told and the concept of Story. *Green Eggs and Ham* is a story; the thing that requires a hero, a goal and an obstacle is Story.

If a word like "Need" is capitalized mid-sentence, know that I am referring to Story Need, and not our general understanding or usage of the word "need."

Also note that throughout you may find sections labelled "Close Up," "Cross Fade," "Writer's Tip," or "The Eternal Story."

Close Ups are a deeper dive example of how a particular topic is applied to a film, play, or TV show.

Cross Fades are examples of how the concept under discussion applies specifically to a theological concept.[14]

The Eternal Story sections, found throughout the bit on Event Points, is the buildup of how each point applies to God's larger history.

Writer's Tips are tips for writers, naturally.

---

14. See what I did there? "Cross" is in the title, it's a film term, but the section is about theology. So, almost a pun. Ah, I'm so clever.

PART TWO

Hero, Goal, and Obstacle

CHAPTER FIVE

Unity

I recently heard on a podcast a common theme from many people who don't like books on writing. The idea is that writing teachers break down writing into component parts — structure, character, dialogue, theme, subtext, images, etc. However, the complaint goes, one cannot separate story into parts — each part works together, so thinking you can create a strong structure without strong characters is lunacy.

In the podcast, the topic came up because Hollywood (the term for generic studios/producers/networks/production companies etc.) will often label a writer by strength in such areas — the "story guy" or the "character woman." The podcast scoffed at the very idea — if you are a "character writer," you can't be a good writer because real writers write movies, not just characters.

He isn't wrong.

He isn't right, either.

A good "character writer" is only good at character because she understands good character (first) and gets how characters interact with structure, how good dialogue reflects character, how theme and character need play on each other, and on and on. I have seen my share of student rewrites that focus solely on dialogue, and without understanding character, proved to be a waste of time.

The same is true in most any field. Let's pick on medicine. A heart specialist knows the heart better than a general practitioner — or should anyway. However, a good specialist will start as a good general practitioner — they will understand the rest of the body. Interaction is key, not superfluous. No one ever looked at a corpse after a heart surgery and said, "His heart looks great, that must be one fantastic surgeon!"

The reverse is true as well. No one ever complained that we shouldn't have heart surgeons because learning more about one area of medicine implies somehow that the heart is not connected to the rest of the body.[15]

So, you will see in this book that I talk about structure, then character, then dialogue, etc. There are teachers out there who think each part is disconnected from the others — I am not one of them. Story works as a whole, the parts working together for one common result.

I am going to start by talking about structure. To start talking about structure, we must first talk about character.

---

15. I don't actually know if no one ever said that. I'm just guessing — and if someone did, it wasn't taken seriously.

CHAPTER SIX

Central Character - Hero

So, you're at a cocktail party (okay, no one has cocktail parties these days, but I need the setting for my point), and you are wondering if you should tell that story of what happened to you today.

You're not going to have much success with it unless it actually is a story. Is it a story?

"Hey, guys, guess what happened today. My yard is next to my driveway."

Crickets. You don't have a story.

Every story starts out with three things, and without those things, there isn't a story.

Hero

A HERO — a central character, someone the story is about. Without that, it is just a description.

"My lawn has grass, and next to that is the driveway, and there is a mailbox out there."

Just a description.

"Want to know what happened to me today?"

Ah — now we have a hero.

Goal

A GOAL — something that the hero wants or must get or do. A quest. Why are we telling the story today and not yesterday? Howard Stein would often say our stories mimic the Passover Seder questions, which each start with "Ma Nishtana" — "Why is this night different from all other nights?"

What action or movement will we add to the description we've given?

"I went outside."

Big deal.

"I went to get the mail."

Not exciting, but at least there is some focused action.

Obstacle

AN OBSTACLE — something preventing the Hero from achieving the Goal. This is what makes the telling have interest, have heart. One can't win without obstacles; all they can do is rack up participation points.

ESPN does not run the Participation Award Games; no one would watch. Instead, they broadcast competitions, where there are teams with goals and opposition.

"I went to get the mail, and there was a skunk in the driveway!"

Now we're curious; now we want to know what happens next; now you have a story to tell at a cocktail party.

Shakespeare started his story about Hamlet on the day Hamlet meets the ghost. If he told the story of the day before, it would have gone like this:

"Once upon a time, there was a guy named Hamlet. He didn't like his new stepfather, but otherwise things were pretty good. Oh, and he's going back to school soon. That should be fun."

Instead, we get:

"Once upon a time, there was a guy named Hamlet. (Hero) A ghost told him that his stepdad murdered his father, so Hamlet set out to prove his stepdad's guilt and get revenge. (Goal) One problem though, his stepdad is the king of Denmark, and has a royal court and an army protecting him. (Obstacle)"

Let's start by talking about the Hero.

"Hero" is a misleading term, as it implies someone heroic. It is a good beginner term; it sticks in our psyche and is easy to understand.

However, in real Story, our Central Character might be heroic (Hamilton, Agent Gibbs, Captain America), or they may be unheroic learning how to be heroic (Jean Valjean, Zoey, Frodo), or they may be downright villainous (MacBeth, Walter White, Joker).

What we are looking for is our entry into the story, the character we will track with — the Point of View (POV). Often the choice of Central Character determines how the story will be received by the viewer.

Jesus chose the non-hero of the man from Jerusalem as the Central Character in "The Good Samaritan." Rather than follow the heroic fellow, the Samaritan, we follow the Israelite as he travels toward Jericho, falls in among bandits, and desperately tries to wave down help.

You will recall that the Samaritans were despised by the Jews — a natural-born enemy. In fact, just one chapter prior to the telling of the parable,[16] a Samaritan town refused to allow Jesus and his followers to stay. John and James, ever the slow-to-anger models, suggested that Jesus rain fire down on the village.

So, a lot of bad blood.

This audience would not identify with a story about a Samaritan who saves the day; they wouldn't listen past the opening lines. But the story of a fellow Jew like them, unfairly victimized and in desperate need? His audience was hooked. They could imagine themselves on the road to Jericho (the same road Jesus was on when turned away from the village); they could feel the noose tightening as "they" were beaten and

---

16. In the Gospel of Luke —— the rejection in Chapter 9, the parable in Chapter 10.

robbed; they would grow in desperation as each passerby looked out to their own interest.

And they would dread the coming of the Samaritan — and the dread would turn to joy as the unexpected happened. Unexpected, yet somehow true.

A simple choice of making the protagonist someone other than the hero of the story, and Jesus made a gateway for his audience to buy into a story they might otherwise ignore.

Rather than "hero," let's use Central Character or Protagonist to describe the core person at the heart of our story.

Central Character

Also known as:
Hero
Protagonist
Main Character
Core Character
Pivotal Character
Principle Character

Cal Pritner and Scott E. Walters sum up the definition of the Central Character: "The character whose motives...and actions...drive the play's conflict from its beginning to its resolution." [17]

"Motive" can be seen as what the character wants — what they seek in the action. They may want to win the girl, catch the robber, escape the killer, uncover the truth, find a cow, a cape, a slipper, and the locks of hair that will reverse the curse.

The motive is the drive that leads into "Action" — what the character does in the story. The Central Character's motives and actions drive the story.

∼

---

17. In their work *Introduction to Play Analysis*

David Trottier would use a similar definition to argue that some-times the antagonist of a movie is really the Central Character — as their actions seemingly drive the story.[18]

Before I take on the arrogance to disagree, please know that Trottier is an expert who has earned that standing. His book on screenwriting is one of three that I consistently require my own students to read, and one that has shaped my own view of the craft. The guy really, really knows what he is talking about.

So, with Icarus' hubris, I will say that I think he got this one wrong.

Trottier points to the Joker in *The Dark Knight* or Professor Dorr in *The Ladykillers* as examples. Batman would have nothing to investigate if Joker didn't rob banks, steal mob money, kidnap citizens, etc. Batman is merely reacting rather than driving the story.

True to an extent. But here is where I think Trottier is conflating "protagonist" with "heroic," and to do so muddies the waters unnec-essarily. His argument is that the "protagonist" — who in this view is defined by being heroic — may not be the Central Character, and the Antagonist (defined as being villainous) may be the Central Character.

However, the definition of "protagonist" is dependent not on hero-ism, but rather story point of view.

Let me explain this a bit more.

Aristotle makes a distinction between "Story" and "Plot."

"Story," for Aristotle, is the whole event, everything that happens from all angles.

"Plot" is the selection of what the author chooses to show, the Point of View (POV) of the creator as it were. [19]

Our concern, in these definitions, is the Central Character of the Plot, not of the Story — regardless of whether that character would be a villain or hero in the grander scheme.

The Gospels, told from Jesus' POV, would have Jesus as the protago-nist; Judas would be a potential antagonist. *Jesus Christ Superstar*, told

---

18. In *The Screenwriter's Bible* — in my opinion, one of the best books for screenwriters on the market.

19. In *Poetics*

from Judas' POV, presents Judas as the protagonist, and Jesus, therefore, as the antagonist.

In *Dark Knight*, the Joker may kick-start the action, but the plot is Batman's — we follow his goal of stopping the Clown Prince of Crime.

Therefore, Batman is the Protagonist; and being the Protagonist, he is the Central Character.

Most horror and thrillers follow this same logic. The antagonist in a sense is forcing the action of the protagonist (the drug dealers in *Wait Until Dark*, the kidnappers in *Taken*). However, it is the Protagonist whose plot we are following (Susy Hendrix, Bryan Mills). Even with "reactive" protagonists, we still follow their motives and actions.

The Ladykillers is interesting because here Trottier and I are in full agreement — at least on Central Character. Professor Dorr drives both the story and the plot — so while he is the villain, he is the Protagonist/ Central Character of the movie. The Antagonist, then, is the sweet old Marva Munson.[20]

Tragedies will typically have the villain as the Protagonist (Macbeth, for example), and the hero as the Antagonist (Macduff). The shift of expectation pulls the audience out of an automatic comfort zone and allows the story to play with ideas in a way that may be glossed over in the story with the heroic as the center.

Whether to have the audience see the "other" in a better light (Jesus' "The Good Samaritan"), to give a cautionary tale (Walter White in *Breaking Bad*), or simply to challenge our own take on morality (do we find ourselves rooting in favor of the home invaders in *Parasite*?), choice of Central Character can shake up an otherwise straightforward tale.

These distinctions make it even more important to be able to properly identify our Central Character and understand his/her role. More on that after a brief sidebar into Reluctant Heroes.

---

20. Or Professor Marcus and Mrs. Wilberforce, if we go with the 1955 movie.

WRITER'S TIP:
Reluctant Hero

To add instant depth to your story, make your Central Character a reluctant one. Someone who doesn't think they are right for the job — not special enough or equipped. Someone who doesn't want to go on the journey.

Think of Frodo in *The Fellowship of the Ring*. While he may have loved the stories his uncle told him, he really doesn't want to leave the shire to go on his own adventure. After some cajoling, he agrees to take the ring to The Prancing Pony. Then he's got to go on to Rivendell, thanks to those freaky black riders.

Once in Elrond's land, Frodo can breathe a sigh of relief — his part of the story is done! He is quite in agreement with the likes of Boromir; if the ring is to continue to wherever the wise ones decide to send it, there are plenty of options for ring bearers: wizards, elves, warrior men, dwarves even.

But darn it! Ugh! Yes, yes, I'll take it. But I won't like it.

And so, he does. It isn't really until the final moments of *The Fellowship of the Ring* (the end of the first movie/book, and a third of the way into the total journey) before the hobbit fully embraces that this is his journey to make.

Of course, a story does not require a reluctant hero. Early James Bond just asks for his next assignment and off he goes. Many an action hero/cop/doctor/superhero/potential love interest doesn't need much convincing before leaping into action.

However, look at the many, many stories where the unqualified, wrong hero comes into play — and how deeply affected audiences are with those characters.

- *The Force Awakens*: the orphan who wants to just wait for her family, and the traitor who just wants to run
- *I and You*: the sick teenager who doesn't want company, and most assuredly doesn't care about a school project due tomorrow

- *Brittany Runs a Marathon*: the overweight woman who hates herself
- *Zoe's Extraordinary Playlist*: the self-involved woman who doesn't know a thing about music (a handicap for someone hearing people's heart songs)
- *Bird Box*: the pregnant lady who doesn't care about people

We have a precedent for this kind of unqualified, reluctant hero. If we go back ten thousand plus years to Moses, we get the perfect example. Moses is chilling with his sheep when God appears as a burning bush.

"Moses," God says, "I need a hero to save your people and bring them out of Egypt!"

And Moses says, "Great! Send me!"

Oh, wait. He doesn't say that. The conversation goes more like this:

"Moses, I need a hero."

"Whoa! Is that bush on fire? It isn't burning up!"

"Focus, Moses. I need a hero."

"Right. Yeah." He looks around. "I'm not seeing anyone. Want me to ask my father-in-law? He might know someone."

"I want you to go and save my people."

"Ha! Oh, you're serious? Who am I to do that?"

"You are the guy I've chosen."

"Yeah, the people aren't gonna believe me."

"Tell them I sent you."

"Sure, but even if they do believe me, the Pharaoh will not, I repeat, not let them go on my word."

"I'll give you miracles to show them."

"Yeah, did you know I killed a guy?"

"Yes, I was there."

"Did you know that I stutter?"

"Yes, I made you."

"Are you sure there's no one else? I'm kinda busy with these sheep."

"Sigh. Hold on a second. Hey, Gabriel — can you rev up the smiting machine?"

"So, Lord, we're going on an adventure. Cool!"

Okay, I may have taken liberties there, but you get the point. There is a very strong principle at work here, deeply rooted in theology.

Donna Partow (*Becoming a Vessel God Can Use*) puts it this way:

> *Every time God intervenes in human history, he does two things: first, he chooses the wrong person. Then, he comes up with a seemingly dumb idea.*

The problem: We need to get the Israelites out of centuries of slavery.

The person: A cantankerous 80-year-old, wanted for murder, hated by both the Israelites and the Egyptians, who stutters.

The plan: Here's where it really gets fun. How does one free slaves? Build an army? Dig a tunnel? Nope. The bright idea here is to ask the leader of the country to willingly undermine his nation's economy for no other reason than as a favor.

You got a giant scaring your army into immobility? Let's find a child and give him a slingshot.

The tens of thousands making up the Midianite hordes have you down? Let's get a doubter (isn't one fleece enough?), whittle down his army to 300, and send them out with pots and torches.

Need to raise the king of the universe? Pick a teenage girl, pair her with a carpenter, and send them to the nation's backwaters. ("Can anything good come from Nazareth?")[21]

Want to get the Gospel to the Gentiles? Let's send a pharisee who is also a Roman citizen (an enemy of all kinds!). Better yet, let's make sure he is mostly known for jailing Christians. Can you think of a better mouthpiece for the cause?

The Bible teems with such examples.

Madeleine L'Engle points out,

> ...as I run over my favorite characters in both the Old and New Testament, I can't find one who was in any worldly way qualified to do the job which was nevertheless accomplished. [22]

And it is a good idea for scriptwriting as well.

~

Here are examples of the principle in action:

- *Serenity*: We need to stop the alliance. Let's pick a failed soldier (from the losing side, just for extra kicks and giggles), wanted by the law, poor as all get out, and barely able to keep a crew together. Plus, he's selfish. Let's give him a team that includes a mercenary ready to sell him out to the highest bidder, a cowardly pilot, a crazy child, a prostitute, and a priest. The great plan? Fly on a suicide mission to a non-existent planet in the hopes of finding information that we don't even know exists.

Wrong person, seemingly dumb idea.

- *Little Monsters*: The kindergarten teacher and the slacker are going to keep an entire class of five-year-olds safe in a zombie apocalypse by pretending they are in a big recess game.
- *Hamilton*: The arrogant, orphaned, son of a hooker, raised in poverty in the Caribbean (so hard to resist rapping right now) brings a new nation into existence by taking on the world's only

---

21. John 1:46, NLT
22. L'Engle, *Walking on Water: Reflections on Faith and Art*

superpower without even having a unified government supporting the move.

- *Gravity*: The woman who isn't even an astronaut is going to traverse a couple hundred miles in space and fix a space station.

- *Finding Nemo*: The dad afraid of the ocean is going to traverse the world to find a teeny tiny fish.

- *The Curious Incident of the Dog in the Nighttime*: A boy on the spectrum who hates leaving the comfort of the known is going to travel to the big city alone to look for random clues.

- *Spider-Man: Into the Spiderverse*: A child who hasn't even figured out how to use his powers is going to take on a team of deadly supervillains and save the multiverse.

- *Battlestar Galactica*: A soon-to-retire commander and the Secretary of Education are going to use a decommissioned battleship to lead the disparate remnants of humanity to a place of safety that none of them believe exists.

- *Les Misérables*: An ex-convict on the run is going to raise an orphan in comfort and style.

- *Slumdog Millionaire*: An uneducated slum dweller is going to go on *Who Wants to be a Millionaire* hoping his girlfriend sees the show and he can use that to save her.

- *Mad Max: Fury Road*: The drifter who just wants to get his freedom will drive with a band of women across a killer desert to a mythical, unknown location.

- *Buffy the Vampire Slayer*: A teenaged cheerleader is going to push back the demons of the Hellmouth.

- *Reservation Dogs*: The indigenous teens who spend their days stealing enough money to run away to California are going to save their community.

- *Star Trek Discovery*: A court-martialed former officer, hated by her crew, will lead a single ship into ending a war raging through all known space.

Wrong person.

Seemingly dumb idea.

Great storytelling.

And there is a good reason for this.

> *But Moses said, 'Who am I to go to the king and lead your people out of Egypt?'*
>
> *And God said, 'I will be with you.'*[23]

Ultimately, it's not about Moses.

God could have sent a hobbit instead of Moses. Or a donkey (He was known for that sort of thing). Or a teenager armed with a stake.

He chose Moses (the wrong person) and gave him a seemingly stupid idea so that Moses would understand that the story is bigger than Moses.

And don't we all want that? To be part of a story that is bigger than us, that is more than we can accomplish, that has significance that ripples out well past our shire.

It is a grand drama — to be part of God's story.

CLOSE UP: Reluctant Hero
1917

One of the things that makes *1917* so compelling (one of the many things) is that our hero, Schofield, is not supposed to be the hero of the movie. He starts out as a reluctant sidekick, then grows into being the Central Character.

In using the script written by Sam Mendes & Krysty Wilson-Cairns to track his progression, we see how the reluctant hero grows into his role.

Page 1: Blake is called up by his Sergeant. Blake wakes Schofield — even though Schofield wasn't called up. From the script: "Schofield grudgingly raises his hand for a lift."

---

23. Exodus 3:11-2 CEV

Page 3: Schofield is looking forward to being on leave soon. "Cheer up. This time next week it'll be chicken dinner." He has a reason to not get involved in anything dangerous.

Page 7: When the idea of crossing to the front first comes up, Schofield is the one to raise objections. "Sir, that land is held by the Germans."

Page 9: Blake, whose brother is in danger, has signed on right away. Schofield registers his doubts with a look. "Schofield eyes flick to Blake: *No questions?* Blake purposely doesn't catch Schofield's eye."

Page 10: Schofield raises more concerns. "It will be daylight, Sir. They'll see us." And "Sir, is it just us?"

Page 11-14: Schofield tries to reason with Blake, arguing that they are on a fool's mission, coming up with reasons to delay. "We should wait until dark." "We won't make it ten yards. If we just wait—" "All I'm saying is that we wait." "The last time I was told the Germans were gone, it didn't end well." "...we've got time to wait until the sun sets."

Page 15-16: Blake is leading the way the whole time, until he gets into a scuffle with a Private. Schofield steps between the two, resolving the problem. Blake takes the lead again.

Page 16: Blake asks Schofield about a prior battle Schofield was in; Schofield pretends he doesn't remember it; claims he lost the medal he was given for his actions. Clearly, he is choosing to not remember; but he has reasons to not want to be back in that situation.

Page 20: As another officer suggests the brass might be wrong about the Germans being gone, Schofield jumps on the idea. "Do you think they're wrong, Sir?" Blake remains focused on mission.

Page 21: Before going over the top into No Man's Land, Schofield gives one more way out. "You sure?" he asks. Then Schofield takes the lead, being the first one out.

Page 25: Blake, the least experienced of the duo, panics when confronting the dead soldiers; Schofield is calmer. Although he is wounded now — hand cut on barbed wire.

Schofield is now clearly leading — out of experience, not necessarily a belief in the mission.

Page 28: Once in the German trench, now on easier terrain, Blake takes the lead again.

Page 30: Moving through the tunnel, Schofield is stopped by a picture of a wife and child. "Schofield stares at it for a beat."

Page 33-37: Schofield is buried in rubble. Blake must dig him out and lead him out of the tunnels to safety.

Page 38-39: Schofield lets Blake know just how angry he is at being chosen. "And I wish you'd picked some other bloody idiot." "Why in G-d's name did you have to choose me?" Blake suggests that Schofield can go home. "At the mention of home Schofield turns on him sharply."

Blake gives Schofield a way out; Schofield says to press on.

Page 42-44: The medal Schofield gave away comes up again. Schofield talks about his trip home after he was wounded. "I hated going home. I hated it. When I knew I couldn't stay. When I knew I had to leave them, and they might never see me—" Schofield has a very realistic sense of the potential cost of their actions; his reluctance is grounded.

Side note: this moment is immediately followed by viewing the cherry trees that were chopped down by the Germans. Blake points out to Schofield that this devastation is only temporary. "...they'll grow again when the stones rot. You'll end up with more trees than before." A vision of hope against Schofield's visions of loss.

Page 46: In examining the farmhouse, Schofield takes the lead.

Page 50-52: Blake takes the lead as the plane crashes near them. It is Blake who rushes to pull the German pilot from the crash; it is Blake who decides to try and save the wounded man.

Page 54: Blake now wounded, Schofield takes charge. "We have to get to an Aid Post." "We're going to get up. We're going to get up."

Page 55: The mission becomes Schofield's argument to keep Blake alive. "You have to try to keep moving." "We have to find the 2nd. Remember? Your brother. We have to go now..." "Your brother. We have to find your brother."

Page 56-58: The mission is transferred from Blake to Schofield. "You'll recognize him. Looks like me...a bit older." "Tell me you know the way." In response, Schofield recites the path he will take to get to Blake's brother...

Page 58: And Schofield makes the big decision — leaving reluctance behind.

"Then, he snaps out of it. With sudden determination, he rummages through the pockets of Blake's tunic — takes the message for the 2nd, blood from his hands smudges on the envelope. He stows it safely in his top pocket".

He collects the map from Blake — unusable. He gets Blake's rings and ID — to pass on to the brother.

Page 60: The decision is confirmed as Captain Smith asks what Schofield is doing there. "I have an urgent message for the 2nd Devons. Orders to stop tomorrow morning's attack."

At the midpoint, Schofield is no longer a reluctant hero.

He is simply the hero.

Finding Your Central Character

I recently heard a director griping during a new play development that the play didn't seem to have a Central Character. The writer responded with, "All my characters are important!"

I should hope so — throwaway characters are a sign of sloppy storytelling. However, there is usually a center, and not knowing that center can be problematic. It was for this play — an erratic mess of constantly shifting goals, random storylines, unfulfilled setups, forced themes and inconsistent character actions.

The play did not know what it wanted to be about or what it wanted to say. At the heart, it didn't know what it was about because it didn't know who it was about.

Certainly, one can argue for more than one protagonist with stories that are truly about multiple characters — dual protagonist, ensemble, and the like. Yet way too often the call of "there isn't one Central Character" is more about the writer (or evaluator) unwilling to make a choice.

And choice matters.

Above, I referred to the parable of the Good Samaritan — a title put on the story by publishing houses and not by the storyteller. The title implies that the Central Character is the Samaritan; as stated earlier, the real Central Character is the victim.

This may seem too subtle of a point to matter — but we have lost something in the centuries of declaring the story to be about a Good Samaritan. Every sermon I have ever heard on the parable puts the audience in the shoes of the Samaritan — when you see someone in trouble, the moral goes, stop and help.

Jesus indeed concurs. "Go and do the same."[24]

Yet there is another layer in the story, one that significantly impacted the first century listeners, that seems completely lost today. Today, we listen to the story as Samaritans, being asked, "Will you help your neighbor, even if they appear to be an enemy."

For Jesus' audience, they listened to the story as the victim, watching for the neighbor.

"There's the priest, is he my neighbor? Will he be my hero? No..."

"There's the Temple Assistant — yes! Here is my neighbor, my hero. Wait, no..."

"Here is my enemy, the reviled, the guy I literally couldn't touch with a ten-foot pole and remain clean. Hold on... Is he...?"

Today, by changing the Central Character, we ask, "Are you willing to be a hero to the 'other.'"

Jesus was asking, "Are you willing to see the 'other' as your hero?"

～

For the writer, knowing your Central Character helps to focus the story (Whose goal is dominant? What Quests are supreme?) and themes (What are we really trying to say? What questions are we asking?).

For the director, knowing the center gives freedom to play with how that center will be presented. Taproot Theater staged a production of *Godspell* set in a cabaret. As the audience arrived, actors performed entertaining bits while waiters served coffee and desserts.

---

24. Luke 10:37, CEV

A busboy worked through the room, clearing dishes, cleaning tables, refilling glasses.

When the play started and it came time for Jesus to appear, the busboy stepped onstage and took the role. Jesus was the servant, the guy wiping up the coffee spills and taking your garbage. A powerful metaphor, established by understanding the center.

The ads for the action movie *Executive Decision* showcased action star Steven Seagal as the main lead, with Kurt Russell playing the supporting nerdy consultant. Terrorists take over an airplane, Seagal and a team head out to stop them, Russell accidentally ends up with them.

And before they can even board the plane, our action hero, Steven Seagal, dies.

What!! This movie is supposed to be about how the flying feet of fury takes out the bad guys — and our lead is dead?

Actually, the true Central Character is (and always was) Kurt Russell. The bait-and-switch is designed for effect — to throw the audience off just as much as Russell's character is thrown. An effective move only made possible by a savvy understanding of Central Character.

Motive and Action

Multiple factors come into play when determining the Central Character of a work. Sometimes the answer is obvious, other times the solution is a bit more nuanced. There may not be an easy or even a "right" answer. The real question becomes: What is the most useful answer?

The dramaturg/evaluator needs to gather the indicators like clues and weigh them to come to a determination. The first clue is our definition from Pritner and Walters:

> *The character whose motives...and actions...drive the play's conflict from its beginning to its resolution.*[25]

Whose motives and actions drive the conflict? If this is clear, your job becomes easy.

---

25. In their work, *Introduction to Play Analysis*

I recommend continuing, however, as the other clues shed light on the script in interesting ways.

Titles

Writers will give their work a title that evokes what the story is about — where is the core. *Parasite, Hidden Figures, The Office, Lost, All My Sons, Wicked*. It stands to reason, then, that the title may also clue us in to the central "who."

The title may be direct to the Central Character — *Buffy the Vampire Slayer, The Tragedy of Hamlet, Prince of Denmark, Black Panther, Picard, WandaVision, The Extraordinary Attorney Woo*.

Sometimes the title is another name or title for the core character — *Hidden Figures, The Two Popes, Mad Men, War Horse, The Godfather*.[26]

And at times it is even more indirect. *Justified* clearly leads us to the man trying to justify his actions (Raylon). *Wicked* is a state of being — one taken on as a veil to hide Elphaba. *Doubt* is the main theme of the play/movie of that title — whose doubt is central?

The Apartment is the critical location; that location leads us to the owner of the apartment. *Frankenstein* (Nick Dear's play) takes the title from the doctor/creator but has fun with the idea that pop culture constantly conflates the doctor's name with his creation (the true Central Character — the Creature).

Be warned: titles can be misleading and shouldn't be assumed at face value. Think of the "waiting" stories: *Waiting for Godot, Waiting for Lefty, Waiting for Guffman*. In each case, the title character (Godot, Lefty, Guffman) doesn't show up. More important than the named characters is the question of "who is waiting?"

---

26. *The Godfather* is interesting in this regard. Hindsight makes it clear that the movie is about Michael becoming The Godfather, something that doesn't happen until the final moments of the film. The audience, however, will start the film assuming it is about Don Vito (Marlon Brando's character) as they are slowly sucked into Michael's story. Another great use of Central Character knowledge to enhance the experience for the audience.

Themed titles (*Knives Out, Parasite, Lost, Doubt, I and You, The Harder They Fall*) couple with Theme (see below) to lead us to the Central Character.

The Fourth Wall

Pritner and Walters offer another clue: the character who breaks the fourth wall and speaks directly to the audience tends to be the protagonist.

This is common in Shakespeare — Richard, Hamlet, Macbeth all speak straight to the audience. Other characters do as well — so it isn't a surefire answer.

TV also uses the bit, clearly in *The Bernie Mac Show*, or with character-as-narrator in *The Goldbergs* and *Veronica Mars*. TV also often changes the protagonist from episode to episode — Adam will narrate every Goldbergs; however, some episodes will feature Beverly, Erica, or another member of the family.

Fourth wall breaks in film are not as common, but used to great effect (Ferris Bueller, anyone?). The *Deadpool* movies elevate the practice to an art form, commenting not just as character to audience, but as a character who knows he is a character to the audience.

Woody Allen, Monty Python, Mel Brooks, and the Marx Brothers mine the fourth wall for comedy like mad geniuses. Even James Bond gets a fourth wall break in *On Her Majesty's Secret Service* to wink at the audience with George Lazenby's replacement of Sean Connery ("This never happened to the other fellow," Lazenby quips to the camera).

A variation on the fourth wall break is the mockumentary styling of a show or movie. *The Office, Parks and Recreation*, and *Modern Family* all use this device, along with the comedies of Christopher Guest (*Waiting for Guffman, Best in Show, A Mighty Wind*).

Like titles, the breaking of the fourth wall is not a definitive marker of a Central Character. As stated, Shakespeare will give monologues to other characters besides the lead. In *Spaceballs* (yes, I am pairing *Macbeth* and *Spaceballs*), Dark Helmet is the one who breaks the fourth wall — yet he is not the protagonist. Still, the breaking of the fourth wall provides a solid clue.

Empathy

The audience's emotions rise and fall with the successes and failures of the Central Character.

Remember, we don't have to "like" the Central Character. You shouldn't "like" the Creature of *Frankenstein* or hope to grab some coffee with Walter White of *Breaking Bad*. Someone with a strong moral center finds little likable about Richard III.

Still, we must find the Central Character compelling, engaging, and worthy of investing in as an audience.

We face the witches with Macbeth, tremble as Lady M seduces him into sedition; our hearts leap out through our throats as the ghost appears at the dinner; we sit in anticipation and dread as Birnham Wood makes its march on Dunsinane.

We are not rooting for Macbeth to win, and yet we are totally invested in his outcome.

Another example is Lester in season one of *Fargo*. I did not want Lester to get away with murder — but that didn't stop me from living in tense fear of him being caught.

Whose story carries the audience's emotional basket? Another clue for our Central Character.

Last Choice

Playwriting mentor Howard Stein suggests that the character who makes the last major decision of the play is the protagonist.

To clarify, Howard was not referring to the last decision of the Climax, but rather the decision that makes the Climax inevitable. The decision that drives us to the final confrontation, and by extension forces the final result.

Jean Valjean (*Les Misérables*) going to the barricade to save Marius. Thor (*Thor Ragnorak*) deciding to call up Surtur (the action is performed by Loki; the decision belongs to Thor). The Baker (*Into the Woods*) opting to fight the giant rather than run. Schofield (*1917*) ignoring the fact that it was too late and racing along the trench.

In TV writing there is an adage: protect the star. What that means is to be sure that the lead character gets the juicy bits. It is really designed to protect the ego of the lead actor, who may not want to be upstaged by a smaller role.

I have a friend who did great work as a one-shot character on a procedural. His scripted daughter dies, and my friend's actions in front of the camera brought the crew to tears. One of the show's leads pulled the director aside, explained that he was the star and not this guest actor, and if anyone is going to cry it will be from the star's brilliance.

And my friend's scene was cut out of the episode.

So, protect the star — a crass reality of the business.[27]

There is another side to the saying, however — one that is good for storytelling. Protecting the star also means keeping your eye on the ball. Giving key moments to supernumeraries can weaken the effect of the decisions that drive the story.

Thor's decision in *Ragnorak* will destroy the thing he has been fighting for the entire movie. Bringing up Surtur is not just a logical battle tactic; it is also a mark of character growth. Surtur could have been awoken by accident or the decision made by another character. And the layers of impact would have been lost.

Giving the final decision to the Central Character has ripple effects through character, theme, and plot.

Thus, a good clue.

---

27. While it is common to have TV leads with fragile egos, there is plenty of anecdotal evidence for the opposite. I hear of shows all the time where the leads encourage the funny/emotional bits be given to the supporting cast. Tina Fey and Amy Poehler both have a reputation of generosity on their sets. This may come from training in improv — where the goal is making your scene partner look good, even at your expense. The sum of the parts is greater than any one piece — a 1 Corinthians theme played out on TV sets.

Theme

Theme is complex, and several characters are likely to be theme-carriers to one level or another. Yet the core of the theme is likely to be found in the Story Need of the main character. The core theme is wrapped tightly around the Central Character.

Doubt. Picard. Get Out. Parasite. Knives Out. Pushing Daisies. Dead to Me. Shrek. Peter and the Starcatcher. Silent Sky. Ms. Marvel.

The trick here isn't finding positive examples (here's the broad side of the barn, now shoot!) but finding a well-written story where this isn't true. I haven't found one yet.

It may not be obvious — theme sometimes is elusive. And very often, as stated above, several characters may carry the same theme. Still, the principle plays out — the Central Character is central to the theme.

The Greatest Showman utilizes many of its characters to explore theme. Pretty much, if a character has a song, they are exploring theme. Barnum himself, however, is the one who goes on the biggest thematic journey, making him the most likely choice for Central Character.

POV

The Central Character is usually our eyes into a situation, so the POV character often becomes synonymous with the protagonist.

Frankenstein (the play) has two major characters. The stunt casting plays into this — for the National Theater run, Benedict Cumberbatch and Jonny Lee Miller alternated who played the doctor and who the Creature. Most of the play is through the eyes of the Creature — becoming our biggest clue that while both characters are critical, one is Central.

For *Jesus Christ Superstar*, it would be easy to assume that Jesus is the Central Character. Yet the Point of View — which separates this retelling from most other Passion works — is given to Judas. It is only through this that we can ask the most evangelical of questions:[28] "Jesus — who are you?" Hence, Judas is the protagonist.

Like the other clues, this one can be misleading. There are times when the writer wants to remove us from the Central Character, keep us from being too close.

Ladyhawke is told through Philippe's eyes, but it is Navarre's story. If we saw it from Navarre's POV, we would know too many secrets. So, to keep us interested and connected, we trail along with Philippe, peeling away the story of the knight and the hawk bit by bit.

The Shawshank Redemption utilizes this idea to brilliant effect — which I will discuss in the next section on Multi-Protagonists.

---

28. Asked by the least evangelical of creators — proclaimed atheists Sir Andrew Lloyd Webber and Tim Rice. Which makes the telling all the more interesting.

CHAPTER SEVEN

Multi-Protagonists

In one of my classes, the students study *The Shawshank Redemption* — which I consider one of the best screenplays of all time.

Traditionally, the students agree that finding the Central Character is obvious. Then half will say it is obviously Andy, while the other half say it is obviously Red.

Obviously.

The confusion is understandable. The title could easily refer to either character — both are redeemed while in Shawshank. Red talks to the audience and we see most of the action from his point of view. Empathy is garnered for both characters — although let's face it, Andy is a bit of a cold fish, so we lean a bit more toward Red.

The theme of hope is articulated and tested most by Red. Final decision — that depends on how you break up the story. Andy chooses to escape, which leads to the plot's Climax. Red chooses to get busy living, which drives the entire New Balance. And there does seem to be an awful lot of story after the escape...

At this point, I would lean toward Red. However, motives and actions driving the plot? The entire plot up to the escape is all driven by Andy. Red is mostly an observer of the action.

So where does that leave us?

This is where a genius writer uses the understanding of the forms of Story to a brilliant end. Frank Darabont takes the function of the Protagonist and plays with it through division.

Andy is the Central Character of the plot.

Red is the Central Character of the theme.

By making this division, Darabont can strengthen the theme; Red's journey is the journey of the audience. By experiencing Andy's plot, Red is changed; just as, hopefully, the audience in the movie theater is changed. Red gets the full character arc experience.

The division also allows Darabont (the sneaky devil) to give us two plots in one: what the audience thinks is happening with Andy, and what is really happening. By giving POV to Red, the writer is able to mask what is going on in Andy's mind.

On the surface (in first viewing/reading), *The Shawshank Redemption* is the story of a man (Andy) who is trying to make life bearable during a life sentence in prison. The climax reveals that this was never the story of a man trying to make life bearable — this was always the story of a man breaking out of prison.

Darabont succeeds in writing a prison break movie without the audience knowing it is a prison break movie until the end of the film. He did this by using a dual-protagonist approach.

Variations on Multi-Protagonists:

Dual Protagonist
Multiple Protagonist
Plural Protagonist
Multi-Protagonist
Ensemble
Parallel Protagonist

The terms for having more than one Central Character each have their own nuance.

Dual Protagonist is for two main characters — *Butch Cassidy and the Sundance Kid* — as opposed to three or more (Ensemble or Multiple Protagonist).

Parallel Protagonist applies when there are multiple, separate storylines — *Big Fish, Avengers: Infinity War*.

Robert McKee uses the label "Plural Protagonist" when all the protagonists share the same goal. *Thelma & Louise* is his prime example. "Multi-protagonist," for McKee, is when the group has differing goals — *Pulp Fiction*, for example. [29]

As seen with *The Shawshank Redemption*, more than one Central Character can be used for great effect. Theme often comes into play — having more than one driver can showcase multiple sides to a theme.

Do lies define you — and should they? Willie and Biff both struggle with this in *Death of a Salesman* — with two distinctive outcomes. *The Big Chill*, *Brownie Points*, *Into the Woods*, *The Band's Visit*, *Greenbook* — each play with theme through the lens of multiple characters.

Three Billboards Outside of Ebbing Missouri (which I will talk more about in our section on theme) is designed to answer its central thematic question in six different ways; ensemble is what allows the film to work so powerfully well.

Ensemble pieces where the characters are on completely separate storylines also tend to revolve around a theme — *Love Actually*, *Valentine's Day*, the multiple plots of a typical *Modern Family* or *Sweet Magnolias*.

Multiple protagonists also come out of plot choices — when a full-length piece is really multiple shorter pieces put together. *Dunkirk* has three separate plot lines, and thus three separate Central Characters. *The Godfather Part II*, *Big Fish*, *Fried Green Tomatoes*, *Once Upon a Time in Hollywood*, *Avengers: Infinity War* are also clear examples.

Ensembles are also used to explore the same event happening through multiple lenses (sort of combining theme and plot explorations at one time).

Come From Away, the musical about the diverting of airplanes to Newfoundland on 9/11 is a breathtaking look at an emotionally driven real-life event. The lives of 7,000 stranded passengers being cared for by a small town is a tour-de-force with twelve actors portraying a broad sampling of town folk and visitors. It is the ensemble nature of *Come*

---

29. McKee, *Story*

From Away that makes it both intimately personal and broadly universal all at the same time.

Central Character Switch

Another variant on the dual/multiple protagonist story is when the Central Character switches from one character to another.

Typically, switching the protagonist is not a good thing. I have seen and read many stories where the change of Central Character comes more from the creators not understanding their story than by design. When a writer (or director) doesn't know who their show is about, they will sometimes try to pass it off as a multiple character piece.

My wife and I watched a play one night. The drive home was a head-scratching conversation, trying to figure out what we just saw. The play jumped from story to story, each scene seemingly changing the Central Character, and none of them ever progressing past a setup for a story. The conclusion we drew: the playwright didn't know what story to tell, so instead he started eight different stories starring eight different characters.

Thus, the Central Character swap can be bad. But it also can be delicious.

Psycho is perhaps the strongest example of such a swap. The Hitchcock classic[30] is about our heroine, Marion Crane. If there is any doubt that she is our Central Character, just check out the poster, featuring a very prominent, underwear clad Janet Leigh, with a much smaller shot of Anthony Perkins off to the side. Marion steals money from her employer to help get her boyfriend out of debt. As she runs away, she slips past cops, trades in her car (with changed license plates) and stops by a motel. After interacting with the motel owner, she decides to return the money and risk arrest.

A gripping heist movie, and a great, sympathetic Central Character, exhibiting all the signs of the full arc expected of our leading lady.

---

30. Yes, I'm giving credit to the director. Hard not to on this one. The screenplay is by Joseph Stefano, based on the book by Robert Bloch.

Then she is murdered in the shower.

Less than halfway into our story, our Central Character, incomplete arc and all, is killed, stuffed in the trunk of a car, and deposited at the bottom of a swamp. We are left without a rudder, and rely on the sister, the boyfriend, and the private detective to take up the slack.

Psycho understands the expectations of Story and uses that understanding to good effect. As a result, the audience is given one of the most terrifying and lasting murder scenes in the history of cinema — more terrifying, I suspect, out of the violent breaking of story expectations than out of the violence of the scene itself.

The passing of Central Character function is also often used to good effect in television, where the storyline is passed from character to character in an ensemble piece.

Parks & Recreation showcased a very clean example of this in their COVID quarantine inspired Special. The event filmed each character passing on a phone chain during self-isolation. Each scene had two or three characters talking via Zoom: then moving on to a new set of characters. The Special told one story through constantly shifting protagonists.

Arthur Schnitzler's 1897 play, *La Ronde*, uses the same technique, showing a pair of lovers in one scene; the following scene showing one of the lovers in a tryst with a new person, and on with each scene until the circle is made complete with the original pair.

Akira Kurosawa's *Rashomon*[31] retells the same incident four times — each time with a different protagonist providing their take on the event. The effect is four completely different tales, all with the same characters and result, all unique just by the shifting point of view. "The Rashomon effect" — a term for the unreliability of eyewitnesses, is taken from the film. The animated film *Hoodwinked* plays tribute to this storytelling style.

---

31. Screenplay by Akira Kurosawa and Shinobu Hashimoto, from "In a Grove," a short story by Ryūnosuke Akutagawa. That story was based on Ambrose Bierce's short "The Moonlit Road."

Television and serialized stories will often switch protagonists between episodes. *This Is Us* plays with its ensemble in a variety of ways and will often use individual episodes devoted to just one main cast member (and occasionally even devoted to a supporting character). *Lost* employed this technique with its ensemble cast, generating several seasons of story arcs from the same people. Even shows with clearer leads will pass off the protagonist torch on occasion. *Star Trek: Discovery* may have a Saru-centric episode; *Doctor Who* was notorious for one episode a season devoted to the companion or another minor character.

~

Other variants are the subplot and bookend storylines. Each subplot will have a mini protagonist (sub-protagonist, if you will), a character to drive the subplot.

One should be careful to not conflate a subplot character with the Central Character of the whole. A subplot has a lesser structure and is there to support the main story. Just as too much devotion to a subplot can undermine the central story, too much emphasis on a sub-protagonist can steal the thunder from the Central Character.

We will discuss the idea more in our section on Supporting Characters.

Bookends are similar to subplots — often a mini-story used to convey the main story.

The grandfather reading to the sick boy in *The Princess Bride* is a perfect example. The grandfather drives the action of the wraparound, but in a minor story with more cerebral stakes, to add to the main story (and not detract).

When a wraparound gets a main story level of complexity, the story should take one of two steps: cut the bookend way back or elevate the wraparound into a full plot.

Big Fish and *Fried Green Tomatoes* both take the second route. The wraparounds are similar to *The Princess Bride* — an excuse to tell the main story. *Bride* uses the story within a story to make a small movement in the present day — a grandson learning to appreciate the action of love in his grandfather.

Fish and *Tomatoes*,[32] on the other hand, have much more complex wraparounds. In the first, a son goes from complete disconnection with his dying father to deep relationship. In the latter, a timid woman finds her true self and the strength to act on her new identity.

In each one, the wraparound is given enough weight to be a dual story, creating an interesting phenomenon. The past stories are stand-alone — enough weight that they only need the wraparound as a story device.

The wraparound story is also complete, using the past as flashbacks that move the present-day stories forward. The wraparound in both cases would not be complete without the past, while the past stories stand alone.

Many of Jesus' parables can be viewed as stories with a wraparound. A lawyer asks Jesus a question, Jesus responds by taking us into a story, and then we return to the lawyer to see the results of that story on the audience. The Parable of the Lost Son stands alone; the story of the lawyer and Jesus is made complete by the tale told in the middle.

CROSS FADE: The Lost Son

Now let's apply our system to try and find the protagonist of the parable of the Lost or Prodigal Son[33]. (Luke 15:11-32)

The Title doesn't help since the author (Jesus) did not provide the title. The Prodigal or Lost Son was added by publishers and tradition — on the evaluation by other publishers and scholars.[34]

---

32. "Fish and Tomatoes" — sounds like an order at a British pub, doesn't it?

33. This academic exercise has the additional value of forcing a closer examination of the scriptural story as a whole — and may even shift some of our own views in the process.

34. I am not saying that we ignore the scholarship of others, just that we do not rely solely on their work. The title given to the text often comes with an emphasis on a particular side of the lesson that the scholar wishes to push forward. For example, "prodigal" means "wastefully extravagant" (per Oxford

There are five active characters in the text:

- Father
- Younger Son
- Older Son
- Farmer
- Servant

The Farmer is easily eliminated — he has no lines and is there only to move along the Younger Son's motives and actions.

The Servant, in a similar way, is there to move along the plot — so the Father would have someone to order party supplies from, and the Older Son would have a news bearer (Herald) function.

We see different parts of the story from shifting Points of View — the Younger Son, the Father, and the Older Son.

Looking at the structure: the final bit with the Older Son seems to be a Tag (see chapter on Events). In essence, it is a start of a new story, and Jesus doesn't tell us much past the midpoint of that new story. In some ways, Jesus is telling two separate stories with the same inciting incident — the story of the Lost Younger Son, and the story of the Lost Older Son. For purposes of this exercise, we will treat the story as one story with an added Tag at the end.

As the Older Son only appears in this coda, I am going to take him out of the running as Central Character.

Only one character speaks when no one is around to hear him — the Younger Son soliloquizes while coming to his senses at the pig farm. The author (Jesus) does say that the young man was talking to himself, so not a clear breaking of the fourth wall.

The Father makes the final choice that leads to the result — the reconciliation of father and son. However, it could be argued that the

---

Dictionary). This title suggests that the defining trait of the boy is his sinful waste. Another title sometimes given is "The Lost Son." This titling puts the emphasis on the cost of the sin — and thus more emphasis on the finding of the lost, rather than the punishing of the prodigal. The story has also been called the "Parable of the Two Brothers," "The Loving Father," and "The Forgiving Father." Each one pushing to the forefront a theme — each a different angle.

true climax is the confrontation between father and son — and it is the Younger Son's choice that drives to that conflict.

Much of the Empathy is with the father — once the Younger Son heads home, at least. This comes late in the story with the Empathy clue riding with the Younger Son up until the return.

I would buy a case for a dual protagonist; however, my choice would be for the Younger Son as Central Character.

Evidence:

1. His goals drive most of the plot (to get the money, to get a job, to restore his fortune).

2. As do his actions (splitting the inheritance, going to a foreign land, spending the money, getting the job, returning home).

3. Our empathy is mostly with the Younger Son, watching him lose everything and sink to the lowest position.

4. Theme — what once was lost, now is found — is carried by the Younger Son (and the Father).

5. Point of View is primarily with the Younger Son (except for the Tag), including journeying with him to the distant land. (We travel with the Younger Son, rather than wait on the farm for his return with his Father.) Even the Father's final act of acceptance is done within the Younger Son's POV.

WRITER'S TIP:
The Gunderson Principle: The Single Protagonist

Lauren Gunderson, one of the most produced playwrights in recent years, proposes that no script really has multiple protagonists.[35] She feels that a story will always have a character that is more the writer's

---

35. I was able to hear Gunderson's theories on writing through free Facebook seminars she offered during the coronavirus shutdown. Lauren's work is produced so often because she really knows her stuff. I have seen a couple of student productions of *Silent Sky* — and it always leaves me in wonder of the Cosmos.

point of view. And consciously or subconsciously, the writer will imbue that character with "more" than the others.

She cites *Romeo and Juliet* as an example. As important as Juliet is — critical even — Romeo is the driver of the story. It is his play.

I can see her point — this author bias toward one protagonist can be seen in many multi-protagonist stories.

In *Butch Cassidy and the Sundance Kid*, the Kid is more partner than driver. *Into the Woods* is an ensemble piece; as the night progresses, the Baker and Cinderella emerge as more core. And by the final confrontation with his father, the Baker is clearly the more Central-er Character.

In *Hidden Figures*, Katherine is more central; *Frankenstein*, it is the Creature.

The Avengers is another clear ensemble piece, yet Tony Stark emerges with the cleanest character arc. This is true of all the *Avengers* films — Tony's spotlight being just a bit brighter. Which clarifies the question of why *Captain America: Civil War*, featuring all the Avengers, is not labeled an *Avengers* movie.

I wouldn't be as definitive as Gunderson; while the writer-bias may be real, for evaluation purposes, the multiple protagonist tag is an important and useful tool.

That said, Gunderson was speaking to writers, and this is a good tip for creators. The risk in stories with multiple protagonists is clarity of vision and storytelling. Good characters have a mind of their own; if they all are allowed in the driver's seat, the car will veer wildly throughout the ride.

To continue the metaphor, as a writer, you have a destination in mind. One can weave a bit along the way, but too much so and the audience gets lost.

Know that, as a writer, you do have a point of view, and likely have chosen a character for that point of view. That character is your guide through the plot, and realizing your bias may help prevent you from getting lost.

So let the post-show evaluators like Gaffney talk about the ensemble or duo-protagonist; you keep your eye on your true Central Character.

CROSS FADE: Ensemble and Theology

"In life," he said, "there are no essentially major or minor characters. To that extent, all fiction and biography, and most historiography, are a lie. Everyone is necessarily the hero of his own life story.

Hamlet could be told from Polonius's point of view and called The Tragedy of Polonius, Lord Chamberlain of Denmark. He didn't think he was a minor character in anything, I daresay."

The above quote from a John Barth short story[36] contains a common thought — we are the Central Characters of our own lives. Or at least we play out our lives as if we are. As we move through the scenes of our day, our natural temptation is to assume that they are "our" scenes.

And why not? One of our keys to Central Character is Point of View; we are by nature and physics viewing our lives from our own POV, and we must consciously try to see from another's POV.

Seeing ourselves as Central Character is not a bad thing (or a good thing) in and of itself. It is simply natural. Just as being tempted is natural. The problem is when you allow that temptation to become action.

The Bible suggests that making the effort to see others as a Central Character is a worthwhile venture. Whether acknowledging that there are stories going on that aren't one's own, or even allowing ourselves to be supporting players in the lives of others, expanding our view outside of self is a good thing.

Negative examples abound of Biblical characters who look at themselves as the Center — and the consequences of that view. King Herod the Great refused the very idea of multiple protagonists — and woe to anyone eligible to take the central role from him (for example, the

---

36. "The Remobilization of Jacob Horner" by John Barth, published 1958. I found the quote in Quote Investigator (quoteinvestigator.com) along with the likely source of Barth's inspiration: Charles Dickens' "David Copperfield" opens with, "Whether I shall turn out to be the hero of my own life...these pages must show."

famed slaughter of the innocents in an attempt to end the life of the Christ Child).[37]

And it isn't just the villains of the Bible that stand as negative examples. Samson, great strongman and lousy judge, made poor choice after poor choice based on his "me" centric lifestyle.[38] King David, for at least one scene, let his own Want (see the section on goal below) outweigh the possibility of Uriah having a story worth living out.

John the Baptist showed a better way — a willingness to be the supporting player in another person's story. When John's disciples griped that Jesus was taking away John's following, the baptizer said:

> At a wedding the groom is the one who gets married. The best man is glad just to be there and to hear the groom's voice. That's why I am so glad. Jesus must become more important, while I become less important.[39]

Paul takes an even more ensemble approach. He constantly refers to the believers as being in one body,[40] and seeks to eliminate the mindset that the individual is supreme over the whole.

> There is no longer Jew or Gentile, slave or free, male and female. For you are all one in Christ Jesus.[41]

Individuals have roles to play, yet to Paul, the church is an ensemble. Being an ensemble player is to realize that our piece is just a part of a larger, more significant whole.

This is the power of the climactic scene in *Mr. Holland's Opus*. The composer-turned-teacher had always felt that his lasting impact would be the brilliant piece of music that he would create. In the end, he is

---

37. Matthew 2:16-18

38. I have heard complaints about the use of anti-heroes in our movies and television shows. The argument seems to be that our central characters should be positive role models — not these conflicted, confusing messes of morality. Maybe. But how then do we explain the use of anti-heroes like Samson and Paul of Tarsus?

39. John 3:29-30, CEV

40. 1 Corinthians 12, Romans 12, Ephesians 4

41. Galatians 3:28, NLT

faced with an auditorium full of Central Characters with their own stories to tell — and the realization that by playing into their lives instead of his own goals, he created his true masterpiece.

CHAPTER EIGHT

Goal

Once you have a Central Character, the next thing you need for a story is a goal — the character must want something.

The boy wants to win the heart of the girl.

The detective wants to solve the murder.

The victim wants to survive the attack.

The Story Want is going to drive the plot of the story. Act One sets up the Want; Act Two is the pursuit of the Want; Act Three is the result of the pursuit.

Therefore, the Want must be strong enough to propel the action. To clarify, it must be strong for the Central Character, and the audience must believe in that strength.

The Want can be something personal, with meaning only to the Central Character ("I want to take my wife's house to Paradise Falls" / *Up*), or something that has consequences for others ("I want to stop Thanos from destroying half of the universe" / *Avengers: Infinity War*). The important thing is that the Central Character really, really wants it.

The first half of *One Man, Two Guvnors* is driven by the want of sandwich. And, boy-o-boy, does that man want that sandwich!

My wife is an actress. She tells me that whenever she is unsure of what to do in a scene — how to hold her hands, how to interpret a line — she goes back to asking, "What does my character want in this scene?" Once she knows what her character wants, her actions and lines come naturally.

This is a good tip for writers as well: when you are blocked on what to write next, ask: "What does my Central Character want?" Then write what the character does to get that want.

Stories without a strong Want tend to lose steam and meander. The Want keeps the story focused and moving.

Young writers will sometimes tell me that their main character doesn't know what he wants — as if that is justification for an aimless storyline. Good stories have a Want, even if the Want is to find themselves or their place in the world. In that case, the character may not be able to articulate their end goal — as the end goal is a mystery; but they are still driven to go on the search.

It may seem that stories that cover decades of time or myriads of locations aren't driven by Want. I would argue that the well-told ones do.

Forrest Gump — it all comes back to Jenny. *Mr. Holland's Opus* — wanting to compose something great. *Johnnie Pye and the Foolkiller*[42] — to outwit death. In each case, the Central Character gets absorbed in actions that distract him from the goal, reacting to life; but in each, the Want is the reason they tackle the distractions.

Many biopics suffer from a lack of goal — they are textbook cases of "this happened, then this happened, then this happened..." As pieces of history, they may be interesting. As stories, they fall short.

When I hear as a criticism that a story based on true events didn't tell all of the story, I tend to be more interested in seeing that movie. It indicates that the creators weren't trying to replace a historical text-book as much as focusing on one angle of the subject matter.

So, *Walk the Line* focuses on Johnny Cash finding his voice, and the cost of his soul in doing so — and the re-finding of that soul (while keeping his voice). The classic structure of "boy meets girl, boy loses girl, boy gets girl," replacing "girl" with "soul". That story is driven by Johnny's Want — to be a star. (See below for Want versus Need, and how they interact.)

---

42. Musical by Mark St. Germain and Randy Courts. A gem that deserves more recognition.

The complaint that Johnny's life traveling with Billy Graham was not in the movie isn't a valid complaint about *Walk the Line* — this movie isn't about all of Johnny Cash. This movie is about one aspect of Johnny Cash.

Let the sequel cover the rest.

~

Strong Story goals are clear and tangible. If by the nature of the story the goal is at all unclear, a good story adds a marker, a way of clarifying if the goal has been achieved. (Or at least how the Central Character believes they will achieve the goal.)

For example, suppose the character wants love — sure, don't we all? But a vague want of love will not drive a story. The story itself then isn't following an arbitrary attempt to be loved; the story follows the tangible Goal of convincing a specific girl/boy to date/marry/go to the prom with the Central Character.

We track the progress of our hero by how close the girl is to saying yes.

- In *The Glass Menagerie*, Amanda wants her daughter to be set up for life; the play is about the Goal of getting her daughter a successful date.

- In *Green Book*, Dr. Shirley wants to prove that white America is wrong in its view on the races, and Tony wants some cash. The Goal is to successfully navigate a classical music tour through the South.

- Buffy in *Buffy the Vampire Slayer* wants the world to be safe; the tangible Goal each episode is to kill the monster of the week.

Note this exchange from Lewis Carroll's *Alice in Wonderland*:

"Would you tell me, please, which way I ought to go from here?"

"That depends a good deal on where you want to get to," said the Cat.

"I don't much care where—" said Alice.

"Then it doesn't matter which way you go," said the Cat.

"—so long as I get SOMEWHERE," Alice added as an explanation.

"Oh, you're sure to do that," said the Cat, "if you only walk long enough."

Goal is the driver of the plot. A tangible Goal means the story is going somewhere. With intangible Goals — who knows where one might end up.

We should make clear at this point that there is a main Want as well as micro-wants. Every character should want something from every scene — not just the Central Character. In fact, much of the drama come from the conflict of various wants.

This may mean the overarching conflict of the story — Thanos wants to destroy; the Avengers want to stop him.[43]

Or it may be a want (lowercase) for just the scene — Steve Rogers wants Tony to join them; Tony wants to be left alone.

Moreover, the main Want may change throughout the story. (We will discuss that in more detail in our section on Characters.) In fact, in most stories the main Want doesn't appear until the Catalyst (Inciting Incident). Bryan Mills in *Taken* wants to rescue his daughter from her kidnappers. He doesn't want to save her until she is taken; it would be nonsense to want to save her before she is in peril.

And often the Want is altered by the Midpoint and/or shifted in Act Three. Need overtaking Want (see below) or circumstances redirecting the importance of Want is common. Think of the RomCom trope where the guy focuses his attention on getting the girl, only to realize in Act Three that he was chasing after the wrong girl the whole time. *Pride and Prejudice, While You Were Sleeping, The Proposal,* and *My Fair Lady* all play on variations of this trope.

For now, the focus should be on the main Want, the thing that drives the show.

---

43. *Avengers: Infinity War*

Understanding Want

Identifying that Want for a writer helps craft a better story. Identifying that Want within an existing script helps understand what is really happening in a tale. Characters speak and act because they want something; understanding the Want helps us understand the character's words and actions.

I mentioned earlier that *The Shawshank Redemption* has dual protagonists. The structure of the plot leads the audience into thinking Andy is trying to make a more peaceful existence during his life sentence; it is revealed that he was planning an escape the entire time.

The audience misunderstands Andy's Want — and that is what leads to the brilliant double storytelling. To really understand the movie, rewatch it knowing his true intentions.

For example: the opera scene. Andy has just gotten (at long last!) the shipment of books and other materials from the State to build his library. Andy finds a recording of an opera aria; he locks the guards out of the warden's office and plays the opera over the loudspeaker.

This powerful scene gives hope to the entire prison population — hearing the beautiful music within the ugliness of their setting. The guards break into the office and Andy is punished for his prank. It is worthwhile, though, because Andy was able to give hope to his fellow inmates.

At least it looks that way. Stop and think about what Andy did, and what it got him. If his goal was to maintain a comfortable life, why risk it by playing a song over the loudspeaker? The record would still be available to anyone who wants to hear it in the library. Andy had to know that he would be punished for this act.

And why now? Andy just had a major victory; his library was coming true! He was on the warden's good side; he was on the guards' good side; he was on the inmates' good side. If Andy's goal was a comfortable ride through a life sentence, this is the moment of Andy's final victory.

However, if Andy wants escape, a comfortable ride is his enemy. His goal isn't easy imprisonment; it's freedom. And if he gets too comfortable, he will lose his hunger for freedom.

Andy plays the music for the inmates — yes. But his main reason for playing the music is to reverse his victory, to remind himself that he is in prison, to fuel his fire to get out. To let his punishment remind himself of the reality, not the fantasy.

To get what he Wants.

Television (and any other serialized format) plays with two main Wants — the Want of the series (or season) and the Want of the episode.

The Want of *Fresh Off the Boat* as a series is to successfully integrate into Florida society. An individual episode might be a subset of that Want (to make the restaurant opening successful) or a tangent (to get out of going to Chinese school).

Some shows break down the main Want into seasonal arcs. Daredevil (*Daredevil*) wants to end corruption in Hell's Kitchen, and by the end of the season he takes down Kingpin. For an individual episode, the want is a micro of the main — to save a kidnapped child, for example.

As I said up above, the Want must be strong enough to drive the plot. The strength of the Want can be tied to Stakes: what happens if the Want is not achieved?

The bigger the stakes, the more compelling the plot.

If the hero fails:

- The son will die alone. ("The Parable of the Lost Son")
- The boy will never find his soul mate. (*Pushing Daisies*)
- The Nazis will win. (*Casablanca*)
- The nation will be run by a murderer. (*Hamlet*)

Some stories amp up their power by clarifying and defining the stakes. We all want money, right? But what if not getting the money means that your child can't get the treatment she needs (*Good Girls*), or the villain gets away with stealing your retirement (*Tower Heist*), or the orphanage closes (*The Blues Brothers*)? Much more interesting than simple greed. Such stakes add the oomph to keep the story focused and the audience riveted.

Note that stakes must be meaningful for the character, not necessarily for the audience. We all know that teen love is fleeting, and in the big scheme tends not to matter that much. Unless you are a teen in love; then it is the whole world.

Romeo prattling on about Juliet is laughable, especially to Mercutio who had to listen to the same exact drivel over Rosalind just hours before taking Romeo to Juliet's party. The stakes aren't serious for Mercutio, nor for any adults in the audience. But for Romeo and Juliet? Young love is life and death.

And that is enough to make a compelling, driving story.

✛✛ CROSS FADE: Stakes at Cana ✛✛

In his sermon "Lord of the Wine,"[44] Tim Keller looks at the account of the wedding in Cana,[45] and brings up an interesting notion about stakes: they are too low in this story.

White would go better with fish.

---

44. The sermon can be heard at gospelinlife.com, "Lord of the Wine," 1996
45. John 2:1-11

Transforming water into wine is to be Jesus' first miracle, the first sign that sets up his ministry. The opening event of a movement should be something monumental, mission-defining, something that makes a splash.

Instead, Jesus helped an unknown couple in a backwater town avoid a little social awkwardness. Sure, the days of partying are important in the short run to the groom — but beyond that? Would word of this party shake up the religious powers? Would it make Herod lose sleep? Would it rival the parting of the Red Sea, the fall of Jericho, the survival of the fiery furnace?

Keller mentions that author Reynolds Price[46] points to the low stakes as the reason he knows this event happened. Any author worth his salt wouldn't choose as the inaugural sign of this movement a miraculous solution to a mere social embarrassment.

I can hear the network notes on this one.

"Love the party scene, perfect. Just one thing. Does it have to be a party in Cana? How about setting it in the temple instead — or maybe Herod's palace? And this whole water to wine thing — can we up the stakes? What if the groom is a visiting dignitary, and he has leprosy, and Jesus heals him? Or the bride is demon possessed and starts killing all the guests, and Jesus steps in and crushes the demon? Yeah, that would do it!"

So, we have some not-so-great story telling in the Bible — low stakes.

I have a rule: "If you find what looks like poor storytelling in the Bible, look closer. You are probably missing something."

The stakes do seem low, and Jesus knows that. Yet he chooses to perform this miracle anyway — and use it as the launch to his entire ministry. He even makes clear that this miracle is to become the first step in a road that leads to the cross, to his hour.

Jesus said to her, "Woman, what does your concern have to do with Me? My hour has not yet come."[47]

So why make this the prime miracle?

---

46. In his introduction to John, Reynolds Price, *Three Gospels*
47. John 1:4, NKJV

Keller has a sermon's worth of answers, and it is well worth the time to listen. I'll pick up on a few of my own.

The stakes are low — for Jesus, for the ministry of the Messiah, for the salvation of mankind. However, the stakes are important to his mother — and therefore, to Jesus. He is a personal messiah — what is important to his followers is, via the transitive property, important to Jesus.

To put it another way, what is important to you is important to Jesus. And it was critical that this be said at the top of the ministry.

Also, the very nature of a party is important to the ministry. There is going to be a long road ahead, with persecution, suffering, even death. It will become easy to forget that the journey ends in celebration — in resurrections, salvation, and a heavenly feast to blot out all wedding feasts.

Jesus is using Setups and Payoffs — he is saving a party here to set up a wedding feast to come. The Master Storyteller is using seemingly low stakes to underline this story, to make us ask why it is included in the Gospels, why this event is the kickstart event.

He is drawing our attention to the fact that he is the Lord of the feast.

CHAPTER NINE

Want versus Need

N ow that we have established the idea of Want, we must address its companion: Story Need. To do so, let's start with the examples.

The movie and musical play *Shrek / Shrek the Musical*: in the story, we have our Central Character (Shrek) with an obvious, measurable Goal (to be left alone). Everything he does in the first two-thirds of the movie is to achieve this goal — from chasing people away in the Hook, to going on his Quest. If he can deliver the princess Fiona to Farquad, Shrek's swamp will be emptied, and he gets what he wants.

Shrek succeeds — he delivers the princess and is left alone. Woohoo! But wait, why is this point of victory the saddest part of the movie, complete with Rufus Wainwright's mournful take on Cohen's "Hallelujah?" Shouldn't we be celebrating?

No, because there is a difference between getting what you want and winning. In addition to Shrek's Want, he has a deeper Need. He wants to be left alone; he needs to understand the value of community.

Want is the body of a story; Need is the heart and soul. And we all understand what Jesus meant when he said:

> *"And what do you benefit if you gain the whole world but lose your own soul?"*[48]

---

48. Mark 8:36, NLT

Another perfect example is *The Wizard of Oz*. Our Central Character, Dorothy, has a clear, measurable Want: to go home. Everything she does once landing in Oz is designed to get her home — following the yellow brick road, encountering danger along the way, confronting the wizard, going on the side quest to get the witch's broom, dealing with those (brrr!) freaky flying monkeys.

When it comes time for her to go home, she uses the ruby red slippers. The slippers she got as soon as she landed in Oz. The slippers she had before following the road, encountering danger, confronting the wizard, seeking the broom, and dealing with those (brrr!) freaky flying monkeys.

In other words, plot-wise, Dorothy did not have to endure any of that to get her Goal. Glinda, the allegedly "good" witch, plays one of the meanest practical jokes in the history of cinema on this poor girl. Is the audience angry? Do we leave the theater mad as all get out over this fairy's meanness?

Nope. We leave happy, elated. We like the ending.[49] Why?

To answer that question, we need to back up. Our Central Character, Dorothy, has a clear, measurable Want: to go home. So why wasn't Dorothy at home when the tornado first hit? How come she didn't make it to the storm cellar in time?

Because Dorothy had run away from home.

And if Glinda sends Dorothy back home as soon as she gets to Oz, Dorothy will run away from home tomorrow. Dorothy wants to go home; she needs to understand the value of home first. She is not ready to go back at the start of the film, and somehow the audience subconsciously understands that.

And we applaud when she goes home only after fulfilling her Need.

---

49. Most people like the ending, if my informal polling of students over the years has any weight. Every now and again I encounter someone who says they did not like the ending; after prodding, we usually discover that they were actually just too scared of the freaky flying monkeys to enjoy the movie.

Story Want versus Story Need

Also known as:
Goal/Want v Need
Physical v Psychological/Spiritual
Outer Journey v Inner Journey
The Action Story v The Emotional Story

Don't copy the behavior and customs of this world, but let God transform you into a new person by changing the way you think. Then you will learn to know God's will for you, which is good and pleasing and perfect.[50]

When talking about Story Need, we must differentiate from "need" in its typical sense. Story Need refers specifically to a psychological/ spiritual lack. Story Need is not a physical object. While in real life we all need oxygen to breathe, oxygen can never be a Story Need.

Story Need will never be riches, or a job, or a girl, or winning a competition, or defeating an enemy. All of those are Wants. Need delves more into the spirit of man, into our psyches and emotions.

Want and Need are never the same thing in a story. They may be related, as we will see below. But they aren't the same.

Think of Need as what God would want for a character to help that person become more whole. Need is never bad for the Character — only the rejection of the Need is bad. Macbeth rejects his potential lesson, as does Mark in *The Social Network*. That is why they are tragedies — why their stories end at Cohen's "Hallelujah." If they embraced their Need, they might have continued the story to save Fiona from Farquaad (figuratively speaking, of course — not that I wouldn't watch a movie about Zuckerberg and Mackie teaming up to take on Farquaad).

The character is usually unaware of Need. Rarely are they striving for their Need — just as we must be constantly reminded to strive for our own improvement over the race for objects.

Some examples of Want and Need:

---

50. Romans 12:2, NLT

- In Gunderson's *I and You*, Caroline wants to be left alone; she needs to accept that she is part of a greater whole.
- Thor in *Thor* wants to get back to Asgard; he needs to learn humility.
- In *The King's Speech*, Bertie wants to get through his speeches; he needs to find his own voice.
- *Dead to Me*'s Judy wants to please everyone; she needs to love herself.
- Lloyd Vogel in *A Beautiful Day in the Neighborhood* wants to expose Fred Rogers; he needs to be healed of the wounds that keep him from experiencing joy.
- *Inside Out* — Joy wants her person to be happy all the time; Joy needs to learn the value of all emotions.
- *Reservation Dogs* — Elora and Bear both want to escape their community; they need to learn their place in their community.
- *Death of a Salesman* — Willy Loman wants to live in the fantasy where he is considered important in everyone's eyes; he needs to face reality.
- *Ms. Marvel* — Kamala wants to be Carol Danvers; she needs to discover/embrace her own identity.
- *Lost* — Jack wants to save everyone else; he needs to put his own life in order.

As you can see, Need is often in conflict with Want. Not always, but often — which plays out for great dramatic effect. Thor isn't worthy of his hammer until he learns humility — until he accepts his own unworthiness. What fun for an audience!

In a step further, often a story is amped up when the Want is bad for the Central Character, while the Need is the real deal. We see this in *Shrek, Inside Out, Death of a Salesman*, and on.

What they want is the very thing that is preventing them from true joy. The moment of "success" is the low point of the story. There is a Biblical take on this:

Yet when I surveyed all that my hands had done and what I had toiled to achieve, everything was meaningless, a chasing after the wind; nothing was gained under the sun.[51]

Do not store up for yourselves treasures on earth, where moth and rust destroy, and where thieves break in and steal. But store up for yourselves treasures in heaven, where moth and rust do not destroy, and where thieves do not break in and steal.[52]

Seek the kingdom of God above all else, and live righteously, and he will give you everything you need.[53]

Life is chockful of us trying to get things that don't matter, all while ignoring the things that do, driving our stories with Want, only stopping when forced to confront Need.

- Want drives the plot.
- Need drives the theme.[54]

Until it doesn't. Often in the late stages of the story, the character's choices become less about pursuing the Want, and more about fulfilling the Need.

Shrek decides that being alone is overrated and puts himself at risk to restore his community with Fiona and Donkey.

Sondheim's *Into the Woods* is really two stories. Act One is all about the Central Characters chasing (and getting) their selfish Wants. Act Two is paying the consequences of winning. Those who come out well at the end do so by choosing others over themselves. (The witch and court live to the end by choosing to save themselves — but I wouldn't say that they come out well.)

The Bond reboot *Casino Royale* plays with this in a very interesting way. Bond gets what he wants (Le Chiffre captured — so to speak); and he gets what he needs (to not be dead inside due to his job). The movie should be over at the end of the Le Chiffre storyline; but it rather awkwardly isn't done yet. Bond must now face the consequences of his

---

51. Ecclesiastes 2:11, NIV
52. Matthew 6:19, NIV
53. Matthew 6:33, NLT
54. Trottier refers to this as The Action Story and The Emotional Story.

win — and in doing so, loses his Need/soul once again. A Bond movie that is a tragedy (a deeper tribute to *On Her Majesty's Secret Service* — revisited in *No Time to Die*).[55]

Ultimately the Want — the driver of the plot — can be irrelevant. It is a device for the story, the ostensible reason for telling the tale, the reason the audience comes to see the show.

However, the Want is not the reason the audience leaves satisfied. We come for plot; that is the Want of the audience. The audience has its own Need, usually subconscious — and that Need is all about the Need of the characters. When the character's Need is met, the audience's Need is also met.

Emilio Estevez's *The Way* makes the irrelevance of Want a part of the story. Each character walks the Camino Santiago for their own reason — Sarah to quit smoking, Joost to lose weight, Jack to control his writer's voice again, and Tom — well Tom struggles to find his reason. To say goodbye to his son? As good a reason as any.

And at the end of the journey, as the quartet look out to sea, they all admit that their Want was irrelevant; the journey gave them their Need. Sarah still smokes, Joost has lost no weight. Jack has indeed found a voice — but with the realization he has no control. And Tom, rather than saying goodbye to his son, becomes his son.[56]

The Want gets us on the journey to the destination of the Need.

Character Flaw

Here's another bit of structure to draw from our look at Want vs Need. Want is blocked by the antagonist.

Need is blocked by the Central Character's main flaw.

---

55. If you want to revisit the original books, I recommend David Tennant reading *On Her Majesty's Secret Service*. Bond goes from misogynist to a man capable of true love, even partnership. And then it is taken away. "There's no hurry, you see. We've all the time in the world."

56. Ishmael, the gypsy father, tells Tom that our sons are the best and the worst part of ourselves. Tom's journey is in seeing the best part of his son and embracing that part of himself.

As we have seen, Need is the real deal. The audience will not cheer unless the Need is satisfied, no matter how much winning our hero accomplishes. And as the Need is an internal item, the battle for Need is an internal battle.

This is where Character Flaw comes in.

The Flaw is that character trait (or weakness) that prevents the Central Character from getting their Need — it is the internal antagonist.

If the Flaw is not confronted, the story becomes a tragedy.

Macbeth's flaw is ambition. ("I have no spur to prick the sides of my intent, but only vaulting ambition, which overleaps itself and fall on th' other.")[57] His ambition blinds him to the power of working with others and replaces it with the desire to rule.

- Joy (*Inside Out*) is controlling — which blinds her to the usefulness of the other emotions.
- Shrek and Alan Turing's (*The Imitation Game*) antisocial self-reliance keeps them from seeing the value of community.
- Lloyd's cynicism (*A Beautiful Day in the Neighborhood*) keeps him at arm's length from the healing power of forgiveness.
- Caroline's (*I and You*) snarky defense mechanism is the wall between herself and acceptance of others.

Ambition, pride, self-reliance, defense mechanisms — these traits aren't necessarily negative things. Joy's controlling nature has saved her girl on many occasions. Turing's self-reliance has allowed his genius to develop in a society that otherwise may have crushed him.

One of the lovely paradoxes of story and character is that our greatest strengths are often also our greatest flaws.

The eponymous Hamilton's pride and determination are key factors in the liberation of a nation. And his pride and determination are what makes him insist on publishing his affair — leading to his professional and personal ruin.

---

57. *Macbeth* Act One, Scene 7.

Dead to Me's Judy has optimism to spare — and this is what allows her to survive (relatively sanely) the abuses of her childhood. That optimism is also what propels her into a series of abusive relationships and situations.

Marta (*Knives Out*) has a sense of trust and selflessness, which is what allows her to be a shining light in a den of darkness. It is also what allows the initial death to occur, allows her to compromise her integrity to cover things up, and allows her to let a villain control the narrative of the action.

This is true in life as well as in story.

For example, attentive parenting is good; helicopter parenting adversely affects the child and puts one at risk for arrest in a college admissions scandal.

Character traits, then, are a bit more complicated than the labels of good and bad. They come in layers, which is a great storytelling tool — as well as a faith tool. Traits are strengths or weaknesses not based on the trait, but the action applied to the trait.

Is Saint Paul's zeal a good thing? That would depend on whether he is using that zeal to hunt down Christians, or to save the lives of his shipmates on the way to Malta. The very flaw that kept Paul from seeing the true God became the strength that opened the way to pursuing God.

All throughout Proverbs we hear that pride is bad.[58] Well, unless we take pride in our hard work (Ecclesiastes 3:22) or pride in our God (1 Corinthians 1:31, Galatians 6:14), or if it is God himself bragging on his son (Matthew 3:17). If one's pride is about arrogance — bad; if it is focused on others — good.

The key is usage. Any trait used for selfish gains can become a fatal flaw. The same trait turned over to God can become a source of power. Paul, referencing an ongoing conversation with God, says:

> *Each time [God] said, "My grace is all you need. My power works best in weakness." So now I am glad to boast about my weaknesses, so that the power of Christ can work through me.*[59]

---

58. Proverbs 8:13, 11:2, 16:18, 29:23
59. 2 Corinthians 12:9, NLT

So yet again, we see character tied with plot: what is the trait like in action? For it is only in action that we see whether a trait is a flaw blocking our Need, or a strength to help us get past ourselves and fulfill our Need.

CHAPTER TEN

Obstacle

We have looked at the first two elements necessary for story: hero and goal.

Dramatic Obstacle defined: the thing that hinders the Central Character's achievement of the Want

The obstacle can be a person (Voldemort) or situation (life as a convict) or nature (a volcano) or... Well, anything. And it could be (and often is) a combination of the above.

Jean Valjean (*Les Misérables*) has a situation (he is a convict on the run) and a person (Javert) that interfere with his desire to fulfill his promise to Fantine. Jack Dawson and Rose Bukater (*Titanic*) must face Cal Hockley, the class system, and an iceberg to come together.

Obstacles also come from within — a character's own flaw. Iago is the villain of *Othello*, but Othello's own flaw of jealousy is the ultimate weapon against himself.

Rarely is there only one full-on force of antagonism; complex stories require many steps towards a goal, and thus often provide many obstacles along the way.

- Caesar (*Dawn of the Planet of the Apes*) wants his tribe to live in peace. He has forces both within his tribe and within the world of man preventing him from achieving his goal.

- Dorothy has her share obstacles in *The Wizard of Oz* — crab apple trees, poppies, the Wizard, the monkeys, the castle guards, and the Wicked Witch herself.

- Burr is the ultimate antagonist of *Hamilton*; however, Alexander is rarely pitted directly against this foe. Instead, he must battle loyalists, the British army, General Lee, his own ego, Thomas Jefferson, James Madison, Mr. and Mrs. Reynolds, his own ego again — all before facing the final duel with Burr.

- Paul in the Bible had plenty of obstacles, from those opposed to his message to those whose livelihood he threatens to his own team (John Mark, anyone?). In his letters, he downplays the antagonism of flesh-and-blood enemies, plying us with principalities, powers, rulers of darkness, and spiritual hosts of wickedness. Not to mention the sin living inside us![60]

Obstacles, then, do not come in simple form. There often is a "big bad" — we will talk more about that (as well as minor obstacles) in our section on supporting characters. The key for writers is to use all the resources they have available to put their main character through theoretical hell to come out the others side. David Ball reminds us:

The better the play, the more the force of motivation (goal) is irresistible, and the more the obstacle is immovable.[61]

Obstacle is key for character growth — and we will dive into that deeper in our section on Character.

----

60. Romans 7:15-20
61. Ball, *Backwards and Forwards*

PART THREE

Five Part Story

CHAPTER ELEVEN

The Three Stories

Before I dive too deeply into plot, I should point out that every story really has three stories inside of it: Plot, Character, and Theme. Michael Arndt refers to these as Exterior, Interior, and Philosophical.

Each aspect — plot, character, and theme — is happening simultaneously, and weave in and out of each other. And they all develop with a structure — a beginning, a middle, and an end. At times they will travel at the same pace — a character growing at the same speed as he solves his quest, for example. Other times the plot will outpace the character or the theme. Loki is barely starting to understand the questions of the theme of the *Loki* television series before completing his quest; in fact, his lack of understanding *is* the final conflict of the season one finale.

Some stories give more emphasis to one of the three aspects — sometimes to the detriment of the telling (think of heavy-handed propaganda pieces), and sometimes to the benefit of the telling. Theater, with its emphasis on human connection, excels in Character driven storytelling. A piece like Lauren Gunderson's *I and You* has a lovely physical plot to keep things moving (the completion of the assignment); however, the physical plot is just a smoke screen for a much deeper metaphysical plot (the theme of acceptance), and the final requirement is one of character growth, not plot resolution.

Theater isn't exclusive to Character driven work. While film and television are typically more plot focused, several examples draw just as much on human connection — from the more obvious character-driven pieces like *Paterson* to the less obvious but equally character dependent stories like *Parasite*, *Parks & Recreation*, *Modern Family*, and *Jojo Rabbit*.

An understanding of the three stories helps elevate shows beyond their genre. *Die Hard* is a classic not just for its action, but by putting character arc alongside fisticuffs. Some of the best scenes are conversations between McClane and Powell. *Black Widow*, ostensibly an action flick, produces a thoughtfulness beyond the explosions with its themes of gender roles, trafficking, and family.

The play *The Christians* has a plot about a pastor who decides he doesn't believe in hell anymore; audiences who exit the theater debating the existence of hell have misunderstood the real story of the play — the themes of power and authority as they intersect with relationship (professional, partner, and family). The play is so much more than plot and character; it balances the three stories to provoke all the more (in such a good way).

And when the Plot, Character, and Theme intersect — well, you have beautiful moments of storytelling. Michael Arndt reminds us that the most effective endings are when the storylines of the plot, character, and theme resolve close to each other. Think of the penultimate conflict of *A Quiet Place* — what I will call the battle of the pickup truck. The Abbott family has been dealing with the guilt each carries over the death of Beau, each blaming themselves. Lee is so wrapped in guilt, he can't see the emotional needs of his remaining children.

Lee's character Need is to see his daughter (all his family really) — to really see her, not through a lens of protector or father. His arc has a beginning (distance after the death of Beau), a middle (being confronted by his son — this is how Regan thinks you see her), and an end (completed with "I love you. I have always loved you"). Lee's Need is resolved at the same time as the thematic question is resolved — choosing love over guilt. The scene sets up the final battle (the battle of the hearing aid squeal). In fact, dealing with her father's resolution helps Regan resolve the plot issue — the final confrontation with the aliens. The three stories come to a head in the same scene, giving a very satisfying resolve.

As I go through the next three sections on structure, keep in mind that while I am exploring plot, those same structure forms can be applied in the progressions of Character and of Theme.

CHAPTER TWELVE

The 5 Sentence Story Game

I want to start with a simple structure form that works for virtually every story. This structure applies to most of your favorite movies, plays, TV shows, and bedtime stories. I use this model for all my writing and teaching — the simplest insight into classical story structure I've yet to encounter.

Confession and lesson for us all: my big breakthrough in understanding story structure did not come from a class, seminar or even by studying scripts. It came from being in an improv company.[62]

As part of Taproot Theatre's improv team, I learned a training game called, "The Five Sentence Story." The game was designed for rehearsal to ingrain the progress of story into the players, so when we were in performance, we would always know how to move a story forward.

The game goes like this. The team stands in a circle. One player starts by giving an opening sentence to a story. The next person in line gives the next sentence, the next adds a third. Another gives the fourth, and then the fifth person wraps up the story with one more sentence.

Then the team politely applauds — because the heart of improv is support of each other.

---

62. Note that I did due diligence, applying the theory to countless scripts, developing it through multiple classes, and vetting it with professional writers and teachers. But the breakthrough "aha" moment came from improv.

The next person in line starts a new story, moving through five players. Applause, and repeat until the team gets tired of the game and wants to move on.

The key here isn't just to come up with five random sentences in a "stump the fifth guy" kind of way. Rather, each sentence has a specific function and must fulfill that function to make a strong story.

Each sentence has a name:

1. Balance
2. Unbalance
3. Quest
4. Crisis
5. New Balance

Balance

BALANCE: Establishes the Central Character and the normal situation

The opening for the game is meant to be very simple — the game is not designed for cleverness or trickery.

Who is the story about, and what are they doing? A Want may be introduced, or not.

The keys for success in a Balance:

1. The Central Character appears

Pretty straightforward, right? Yet you would be surprised at the number of scripts that I've seen where the writer doesn't quite figure out who their Central Character is until somewhere in the middle of Act Two.

2. Normal for this story is established

The "Normal" should be the normal for *this* story — not necessarily normal anywhere else. The Balance in *The Addams Family* will show that loving monsters enjoy killing and gently terrorizing the neighbors. That may not be normal for you and me, but it is normal for the Addams'.

War stories usually start with the normal of being at war; a western may show that the gang of bank-robbers runs the town; a romance may start with the notion that everybody has someone — except our hero.

~

I will track with two simple "Five Sentence Story" tales:

The Dog Story

Balance: Suzie walks down the street with her dog.

Very clean — we have a Central Character (Suzie) and a normal world (she walks her dog).

The Lunch Story

Balance: Ted walks to his favorite diner for lunch.

Note how simple the Balance can be. Central Character (Ted) in the midst of the story's normal (going to a diner for lunch).

Unbalance

UNBALANCE: Something happens that unbalances the normal world

There are three keys to a good Unbalance:

1. The Unbalance is an event

"Something happens." The Unbalance is going to be an intrusion into the life of the story — so it won't be a random thought ("Suzie wondered if she should get a cat"), rather it will be something that happens.

2. The event happens to the Central Character

The Central Character is the one who is going to go on the journey as a result of the Unbalance, so the event should affect them. Otherwise, we are telling the wrong story. In the Dog Story, "Suddenly Frank realized his pants were on fire" would be an exciting twist, but not relevant to Suzie's story.

3. The Unbalance unbalances the normal world

As the title implies, the normal must be upset at this point. An event that happens that involves Suzie but doesn't apply to the established normal world is a distraction not an Unbalance — and a sign of a poor Balance or Unbalance. If the Unbalance happens to Suzy and she can continue walking down the street with her dog, then not much has been unbalanced — and we have the low stakes talked about in the prior section.

Often an Unbalance that does not unbalance is an issue with the Balance and not the Unbalance. Often, we writers start our story following the wrong thing. When working with authors, I often encourage them to relook at the Balance before tossing out an Unbalance that isn't working.

The Dog Story

Balance: Suzie walks down the street with her dog.
Unbalance: Suddenly, the dog breaks the leash and runs into the park.
Something happens (dog breaks the leash) to our Central Character, and her world is thrown a curve.

The Lunch Story

Balance: Ted walks to his favorite diner for lunch.
Unbalance: The diner is closed!
This is a very simple yet effective Unbalance. Ted's day is about lunch at the diner — and that day has been foiled.

Quest

QUEST: The Central Character does something to restore balance

The keys, as you can guess the pattern:
1. The Quest must be an action

We are using this model to move the story forward — a Central Character with nothing to do does not move the story forward, hence we are looking for an action.

2. Quest must be done by the Central Character

And again — let's keep the Central Character central. I recently worked with a student who had a script that followed a format you might be familiar with: A woman living out her life (Balance) is captured by an evildoer (Unbalance). Then a young, heroic male sets out to save her!

See what happened there? We had a story about a woman who is now a story about a man. Sexist, misogynistic? Maybe. But the real point is that this is bad storytelling.

3. The Quest must be direct to restoring the problem of the Unbalance

The third key is a very, very common trap that undermines many a story: forgetting about the Unbalance. The dreaded Act Two problem (how do I fill out my story?) is often solved by finding things for the hero to do. Which can be good — if those things are moving the story forward rather than starting new stories.

Suppose in the Quest of the Dog Story, Suzie decides to go and see if Frank's pants are on fire and help him put out the blaze. That may be interesting; may even be more exciting than dealing with a runaway dog. But it would not be right for this story.

Not to say that one can't find a variety of actions and still stay focused. In fact, the job of the writer is to find focused variety.

Shrek has a bunch of mythical creatures dumped into his forest (Unbalance) and he sets out to get them gone. Soon he will be on a quest to save a princess from a dragon. Note, however, that the writers have indeed kept us on track: Shrek is on quest to save a princess because this action will restore balance; succeed and Farquaad will remove the creatures from his swamp.

The Dog Story

Balance: Suzie walks down the street with her dog.
Unbalance: Suddenly, the dog breaks the leash and runs into the park.

Quest: Suzie runs after her dog, yelling, "Fifi, Fifi! Come back!"

The Central Character (Suzie) does something (runs and yells) to restore balance.

The Lunch Story

Balance: Ted walks to his favorite diner for lunch.

Unbalance: The diner is closed!

Quest: Ted breaks into the diner to make himself lunch.

Crisis

CRISIS: Something happens that prevents/blocks the Quest from working

In some variations of the game, the word "Climax" is used instead of "Crisis." I prefer the latter, as it helps avoid skipping an important element in the storytelling: the hero must lose. We will get into that later; for now, it's enough to know that writers who are nice people struggle with putting real conflict into their stories.

Forcing oneself to put in a full block to the Quest helps us to keep the story from being undermined by niceness.

The keys for the Crisis:

1. It is an action — something happens

A common key — but important. Let's not run out of steam just when the action is heating up! The hero doesn't just stop, or peter out, or lose focus. There are forces of antagonism at play; let them play!

2. The block is direct to the Quest

The Crisis isn't just an inconvenience or distraction; the Quest is blocked. In the Quest, the writer may be tempted to give unrelated tasks to the Central Character to fill out the story. Here is the Crisis-temptation: filling out the story by creating unrelated problems.

Each step should lead naturally to the next step: because of the Unbalance, the Quest happens; because of the Quest, the Crisis comes into play. Anything else, and we are just meandering, rather than following a plot.

3. The block works

Another temptation is to introduce false or weak blocks. As has been said and will be said again before this book is over — a weak obstacle equals a weak story.

How the Central Character comes out of the Crisis is going to determine how our story ends. We shouldn't be afraid of earning that ending! So, the Crisis works, and the hero is blocked.

The Dog Story

Balance: Suzie walks down the street with her dog.

Unbalance: Suddenly, the dog breaks the leash and runs into the park.

Quest: Suzie runs after her dog, yelling, "Fifi, Fifi! Come back!"

Crisis: A policeman grabs Suzie and says, "You can't walk on the grass!"

An action that directly blocks Suzie's attempt to run after her dog.

The Lunch Story

Balance: Ted walks to his favorite diner for lunch.

Unbalance: The diner is closed!

Quest: Ted breaks into the diner to make himself lunch.

Crisis: The police show up and arrest Ted.

Ted doesn't get lunch — can nothing go right? Let's see in the:

New Balance

NEW BALANCE: As a result of the Central Character's actions, a new balance is put into place

My additions to the game are the words: "as a result of the Central Character's actions..." We are putting the Climax into the New Balance, which keeps the idea of Climax in Act Three in our brains — but I am getting ahead of myself. For purposes of this game, what the Central Character does in response to the Crisis is what leads us to the resulting new world.

Keys:

1. There is some sort of balance put in place

Note the wishy-washy language: "some sort of". This is reflective of what we talked about with Balance — the Balance is normal for this story, not necessarily normal in another setting.

This is true of the ending as well; the new world does not have to conform to any expectations of the audiences (or studios, publishers, teachers...). The point is that the world has its new normal — the story set into motion in the Unbalance has concluded its pattern.

This may mean that the guy gets the girl, or the guy loses the girl, or the guy and the girl both commit suicide and the feuding families must deal with the mess.

Mark Twain's short story "A Medieval Romance" puts his main character into an impossible situation. So impossible that Twain abruptly ends his story with:

> *[The remainder of this thrilling and eventful story will NOT be found in this or any other publication, either now or at any future time.]*

> *The truth is, I have got my hero (or heroine) into such a particularly close place, that I do not see how I am ever going to get him (or her) out of it again—and therefore I will wash my hands of the whole business and leave that person to get out the best way that offers—or else stay there. I thought it was going to be easy enough to straighten out that little difficulty, but it looks different now.*

Needless to say, this is not a good New Balance. The story is abandoned rather than fulfilled. The idea is to complete the pattern. (Twain is aware of this and is thus having fun tweaking the noses of his readers.)

Trilogies are a good place to look at this principle in action. At the end of *The Fellowship of the Ring*, there are many issues unanswered. However, this is not the story of "The Final End of the Ring," rather it is the story of "The Fellowship." The Fellowship is abandoned; Frodo and company are now in a new normal; the pattern is complete.

If Peter Jackson and company opted to end the movie in the mines of Moria, you know, for a real good cliffhanger — that would have been a poor New Balance.

Star Wars: The Empire Strikes Back ends with Han captured, Leia on the run, and Luke handless. (He lost a hand, but gained a father. What, too soon?) Perhaps a lousy ending if the movie were called *Luke Defeats the Dark Side*. However, this is the movie about Luke confronting Vader; he confronted Vader and lost. Pattern closed, new normal in place.

The television show *Alias* (and many others, but *Alias* does it well enough for the shout out) would often mess with the pattern by ending an episode in the peak moment of the Climax. The next episode would pick up exactly where the prior left off and play out through the New Balance before starting in on the new storyline. J.J. Abrams (creator of *Alias*) could get away with this as the audience knew the story pattern would be complete within a week.

Not completing a story creates unrest in the audience — if you don't believe me, stop reading to a child before Sam-I-Am gets his friend to try green eggs and ham. This unrest, so the theory goes, drives the audience to see the next episode.

If the audience is patient enough. Waiting a week can be hard (binge TV has figured this out), waiting until next season even more so. Personally, I have lost interest in who shot who over the summer months on many a show. Waiting a few years? This is why movies that seem to end on cliffhangers really complete the pattern — just leaving another chapter in the story to tell.

The Fellowship of the Ring, then, finds that just-right balance — giving us a complete journey *and* a yearning to see what happens next.

2. The New Balance must be New

This is the key of all keys. We have gone on a journey, and therefore must land in a new place. New circumstance, character growth, character decrease, new understanding... Without the "new," the journey has lost its value.

We start with Claudius as king of Denmark, the old king dead, and Hamlet all mopey. We end with the old king revenged, the new king dead, and, well...everyone including Hamlet also dead.

We start with Shrek alone, Fiona imprisoned, and the kingdom under the thumb of an evil ruler. We end with Shrek in community, Fiona free (of the dragon and Farquuad), and the kingdom free of tyranny.

We go from normal to new — that is the journey of story.

The Dog Story

1. Balance: Suzie walks down the street with her dog.
2. Unbalance: Suddenly, the dog breaks the leash and runs into the park.
3. Quest: Suzie runs after her dog, yelling, "Fifi, Fifi! Come back!"
4. Crisis: A policeman grabs Suzie and says, "You can't walk on the grass!"
5. New Balance: Suzie gazes into the policeman's eyes, he gazes into hers, they fall in love, get married, and buy a new dog!

Note the newness — we do not end with Suzie walking down the street with Fifi; we have gone on a journey.

When I use this story, I am often challenged, "But what about Fifi?" What happened to Fifi is not at issue; this is not Fifi's story. Fifi's story will have to wait until the sequel. (One class dubbed that untold sequel, "Fifi's Revenge." I can only imagine what those students were thinking.)

The Lunch Story

1. Balance: Ted walks to his favorite diner for lunch.
2. Unbalance: The diner is closed!
3. Quest: Ted breaks into the diner to make himself lunch.
4. Crisis: The police show up and arrest Ted.
5. New Balance: Ted has lunch in his prison cell.

Ted finally gets lunch, just not in the way he planned. New Balance established; story complete.

CHAPTER THIRTEEN

Five Part Story

The Five Sentence Story game gives us a simple view of classic story structure. Most every story fits into this pattern: Balance, Unbalance, Quest, Crisis, and New Balance. In a moment of extravagant creativity, I call this the Five Part Story. Here are a few examples:

The Parable of the Persistent Widow[63]

A widow lived in town (Balance)
and had a grievance. (Unbalance)
So, she pestered the judge to give her justice, (Quest)
however, he refused. (Crisis)
She persisted in pestering, until she was given relief. (New Balance)

Green Eggs and Ham

Guy-I-Am[64] lives a life free of trying new things. (Balance)

Sam-I-Am interrupts that life, pressuring Guy-I-Am to try green eggs and ham. (Unbalance)

Guy-I-Am provides argument upon argument against trying said meal, (Quest)

---

63. Luke 18:1-5

64. Not named in the book, but for convenience I'll use the character name given in adaptations.

to no avail, as Sam-I-Am keeps coming at him. (Crisis)

Guy-I-Am breaks down and tries the dish, and decides he really likes this new thing. (New Balance)

Hamlet

Hamlet is a prince in Denmark, under rule of his uncle, the king. (Balance)

A ghost appears to Hamlet and accuses the king of murdering Hamlet's father. (Unbalance)

Hamlet sets out to prove his uncle's guilt and exact revenge. (Quest)

Hamlet is banished for murder before he can get his revenge. (Crisis)

Hamlet returns, and in a duel kills the king — while also causing the death of his mother and himself. (New Balance)

Zoey's Extraordinary Playlist "Pilot"

Zoey is struggling to get a promotion at work, as well as deal with her dying father. (Balance)

During a freak accident, Zoey is given the power to hear the private thoughts and feelings of others through song. (Unbalance)

Zoey sets out to help those whose songs she hears, including coworkers and her own father; (Quest)

however, her coworkers and family reject Zoey's offers of help. (Crisis)

Zoey insists, pushing through their arguments, and gives her father a day of happiness and secures the promotion at work. (New Balance)

Toy Story

Andy's favorite, Woody, rules over Andy's toys. (Balance)

Buzz arrives, threatening Woody's position, and Woody is accused of murdering Buzz when the space man gets knocked out of a window. (Unbalance)

Woody heads out to return Buzz to prove he is a good person. (Quest)

Woody and Buzz get captured by Sid. (Crisis)

After escaping Sid, Woody gets Buzz back to the family as they are moving, ready to share the spotlight. (New Balance)

~

Of course, story has more complexity and nuance than shown here. The Five Part Story is just a set of building blocks, a starting point to help our overview of story. In the next two sections, I will use those building blocks to look at short form and long form storytelling. Then in the next part, we will start adding the much-needed detail and distinctions of more mature story structure.

Five Part Story for Shorts

The Five Part Story is a great outline for creating short films and plays, mostly following our standard form with a simple expansion in the middle. Rather than a single Quest and Crisis, the typical short adds a series of tactics (ways to achieve the Quest) each of which is blocked or only partially succeeds (Crisis), until the story reaches a climactic moment that forces a New Balance.

The structure for a short would then look like this:

1. Balance (normal world and Central Character)
2. Unbalance (something happens...)
3. Quest One (the first attempt to restore balance)
4. Crisis One (the first attempt is blocked or only partially succeeds)
5. Quest Two (the second attempt)
6. Crisis Two (the second block)
7. Quest Three (the third attempt — often a final push)
8. Climax (resulting in a final block or success)
9. New Balance (where we see the result of the action)

Three is a standard number of attempts (Quests), but there is no hard and fast rule on how many Quests to have. (See Appendix B: The Number Three for more on, well, the number three.)

Examples of Expanded Five Part Story for Shorts format:

The Good Samaritan

- **Balance**: A man travels the road from Jericho.
- **Unbalance**: Robbers attack him and leave him for dead.
- **Quest One**: The man tries to get help from a passing priest.
- **Crisis One**: The priest crosses to the other side of the road.
- **Quest Two**: The man tries to get help from a Levite.
- **Crisis Two**: The Levite passes by on the other side.
- **Quest Three**: The man tries to get help from a Samaritan.
- **Climax**: The Samaritan takes pity on the man, binds his wounds, and takes him to an inn.
- **New Balance**: The man stays at the inn under the care of the innkeeper.

Pretty straightforward. Here is another example using the popular Pixar short "For the Birds" along with my commentary.

"For the Birds" (Pixar)[65]

- **Balance**: Bully[66] and the other little birds come together on the wire, bickering, and making fun.
- **Unbalance**: A big bird lands near them and attempts to join them.
- **Quest One**: The little birds mock the big bird to get him to leave.
- **Crisis One**: The mocking does not work, as the big bird doesn't seem to understand their mocking.
- **Quest Two**: The little birds move away from the big bird.
- **Crisis Two**: The big bird flies over and joins them in the middle of the wire.
- **Quest Three**: The little birds attempt to knock the big bird off the wire.

---

65. "For the Birds," written and directed by Ralph Eggleston, is available on Disney+, and may be found on DVD and other sources such as Amazon.

66. No name appears in the film; Disney.Fandom.com names the lead bird as "Bully."

- **Climax**: They succeed! And as a result, are twanged up into the air.
- **New Balance**: The little birds are now on the ground, featherless, and are objects of ridicule.

A few notes on the nearly perfect "For the Birds." The first important thing to note is that the Central Character is not the likable big bird, but rather the despicable Bully and his cronies. As stated earlier, hero for story purposes is not the most likable character, but rather the character whose actions we follow.

Note that there are three Quests/attempts/tactics. This is very common in Pixar shorts.

The final crisis — the Climax — is marked by success. A wonderful tool for the writer with a Central Character needing to learn a lesson is to give them exactly what they want. The comeuppance is in having to deal with the consequences of their own success.

God tells the Psalmist:

> "Listen to me, O my people, while I give you stern warnings... But no, my people wouldn't listen. Israel did not want me around. So, I let them follow their own stubborn desires, living according to their own ideas."[67]

In other words, God's punishment for not listening isn't God doling out punishment at all. The punishment is that we get to follow our desires. We get what we want! And must suffer the consequences, of course.

Paul reiterates this idea in Romans chapter one. God showed his anger, according to Paul, by letting ("abandoning") men pursue their sinful ways. What we then do to each other is an obvious punishment.

So rather than thwart the actions of our wicked characters, we should strongly consider allowing them to win — and face the consequences.

- Macbeth gets away with killing the king.
- Mark (*The Social Network*) can separate the others from his company.

---

67. Psalm 81:8, 11-12, NLT

- The Kim family (*Parasite*) successfully infiltrates the Park's home.
- Walter White (*Breaking Bad*) can build his crime empire.

One more example of the Five Part Story for Shorts:

"The Present"[68]

- **Balance**: Jake spends his days inside, playing video games and feeling sorry for himself.
- **Unbalance**: His mom presents him with a puppy, a deformed puppy.
- **Quest One**: Jake tosses the puppy aside.
- **Crisis One**: The puppy comes right back to Jake.
- **Quest Two**: Jake kicks the puppy with a "Get lost!"
- **Crisis Two**: The puppy brings a ball to Jake to play with.
- **Quest Three**: Jake kicks the ball away.
- **Climax**: The puppy persists (adorably so), struggling to bring the ball back.
- **New Balance**: Jake gives in and goes outside to continue to play with the puppy.

~

A key to a successful short work is keeping the Balance and the Unbalance as brief as possible. A great advantage to working in shorts is that the audience comes in with lower expectations — so one can get away with a lot.

The downside is that the audience does expect things to happen sooner and faster. Seconds become significant chunks of time in a five- or ten-minute piece. So, with the Balance, give only the information needed to kick-start the story.

---

68. As of this writing, Jacob Frey's short film is available on his Vimeo site and on Amazon Prime.

Linda Cowgill says, "In a short screenplay, every word, every line must advance the action and reveal only what is necessary for us to understand the characters and the story."[69]

So don't linger, don't give extraneous information, and don't give information that can be doled out later.[70]

"The Present" doesn't tell us how the boy (or the puppy) got hurt or how long he has been in this condition. We don't even know that he has a condition until the Climax — and we don't need to know until then. The present is dropped in front of him 30 seconds into the short, and the first 30 seconds include the opening credits.

"For the Birds" gives us a few seconds of the smaller birds landing and bickering before the world is unbalanced. And the Unbalance itself (the arrival of the big bird) takes only a few more seconds. The film gets to the action right away.

Some short films/plays/webisodes start after the Balance — good advice if the Balance can be assumed. A Road Runner/Looney Tunes cartoon rarely gives any Balance or Unbalance — the audience knows that prior to the start, Wile E. Coyote was hungry, and the Road Runner ran by — Balance and Unbalance. Also in the Looney Tunes sphere, "Rabbit of Seville" starts with Elmer Fudd already chasing after Bugs Bunny — no need for a setup.

On the flip side, in "Long-Haired Hare," which pits Bugs against the classical tenor, time is taken to set up the reason for "this means war." We have Bugs playing his banjo, and the tenor breaking his instrument. So, we play out the Balance (Bugs is at his home playing his banjo), and the Unbalance (the tenor stops him). The pattern is repeated with a harp, and a tuba (three times, the number of completion). Michael Maltese (writer) and Chuck Jones (director) know that Bugs is about to prank the poor tenor to extreme lengths; it is important that the audience be fully on the rabbit's side at the start, otherwise the punishment

---

69. Cowgill, *Writing Short Films*

70. For another improv game (CROW) that can help in giving clarity and succinct exposition, see Appendix C.

will come across as mean. The proper Balance instills us with the feeling that the character is getting his just desserts.

The principle of sticking to essentials applies to the New Balance as well — too much time spent here detracts from the story and risks undercutting the power of the ending. What do we need to know to fully understand and appreciate the new world? "The Present" gives us the boy making a throw outside — which is all we need. He is outside, he is interacting with the puppy — he is going to be okay.

"For the Birds" gives us time to see the first bird land and realize he is now naked. A few seconds of the rest of the birds falling and scrambling for cover — and we know that the comeuppance has been delivered.

The length of the opening and closing is a balancing act (apologies for the pun). Too much and the audience is distracted; too little and the audience is lost. New writers tend to err on the side of too much — a distrust of the audience's ability to fill in the blanks. Unfortunately, that distrust comes through, easily offending (and boring!) the viewer.

Five Part Story for Features and Plays

The Five Part Story also works well with full/feature-length works in theater, film, and television. I find it especially useful as a writer in finding the meat of my story. There is an old mantra: "If you cannot summarize your story in a concise way, you don't know what story you are telling." Putting a script I am working on into its five parts is a great way to test if I know what story I am telling.

For features, rather than starting with the Balance it is more useful to start in the middle by finding the main action. What is the core of the story, in a simple sentence? This exercise means cutting away "all that happens" to focus on the one (or two, as we shall see) action that summarizes the plot.

Using *Macbeth* as our example, there are many things that happen in the story, including:

- Mac hears a prophecy from the witches.
- Mac and his wife plot to kill the king.

- The king arrives.
- Mac and his wife kill the king.
- Mac gets nervous about Banquo.
- Mac has Banquo murdered.
- Mac sees Banquo's ghost.

And on and on.

Of the things that happen, what is the action that is the core of the story? To put it another way, if you had one sentence to tell a friend the plot of Macbeth, what would you say? Would you say, "*Macbeth* is the story of a guy who has a king stay at his castle?"

Likely not. Instead, you might say, "*Macbeth* is the story of a man who forces his way to becoming and staying king."

Here are other examples:

- *The Martian*: about a man stranded on Mars who does everything to survive
- *Glass Menagerie*: about a mother desperate to set up her shy daughter with a husband
- *Mad Max: Fury Road*: about a man helping a group of women escape their captors in a post-apocalyptic world
- *Spider-Man: No Way Home*: about a boy trying to collect and return a series of villains that have entered his universe

Note how these simple sentences begin to encapsulate the whole of the story. They are not complete, don't have the juicy details that makes the play/movie exciting, don't contain a lot of character — which is exactly as it should be. Remember, we are working on skeleton; muscle, blood, nervous system, and skin all will come later.

Once we have the core, we can use that to build out our five parts. For this example, let's use a simply plotted movie: *Taken*. I like using this example as it is straightforward, even for people who haven't seen the movie. One can usually guess each piece with ease. If you haven't seen the movie, here is an online description:

Bryan Mills (Liam Neeson), a former government operative, is trying to reconnect with his daughter, Kim (Maggie Grace). Then his worst fears become real when sex slavers abduct Kim and her friend shortly after they arrive in Paris for vacation. With just four days until Kim will be auctioned off, Bryan must call on every skill he learned in black ops to rescue her.

If I wanted a friend to see the movie, I wouldn't start with, "It's about a father trying to reconnect with his daughter." That's just the set up. The core is Mills setting out to save his daughter. Now that we have the core, we have the quest:

- Quest: Mills sets out to save his daughter.

Next, we move backwards and forwards to find the rest of the five part story. We know that the Quest is the Central Character doing something to restore balance. What happens that causes Mills to have to save her daughter?

The title says it all.

- Unbalance: Mills' daughter is taken.
- Quest: Mills sets out to save his daughter.

He only has to save her because she was taken. Note that we keep things in terms of the Central Character. Therefore, the Unbalance is not, "Kim is taken" but "Mills' daughter is taken."

Now we can go forward and ask, "What blocks the Quest from succeeding?" Again, not hard to guess that the kidnappers fight back.

- Unbalance: Mills' daughter is taken.
- Quest: Mills sets out to save his daughter.
- Crisis: The kidnappers fight back and capture Mills.

Since I've seen the film, I'll add the tidbit about Mills being captured. Now we have our middle, so let's ask, "How does it turn out?"

Even if you haven't seen the movie, the fact that there are two sequels suggests an ending:

- Unbalance: Mills' daughter is taken.
- Quest: Mills sets out to save his daughter.
- Crisis: The kidnappers fight back and capture Mills.
- New Balance: Mills saves and reunites with his daughter.

Now we have the last thing, what is the first thing: how did it all begin? We can assume that it starts with Kim untaken, so that she can be taken in the Unbalance. We also know that the opening needs to be in terms of the Central Character (so "Kim is not taken" does not give us a good Balance). Also, the New Balance must be new.

Which is why the "trying to reconnect with his daughter" is a good choice on the filmmakers' part. What makes the New Balance new becomes an emotional rather than physical thing. The plot is going to be about Mills physically saving his daughter. The heart is going to be about Mills emotionally saving the relationship with his daughter.

- Balance: Mills tries to reconnect with his alienated daughter.
- Unbalance: Mills' daughter is taken.
- Quest: Mills sets out to save his daughter.
- Crisis: The kidnappers fight back and capture Mills.
- New Balance: Mills saves and reunites with his daughter.

Simple, streamlined, and ready to add all the elements that make the story exciting and fulfilling.

Well, almost ready.

~

Remember how for short film, we adapted our Five Part Story by adding Quests and Crises to fill out the action? We also need to adapt the Five Part Story for Feature/Full-length works. But rather than focus on the beat by beat, we want to remain at a bird's eye view of the script.

Often our main action summaries only describe half the story. Typically, the Central Character sets out in a direction, then meets with a Midpoint that changes the direction. Note how *Macbeth* is really in two parts: Mac killing to become king, and then the actions he needs to take to stay king.

The pattern we see here is a two-part Quest, a two-part middle sentence: the hero does this, but then this happens, and the hero must now do this. In essence, our Quest sentence becomes a compound sentence: Quest, Midpoint Crisis, New Quest; Central Character does this, but this happens, so Central Character now does this.

- *Toy Story* Quest: Woody sets out to return Buzz, but when they are captured by Sid, he must save Buzz and himself from Sid's house.

- *Three Billboards Outside Ebbing, Missouri* Quest: Mildred tries to force the police to solve the murder of her daughter, but when Chief Willoughby dies, she must find a new way to get revenge.

- *Thor: Ragnorak* Quest: Thor attempts to escape from the Battle planet, and when he discovers Hela has taken over Asgard, he must win his home back from her.

- *War for the Planet of the Apes* Quest: Caesar sets out to get revenge on the humans, but when he discovers his tribe has been captured, he sets out to find a way for them all to escape.

Notice that in each case, the second half of the story relates to the first half. We aren't looking for a new start or new story, but a natural escalation: because of the actions of the first Quest, we now must move into Quest part two.

∿

Other key changes for Five Part Story for Feature/Full-Length are the Crisis and New Balance — and how to fit the Climax in there.

For Crisis, I recommend that you focus on the event that happens that prevents the second action in the Quest from succeeding. For example, in *Top Gun: Maverick*, the first action of the Quest is to train the pilots; the second action of the Quest is to lead the pilots into the danger zone and destroy the base. The Crisis would be the thing that blocks the second Quest; therefore, the Crisis for the movie is Maverick being shot down behind enemy lines.

The temptation is to rush to the Climactic battle; however, we are still in blocking mode. Something should happen that fully defeats the goal of the Central Character. (We will dig deeper into this when we discuss events.) The decision taken by the protagonist coming out of the Crisis will determine the Climax. In our example, Maverick decides to escape, leading to the final battle with the enemy fighters.

We want to put the Climax, then, into the New Balance. Summarize the result of the Climax, add "and now," and summarize the New Balance.

In our *Taken* example, the climax is as simple as "Mills saves his daughter." *Toy Story* might be, "Woody escapes from Sid's house." *Macbeth*: "Macbeth fights the opposing army, losing his life to Macduff." The win or loss then naturally leads to our New Balance, our new normal.

Top Gun: Maverick's full New Balance sentence would read: Rooster returns to save Maverick, and the duo steal a plane and shoot down the enemy fighters; and now Maverick continues his work on his planes with Rooster and Penny at his side.

So, our formula for the Five Part Story for Feature/Full-Length looks like this:

- BALANCE
- UNBALANCE
- QUEST Central Character does this, *but this happens,* so the Central Character does this (In essence: "Quest, Crisis, New Quest")
- CRISIS The block of the second Quest
- NEW BALANCE Climax *and* New Balance

Let's dig into three detailed examples:

Five Part Story: *The Shape of Water*

In the process of breaking down this Oscar-winning Best Picture,[71] I started with a summary of the main plot.

- Elisa plans the jailbreak of the Amphibian Man out of a secret government facility.

Right away, one would notice that this only accounts for half of the film. We don't have the time spent in the apartment, falling in love,

---

71. Among the many accolades, the picture received thirteen Oscar nominations (including Best Screenplay), winner of four (including Best Picture).

and the final escape. So, I revised my summary, providing for our Quest statement:

- Quest: Elisa plans the jailbreak of the Amphibian Man from a secret government facility; once the plan succeeds, she hides the Amphibian Man in her apartment while scheming to get him to permanent safety.

A step backwards[72] provides the next question: "What makes Elisa go on this quest?" The capture of the Amphibian Man would be an obvious answer; however, it doesn't center on our Central Character. So instead:

- Unbalance: Elisa discovers that the government is experimenting on the Amphibian Man.

Now jumping forward, "What prevents the second half of the Quest from success?"

- Crisis: The Amphibian Man becomes ill, and the government agent discovers Elisa has the Amphibian Man and comes for her.

Pushing forward again, "How does this all turn out?" We are looking for the result of the Crisis (the Climax), followed by the result of the Climax.

- New Balance: Elisa sacrifices herself to save the Amphibian Man; he kills the agent, heals Elisa (revealing she is one of his race), and the two swim off for a new life together.

The sacrifice, death of the agent, and healing summarizes the Climax; the two swimming off summarizes the New Balance.

Now all we have left is the Balance — and ensuring that the New Balance is indeed "new" in comparison to where we started.

- Balance: Elisa, a lonely woman who doesn't know where she came from, works as a janitor at a secret government facility.

And now in order:

- Balance: Elisa, a lonely woman who doesn't know where she came from, works as a janitor at a secret government facility.

---

72. Reminder that you can go backwards or forwards. You can even start at any point that might be an easier entry into the story. Most stories will be easier to start in the middle — most not all.

- Unbalance: Elisa discovers that the government is experimenting on the Amphibian Man.
- Quest: Elisa plans the jailbreak of the Amphibian Man from a secret government facility; once the plan succeeds, she hides the Amphibian Man in her apartment while scheming to get him to permanent safety.
- Crisis: The Amphibian Man becomes ill, and the government agent discovers Elisa has the Amphibian Man and comes for her.
- New Balance: Elisa sacrifices herself to save the Amphibian Man; he kills the agent, heals Elisa (revealing she is one of his race), and the two swim off for a new life together.

Hamlet

The play about the melancholy prince is often seen as a revenge play. So, it would be easy to think of the core as about revenge. However, Hamlet waits until the second half of the play to seek his opening for revenge (first instance is at Claudius' prayer closet, scene two of act three). So, what's all that running around in the first half?

From the moment the ghost accuses Claudius of regicide, Hamlet gets busy, mostly setting out to prove that the ghost is telling the truth. Once Claudius' guilt is proven (the play is the thing!), Hamlet can act on his revenge.

- Main action: Hamlet sets out to prove Claudius murdered his father. Hamlet seeks revenge on Claudius.

We are still missing something; what about England, and Ophelia's death — Hamlet seems to be going about getting revenge is a very circuitous way.

Here's where we need to ask — what is the "but when this happens" that interrupts Quest Part One and Quest Part Two? In this case, it is the death of Polonius — which forces Hamlet to rethink his strategy. This is the monkey wrench that alters the direction of the plot.

- Quest: Hamlet sets out to prove his uncle committed murder; he succeeds, but in the process accidentally kills Polonius instead of the king and must evade punishment while finding a new way to get his revenge.

The rest now falls more easily into place: the normal for Hamlet — trying to move on with his life (Balance); the ghosts accusation kicking off the action (Unbalance); Laertes getting between Hamlet and the king (Crisis); the final fight (Climax) and resulting foreign power taking over Denmark (New Balance).

- Balance: Hamlet tries to move on with his life, grieving his father and bickering with the new king, his stepfather/uncle.

- Unbalance: Hamlet's dead father appears as a ghost and claims he was murdered!

- Quest: Hamlet sets out to prove his uncle committed murder; he succeeds, but in the process accidentally kills Polonius instead of the king and must evade punishment while finding a new way to get his revenge.

- Crisis: Laertes challenges Hamlet to a duel, and Hamlet must go through Laertes to get his revenge.

- New Balance: Hamlet defeats Laertes; in the process the king, the queen, and Laertes all die — now Hamlet is dead, and a new king is taking over the throne.

Fences

August Wilson's play is complex in its time jumps and multiple storylines. Troy's ups and downs with his two sons, wife, and brother all mirror each other to an extent, as the father tries to keep his family safe through total control.

Rose's story initially follows just behind Cory's; the first act ends with the midpoint shift of Cory's story (the fight with his father — strike one); act two's first scene ends with the midpoint shift of Rose's story — the admission by Troy of having an affair. The two switch positions as Rose embodies the Crisis for Troy, agreeing to raise Troy's illegitimate child at the cost of her estrangement as his wife. Cory then takes the focus of Troy's Climax, in the final fight leading to the son's expulsion from the home — completing Troy's tragic journey.

Fences in simplified Five Parts plays out like this:

- Balance: Troy works as a garbage man to provide for his son (Cory) and wife (Rose), all the while procrastinating in building the fence around their house intended to protect his family.

- Unbalance: Troy's son (Cory) announces that he is going to pursue a career playing football.

- Quest: Troy tries to protect his son from a disappointing career by covertly preventing Cory from playing football; but Cory discovers Troy's attempts, and soon after Rose learns about Troy's secret affair. Troy shifts to maintaining the family out of force of will, refusing to be distracted by input from his wife and son.

- Crisis: Troy's mistress dies in childbirth; Rose agrees to raise the child, but at the price of estrangement from Troy.

- New Balance: Cory has a final blowout fight with his father, resulting in Cory being kicked out of the home; after Troy's death, the broken family reunites behind the now completed fence to pay tribute to the complex, imperfect man.

Five Part Story for Television

Now let's apply the Five Part Story to television scripts.

Television has two main categories: the one-hour drama and the half-hour sitcom. Of course, variations abound — half-hour-long dramas and hour-long comedies (more common). The Five Part Story can be helpful in either scenario.

Network shows tend to be easier to evaluate, as they are neatly broken into acts to make space for the commercials. Each act drives to a cliffhanger-type moment, something dramatically big to keep the audience engaged through commercials.

The Balance is typically very short in television as we know these characters and understand their world from prior episodes. The New Balance is also short.

The midpoint break is typically a big twist, dividing the action into two parts akin to features. Thinking in terms of the detective procedural, the midpoint is often the place where they realize they were on the wrong trail, and now are heading in the right direction. For our Quest, we would summarize the first set of actions, summarize the midpoint twist, then summarize the second set of actions.

The penultimate break, the act before the end, tends to have a moment of all is lost that will then drive the final act climax.

Our Five Parts might look like this for a six-act drama:

- Balance: short setup, start of Act One (or teaser, if there is one)
- Unbalance: early part of Act One
- Quest Part One: summary of actions of Act One through Act Three
- Midpoint: the midpoint action that ends Act Three
- Quest Part Two: summary of actions of Act Four and Act Five
- Crisis: the actions at the end of Act Five
- New Balance: a summary of the Climax of Act Six and the results of the Climax

Here are some television examples:

Pushing Daisies: "The Pielette"

- Balance: Ned, destined to be alone, uses his gift to make pies and solve murders. (Act One)
- Unbalance: Ned discovers that his first love was killed. (End of Act One)

- Quest: Ned revives Chuck and must hide her[73] from Emerson (Act Two and Three); once she reveals herself (End of Act Three), Ned sets out to solve her murder. (Act Four)
- Crisis: The Plastic Sack Killer — the person who killed Chuck — is going to kill Chuck's aunts! (End of Act Five)
- New Balance: Ned and Chuck defeat the killer; Ned, no longer alone, makes pies and solves murders with Chuck. (Act Six)

Zoey's Extraordinary Playlist: "Pilot"

- Balance: Zoey struggles to keep her life together: working for a promotion at her job and crushing on a coworker, all while dealing with the terminal illness of her near-immobile father. (Act One)
- Unbalance: When an MRI goes awry, Zoey is given the power to hear people's thoughts expressed in song and dance. (End of Act One)
- Quest: Zoey attempts to understand — then ignore — her new situation (Act Two), but when she realizes that she can use the power to make emotional connections with others (Act Three), she works to use the gift to further her relationships — including with her coworker crush (who is also dealing with grief) and her stricken father (Act Three and Act Four).
- Crisis: The revelations are quickly complicated as Zoey learns that her crush is engaged, her coworker is winning in the promotion race, and her dad has a setback. (Act Five)
- New Balance: Zoey's father can communicate with her in his own song and Zoey is able to persuade her family to take him sailing, bringing new vigor to her ailing dad; she is also able to help her crush with his fiancée; and with her newfound confidence, Zoey

---

73. For those who don't know the show, Charlotte "Chuck" Charles is our female lead. And if the name Charlotte "Chuck" Charles doesn't grab your interest, well, I don't know what can.

wins the promotion at work. She is now a superpower manager starting to get a handle on dealing with her father. (Act Six)

~

Han Zhao, a writer from Hong Kong, has developed the Five Part Story as it relates to half-hour comedies. She applied her technique to *Modern Family*, and found it works quite nicely.

She followed the television terms from Sheldon Bull:[74] Cold Open, Goal, Obstacle, First Action, Act Break (Midpoint), Second Goal, Second Action, Second Action Backfires, and Resolution. The points align with the Five Part way of thinking about story thusly:

- Balance: Cold Open & Goal
- Unbalance: Obstacle
- Quest Part One: First Action
- Midpoint: Act Break
- Quest Part Two: Second Goal & Second Action
- Crisis: Second Action Backfires
- New Balance: Resolution

To be honest, while I find Five Part Story very helpful for most stories in most media, Sheldon Bull's breakdown of sitcoms is so simple already, the Five Part way of thinking about it may be nothing more than extra work. Which is a good reminder that as with any tool, the tool is there to help make things easier. And if it doesn't help — ignore it.

---

74. Articulated in *Elephant Bucks* by Sheldon Bull

PART FOUR

The Classic Structure

CHAPTER FOURTEEN

Form Not Formula

> The earth was formless and empty, and darkness covered the deep waters.
> And the Spirit of God was hovering over the surface of the waters.
> Then God said, "Let there be light," and there was light.
>
> — Genesis 1:2-3, NLT

Madeleine L'Engle tells us that the purpose of art is to find Cosmos (Order) in Chaos. Just as God took the formless and empty and filled it with order, the storyteller's job is to take an event (real or imagined) and find its shape.

We call this shape the Plot — the writer's choice of what to show and when to show it. Our scripts then become our point of view, our insight into story. How a story is told is closely tied to what a story means. Aaron Frankel[75] puts it this way:

> *What matters is not what the story is about but what makes it happen. Characters in action, which is the only way an audience will takes sides, is the only way an audience will care about meanings.*

We have a way of getting a broad overview of story (the Five Part Story), now we will take a deep dive into the details. Before we start, we have another critical fact to keep in mind:

Structure is there to serve Story, not the other way around.

---

75. *Writing the Broadway Musical* by Aaron Frankel

116

This is where the formula people go wrong. One idea popular in writing books is that if you follow the structure formula, you are sure to have a hit. Which, of course, is a logic fallacy; if it were true, there wouldn't be so many failed movies, plays, and television shows.

Instead of formula, what we are talking about is form — the shape of story. John Yorke tells us, "All stories are forged from the same template..." and immediately warns, "It's all too tempting to reduce wonder to a scientific formula and unweave the rainbow."[76]

I am put in mind here of Robert Barron's take on formula in creeds. He points out that the "in" from "I believe in..." is about direction and location — not arrival. Believing "in" God means a movement toward. He then explains for those who think belief "in" equals arrival:

> On the contrary, credal formulas are guides, guardrails, indicators on the side of the road that is leading us into God. They point us in the right direction and prevent us from going completely off the path....
>
> ...But the "content" of these great mysteries is not fully given in the formula themselves; we approach that completeness only through repeated narrating of the tale and through the concrete living of the Christian life.[77]

The shape of story is universal; the implementation of the shape is all creativity and Spirit. In a really good story, the audience is unaware of the shape — just as they should be unaware that the actors are putting on an accent, that the costumes were not made in the 18th Century, and that the lead character is actually a puppet. The skill of the artist is used in creating an experience; the script and its structure are the architectural plans, not the building itself.

Sometimes this means moving away from the rules — not discarding the rules but using the rules to enhance expectation. Howard Stein would often lament that some directors want to be seen as rebels, but would admonish them, "You can't break the rules if you don't know the

---

76. *Into the Woods: How Stories Work and Why We Tell Them* by John Yorke

77. Marvelously articulated in *Light from Light: A Theological Reflection on the Nicene Creed*

rules." Yorke puts it this way in discussing modern art pioneers: "They had to know their restrictions before they could transcend them."

Ignoring the built-in expectations of the audience is like changing rules in a spectator sport during game play. The athletes may decide halfway through a game that dribbling is no longer necessary. And the result may be fun for the athletes, but it excludes the audience from understanding and enjoying the game; it shuts the audience out.

Using the shape to play with the audience's expectations is a completely different thing. In fact, thwarting expectation can have wondrous results — if done right. Like surprising the spectators who thought you were going to punt and instead you throw the touchdown pass. Or this limerick:

> *A forgetful old gasman named Dieter,*
>
> *Who went poking around his gas heater,*
>
> *Touched a leak with his light;*
>
> *He blew out of sight —*
>
> *And as everyone who knows anything about poetry can tell you, he also ruined the meter.* [78]

Funny because the writer has a full understanding of, and exploits, the rules of the poem.

So, shape, not formula. Hence, if you find yourself reading a book on scriptwriting that includes page numbers ("...the Climax must happen on page 68..." sort of thing), toss the book out now. This is a boxed-in way of thinking that ignores the actual work of art. *Knives Out*'s Hook ends on the top of page two. *Up*'s Hook goes through the middle of page 14. Both are done brilliantly.

The New Balance in the short film "Hair Love" is longer than the New Balance for the feature film *North by Northwest*. In "Hair Love" we are rewarded by seeing the results of the journey of the film — because of the journey, the mother (not a lead character in the film)

---

78. Reader's Digest, "Laughter the Best Medicine," October 2018

is restored.[79] In *North by Northwest*, most of the New Balance can be easily assumed by the audience, and it would be redundant to show those elements. Each story had different needs, and the skill of the creators is in understanding that filling those needs is more rewarding than following a formula.

So, while I am about to give you a list of required scenes, and the order in which we should experience them, know that structure is not just a list of scenes in a certain specified order. Structure is order, rhythm, and pacing.

In American football, the offense tries to control the pacing — slow things down, speed the action up — all to give their team the best chance at a win. The defense often focuses on upsetting their opponent's rhythm, in effect to destroy the offense's control over the story. While I may give you the pieces of every story, rhythm and pacing belong to the art.

The surface of structure — events — belong to the brain; the rest belongs to the heart. Here, experience becomes the teacher — viewing, reading, and writing. Rhythm and pacing can be learned if one has an aptitude for them. Books like this one won't cut it without experience. View, read, and write!

The Important Plot POV

One more important thing to consider before we dive into the details of structure. But first: a risqué five sentence story!

- **Balance**: Mark sits at the hotel bar, playing with his wedding ring, lost in thought.

- **Unbalance**: Hannah, a vivacious woman wearing an outfit meant to attract, approaches Mark, saying, "What's a handsome man like you doing all alone?"

---

79. The short "Hair Love" is currently available on Sony Pictures Animation's social media sites, including YouTube. Seven minutes of joyous gold.

- **Quest**: With one look at Hannah, all of Mark's previous thoughts fly away; he flirts with her and suggests that maybe they should retire to the room he booked upstairs.

- **Crisis**: As Mark and Hannah tumble into the room in an amorous clutch, Mark's cell phone rings. It's his home calling!

- **New Balance**: Mark answers the phone, then quickly passes the cell to Hannah saying, "It's the sitter,"; Hannah calmly explains to the sitter that Darlene's blanky is in the dryer, and thanks the sitter once again for watching the kids while she and Mark celebrate their anniversary.

We'll come back to this story in a moment. There is a critical understanding of structure that I am going to state here, and then restate a few more times before this book is done. Trust me, you will forget this critical point. In fact, it will seem obvious that I have forgotten this critical point as we move through our discussion of structure.

As we know, Plot by definition is the order in which a story is told to an audience. Not necessarily the order in which the events happen, or even the order in which the characters experience the events. Rather, the order in which it is told. Therefore:

Structure is how the audience experiences the story.

This fact will get lost, as the easiest way to think of story is in terms of the characters, not the audience. The Five Part Story falls into this trap: the character has a balance, then an unbalance, then they come up with a goal... It seems to be completely from the character's point of view that the major points — Balance, Unbalance, Quest, Crisis, and New Balance — happen. And for most stories, this is how the plot unfolds. Thus, the simplest way to get our heads into structure.

However, structure really is about the audience's experience. As I break down Events below, I will walk through what the characters are doing, and how they are affected by the action. What's more important is how the audience is perceiving the actions, and how they are affected. (This becomes much more obvious when discussing stories that are told non-linear.)

For example, let's look at the risqué story that started this section.

In the first reading, the story seems to make sense from the Central Character's point of view: a married man at a bar, unbalanced by the arrival of an attractive woman. He sets out to have an affair, which is interrupted by a reminder of home.

Once we get to the end, we realize we were wrong all along. This is the story of a married man waiting for his wife at a bar. When she arrives, they head up to their room (as planned) — but are interrupted by the babysitter calling.

The Unbalance does not unbalance the life of Mark; he is not on a Quest; the Crisis is just an inconvenience to him; and there really is no New Balance — nothing has changed for him.

Now think of the structure from the audience point of view — we feel a Balance and an Unbalance — worried about what he might do. We see a Quest, and root against this man's seeming desire to have an affair. We feel the "oh no!" moment as the call comes in — is he about to get caught? Have second thoughts?

And the New Balance is 100% for the audience — we started in a story about a married man about to have an affair, and end with the story of a dedicated man celebrating his marriage with his wife.

Keep this in the back of your brain as we go through discussions of structure; it will pay off in the end. Plot is for the audience.

CHAPTER FIFTEEN

The Classic Three-Act Structure

Classic Structure

Also known as:
Aristotle's Structure
Three-Act Structure
Beginning, Middle, End

Y ou may hear among writers and aficionados, "The Three-Act Structure is dead!" And to prove their point, they will show you gobs of plays in two acts, or TV shows in five to seven acts, or films that they have no idea how are broken down.

I'm going to be bold in saying this: they are confused. Virtually every movie at the top of the box office follows the Three-Act Structure; virtually every play on or off Broadway follows the Three-Act Structure; just about every show on cable or streaming follows the Three-Act Structure. (Well, the good ones do.)

The confusion comes with the word "act." An act in commercial television is marked by the placement of the commercial — the more commercials, the more acts. Film doesn't tend to have acts broken out at all. Theater marks acts by intermissions — at least in practice.

John Yorke gives a lovely historical breakdown of the artistic reasons for the change in act breaks throughout time — technology, furniture, and bladders. In Shakespeare's day, a show couldn't progress once the candles burnt out — so the acts were designed to last the length of a candle's burn. Turns out that five acts — four intermissions — was perfect to replace the lighting.

Electricity came about, and we no longer needed to measure our plays in candle units; however, the audiences couldn't sit comfortably in those creaking wooden chairs for long. Hence the rise of the play in three acts. And modern cushions helped eliminate the need for two breaks — so we are in the age of the two-act-with-a-pee-break structure.

Ever attend a full-length play with no intermission? Someone decided it was short enough that you could line up at the restroom after the curtain call.

However, the Three-Act Structure (notice the capitalization) has nothing to do with intermissions — so the word "act" means something different here. The Structure refers to the Aristotelian idea of story having three parts — a Beginning, a Middle, and an End. Or think of it this way: a Balance, a Quest, and a New Balance.

John Yorke explains:

> Three-act structure is the cornerstone of drama primarily because it embodies not just the simplest units of Aristotelian (and indeed all) structure; it follows the irrefutable laws of physics.[80]

Shakespeare's plays all follow such a structure within his five acts — act one corresponding to Act One of the structure; acts two, three, and four meeting the Act Two of the structure, and act five roughly fulfilling the function of Act Three of the structure.

～

There are several terms like "act" that can have multiple meanings in our world. To avoid as much confusion as I can, let's define another term with potentially misleading multiple definitions: the scene.

---

80. *Into the Woods*, again. Yep, I do love Yorke's book.

Scene defined: Continuous action bounded by location and/or time

If in our script, Jim has a conversation with Betty in the living room, then the action jumps to Jim repeating the conversation to Mary in the diner — we have two scenes defined by location.

If Jim and Betty have their conversation in the living room, and continue the conversation out the door, down the street, and end at the diner — that is one scene defined by unbroken time.

Point of confusion: the script would mark each location as a separate scene — this is a technical breakdown of the script, necessary for lighting, cameras and/or scenery changes. For our purposes, we will count that as one scene.

Theater may use an additional breakdown of the scene, as many plays take place in one location without time breaks. The French Scene is a term used to demarcate scenes by character entrances and/or exits. If Jim and Betty have a discussion in the living room, then Mary enters, that would mark the end of one scene, and the following lines would be a new scene.

A combined definition of "scene" might look like this:

A single encounter, composed of beats that combine to result in a change in plot, character, or theme, typically bounded by unity of location, time, and participating characters.

Cal Pritner and Scott E. Waters add another way to define a scene, which I think is helpful. "A scene is a unit of conflict that has a beginning, middle and an end."[81]

From a dramaturgical point of view, this definition helps keep the focus on the functions of scenes, which leads us to a discussion of Events.

~

For, while the tale of how we suffer, and how we are delighted, and how we may triumph is never new, it always must be heard.

---

81. Pritner & Walters, *Introduction to Play Analysis*, p.68

There isn't any other tale to tell, it's the only light we've got in all this darkness.[82]

We started with the notion that we are hardwired for story — that the form we seek in stories we encounter comes embedded in our DNA.

Dramatic structure is not an arbitrary — or even a conscious — invention. It is an organic codification of the human mechanism for ordering information...event, elaboration, denouement; thesis, antithesis, synthesis; boy meets girl, boy loses girl, boy gets girl; act one, act two, act three.[83]

The details in the following sections are that classic structure. As we shall see, the form may be played with in a myriad of ways — even broken for the right effect. Yet it all comes back to this way of telling story — whether dressed up as a mythic journey or the saving of felines or the "mah nish tah nah." Beginning to middle to end: this is the story form we desire in our bones.

I've realized that the underlying pattern of these plots — the ways in which an audience demands certain things — has an extraordinary uniformity.[84]

God did not randomly pluck out this structure. The Creator put it in our minds to seek out this form, this ordering of the chaos in every story we hear or tell, because it is God's story — the story of us and our Lord. The structure of Story is the Eternal Story — the structure of our own past, present, and future.

Our stories parallel the greatest story ever told, all in a search for God.

In the following sections, I will explain the function of each plot point, and then show how that point connects to God's story, labeled The Eternal Story.

He has planted eternity in the human heart, but even so, people cannot see the whole scope of God's work from beginning to end.[85]

---

82. Sonny in the short story *Sonny's Blues* by James Baldwin
83. David Mamet, *Three Uses of the Knife*
84. Yorke, *Into the Woods*
85. Ecclesiastes 3:11, NLT

PART FIVE

Events - Beginning

CHAPTER SIXTEEN

Events

Events

Also known as:
Plot Points
Action Points
Turning Points
Transition Points

I n working our way through the Classic Structure,[86] I am going to talk about the building blocks of story, which I will refer to as "Events." We start with actions (or beats), which build into scenes, which then become Events.

David Ball, in *Backwards & Forwards*, points out that an action is something that happens that causes or permits something else to happen, which he calls the Trigger and the Heap (action and reaction). To build our story, we need a series of actions that "trigger" another action to lead us through the story.

For *Taken* to happen, Kim must be taken.

For Kim to be rescued, Bryan needs to know she's been taken.

Bryan must then go to where she was taken.

Bryan must do some investigating.

---

86. For structures that don't quite fit the Classic Structure, or take a different tack, see Appendix D "Other Structures."

Bryan must take action on his investigation.

And on.

Event defined: a group of actions/reactions that combine to one unified Story goal usually bounded by a scene or sequence of scenes

The goals that define the Events shift throughout the script, progressing through the plot to give the script its shape. The following sections define the Events and their goals.

Breaking a Story defined: choosing the actions to make up the Events that will be included in the script

A writer may opt to combine actions into one scene. In the case of *Taken*, the writers combined the scene where Kim is taken with Bryan discovering the kidnapping — Kim calls her dad, and he listens as she is kidnapped.[87]

In the same way, a writer will exclude actions — which is good, as the movie/play/TV show would get boring awfully fast. (In order for Bryan to go to where she was taken, he must find his car keys. Then he must drive to the airport. Perhaps he must get gas on the way. Then he must buy a ticket. Then he must go through security...)

The key is to ask if a scene is fulfilling its goal — is it moving the plot forward, developing character, exploring theme — at the right time in the right place. If not, the scene should not be included in the Plot.

On we go to Events.

---

87. "I don't know who you are. I don't know what you want. If you are looking for ransom, I can tell you I don't have money, but what I do have are a very particular set of skills. Skills I have acquired over a very long career. Skills that make me a nightmare for people like you. If you let my daughter go now that'll be the end of it. I will not look for you, I will not pursue you, but if you don't, I will look for you, I will find you and I will kill you."

CHAPTER SEVENTEEN

Hook / Teaser

Hook

Also known as:
Teaser
Cold Open

The first Event that the audience encounters is the Hook. This is an optional Event — not all stories call for this scene or sequence.

The Hook defined: An opening scene or sequence outside of the core plot designed to catch the audience's attention and attract them to the rest of the story

The Hook almost always opens the movie/play/television show; it is the introduction of the world to the audience. For the most part, this Event does not start the story itself, but exists outside of the story. The function of the Hook is to get the audience engaged and leaning forward. We would like the audience to be active in the story, taking ownership as participants in the project.

- *Raiders of the Lost Ark* has a memorable hook, as Indiana Jones evades the traps of a temple to steal a golden idol. The sequence of scenes from the opening shot through the plane flying off (and Indy's iconic discovery of the snake in the plane) all constitute the Hook. There are two elements that play into our story — the characters of Indiana and Belloq. However, the movie is not "Indiana Jones and the Golden Idol" — this Event is just a setup to the story, not the story itself. (Here is one place where the Five Part Story helps differentiate Events — the Hook will not appear in the Five Part Story.)

- The Hook for *LaLa Land* is a good example of existing outside of the story. The dance sequence on the stalled 405 freeway draws us in — "Oh, it's that kind of story!" And yet the leads don't appear at all in that opening number; the story starts after the dancing ends, and our two leads meet-without-meeting in their separate cars.

- *Phantom of the Opera* plays with time in its hook. The musical starts with an auction of items from the now decrepit Paris Opera House. An old Raul bids on an item, and as he gets lost reminiscing about that music box, the broken chandelier is put on the block. Before our eyes, the chandelier rises off the floor, transforming into a working light fixture that floats into place above the audience as the scene transforms to the past — and the story of the Phantom and Christine.

Hooks do not need to be long. *Citizen Kane*'s hook lasts barely past the opening credits, consisting of a moving camera shot through the ramshackle grounds of an estate, up to the one lit window, to a bed, to a closeup of lips — "Rosebud" — then the fall of a snow globe. That's it. Who was that man? Why is the estate in such disrepair? What is Rosebud? Stick around for answers.

Television will often have a hook take place before the opening credits (called a "cold open"). For sitcoms, it might be a funny action — something to makes us laugh, to let us know this is a funny show. *Castle* would often have a two-scene hook — a setup of the discovery of the body of the week, followed by a scene of Castle at home — reminding us how much we like that character. Now we are set to jump into the plot — the solving of the murder.

Avengers: Endgame pulls us in with an emotional hook. This is a sequel — the audience already knows what happened at the end of *Infinity War*. So rather than tell us about the important things that are going to happen, we are drawn in by the emotional stakes: Hawkeye, at peace at home, loses his family to Thanos' actions at the end of the last movie. Heartbreak.

Again, the Russo's[88] make this a pure hook; we will not see Hawkeye again for some time. The Hook doesn't kick-start the story, it pulls us into the story.

Contrast *Endgame* to *Avengers: Age of Ultron*. The Hook is the attack on the Hydra base in Sokovia. Little in the way of emotion; lots in the way of action, cool effects, and danger mixed with humor that is a marker for these movies. *Age of Ultron* pulls the viewer in with action — it is this kind of movie. *Endgame* pulls the viewer in with emotion — you've been through a lot with these characters, let's see where we go from here.

42nd Street, the musical play, has a fun Hook — an audition tap dance number to an orchestral version of the title song. The Hook starts in darkness, as voices chime out that there is to be a new Julian Marsh

---

88. Directors of *Endgame*, written by Christopher Markus and Stephen McFeely

show with auditions coming up. The music starts and the curtain rises — and stops at knee level. The stage is jam packed with dancing feet, an overwhelming amount, giving the audience a taste of what is to come.

It is a breathtaking moment — and one discovered by accident. Apparently in tech rehearsal, the show started, the curtain began to move, and the director yelled, "Hold!" He wasn't ready. The guy on the curtain heard him and stopped at knee height. The dancers did not hear him and kept dancing their hearts out. The director and crew watched those "dancing feet" for a few moments, and knew they had their opening.

While Hooks are outside the story of the script and do not need to include our Central Character, many times the Hook doubles as a way to create sympathy for our hero. *Raiders of the Lost Ark* makes us want to follow Indy through the action. *Butch Cassidy and the Sundance Kid* has two hooks, both are pure character introductions. We watch as Butch cases a bank, complaining about the new security features. ("That's a small price to pay for beauty.") We then meet the taciturn Sundance, and get a deep dive into the legend of the man. ("Kid? Hey, how good are you?")

Creating mystery is another way Hooks can draw the audience in.

- *Sunset Boulevard* opens with a spoiler — a dead man floating in a pool. Not just any dead man, but the narrator and soon-to-be lead of our movie. How did we get here?

- *Cabin in the Woods* is supposed to be a horror movie about, well, a cabin in the woods. It opens instead in a concrete building with two guys talking about baby-proofing a house and something about it being down to Japan and us. What does this have to do with horror at a cabin? Stick around to find out...

~

Additional Examples of Hooks:

- Shakespeare loved a good Hook. *Hamlet*: Horatio and friends lie in wait to try and catch sight of a ghost. *Romeo and Juliet*: members of the opposing houses of Capulet and Montague brawl in the street. *Macbeth*: three witches meet in an ominous storm and tease a significant upcoming encounter with one Macbeth.

- *Brooklyn 99* has fun with its cold opens, from a contest to see who best mimics Captain Holt eating a marshmallow, to a competition to see if Jake can skid the full length of the squad room, to Jake forcing a suspect line-up to sing a Backstreet Boys song. All hilarious, all signaling that the rest of the show (having nothing to do with the cold open) will be equally as funny.

- *Toy Story* opens with a montage of Andy playing with an inanimate toy, Woody. The sequence ends with Woody coming to life.

- *Get Out* opens with a kidnapping of a character named Andre on a creepy suburban street. Then the movie "starts" as we meet our Central Character — knowing that despite the breezy flirting between our lead and his girlfriend, there is something not quite right in this world.

- The *Breaking Bad* pilot opens with an RV racing through the desert, driven by an underwear and gas mask clad man. The RV crashes, the man makes it out of the RV, gets a gun and a camera, confesses to his family, then awaits the deadly shoot-out with the police to come. Then the show backs up for its core story about a high school teacher with cancer, who is in no way the drug dealer seen in the tease.

- *Black Panther* opens with an animation, as a man tells his son the story of Wakanda, ending on the questions: "And we still hide, Baba?" "Yes." "Why?" The last question is to be answered by the movie.

That is, in fact, the main function of the Hook: a promise to answer the question, deliver on the action, fulfill the emotion. The Hook is a covenant between the artists and the audience: "I tell you this is what you are here for. And you will receive the journey promised."

Or as Isaiah says it:

From the very beginning,

I told what would happen

long before it took place.

I kept my word.[89]

A good hook, then, is more than just scenes that draw in an audience; it is a foretelling of the future.

John's Gospel has one of the best Hooks[90] I've ever encountered.

The Gospel, at its core, is about the life, death, and resurrection of Jesus Christ. The core story starts with John the Baptist preaching in the desert, then encountering the one he was announcing.

The Gospel writer starts before introducing the Baptist, though. He tells us that although this story is captured in time (around the change-over from BC to AD), it started long before.

In the beginning ...

The tale we are about to hear stretches through — and is the culmination of — history. The center of creation itself is coming. The light is about to become man; the Word is about to become flesh.

Someone is coming after me who is far greater than I am, for he existed long before me .

This coming one, this intervener in history is going to change everything. He is going to completely rearrange how humanity interacts with God.

For the law was given through Moses, but God's unfailing love and faithfulness came through Jesus Christ.

---

89. Isaiah 46:10, CEV
90. John 1:1-18, NLT

The Gospel writer tells us that no one has seen God — until now. Now we have the one who can reveal God to us. This is a story of blindness, rejection, suffering, and beautiful rebirth.

So — ready to meet the Word?

Then the Gospel of John gets underway.

This was John's testimony ...

The Eternal Story: Hook

HOOK: In the beginning, God created

Before our story begins, there is a void — nothingness. Then — God creates! The making of the universe is our hook into the story. We have not yet met the central characters around which our story will revolve; our hook will end with their introduction.

We start with dynamic action, action that only leads to questions that will drive our interest:

Why create? What is the purpose of this new world?

With a God who can do all this, what else will be done?

What story is about to happen that requires the creation of such an elaborate set?

What next?

CHAPTER EIGHTEEN

Balance

Balance

Also known as:
Normal World
Setup
Stasis
Ordinary World
Status Quo

Now that we've hooked our audience, the story moves on to establish the Balance.

Balance defined: After the Hook, the opening scenes and sequences that establish the normal world of the Central Character, laying the groundwork for the Unbalance

In a short piece, the Balance could be done in a few seconds — or even in a single image. Some short works start in the Unbalance, requiring the audience to assume the Balance.

For longer works, the Balance will be a series of events. The Central Character is introduced and the nature of who they are is established. We understand the relationships and things that are important to our hero — what will soon be at stake. The world of the story is set up — location, time, and history.

Raiders of the Lost Ark combines the Hook and the Balance to show-case both sides of Indy's character — the brawn and the brain. From the opening idol in the Peru adventure (Hook) and the life of Indiana as a professor (Balance), we get a clear glimpse of his world. The importance of artifacts for history's sake is set up (which resurfaces when Indy gives up near the end rather than sacrifice the ark). The plot hasn't started yet — Indy won't be on his journey until hired by the government agent — yet we have a clear vision of who this man is.

The rules of the arena are put into place during the Balance. This is an obvious need in sci-fi and fantasy: can we planet hop? Does sound travel in space? Do aliens speak English? Do aliens even exist? Are we in *Star Trek* or *Battlestar Galactica* or *Arrival* or *The Martian*? The rules of each movie are critical to understanding the journey of the story. Otherwise, Mark Watney should just beam up to his ship; or Louise Banks should just use her universal translator to chat up the aliens.

And not just for sci-fi; it is just as critical to establish the rules of the world in any genre. Broad social constructs come into play — either centrally or subtly, such as the state of race relations (*Clybourne Park, Blackish, The Band's Visit, Knives Out, Hidden Figures, Get Out*), gender roles (*Jane Eyre, A Doll's House Part 2, Mad Men, The Favourite, Silent Sky, Some Like It Hot*), or economics (*Death of a Salesman, Reservation Dogs, Fences, This Is Us, Downton Abbey, Parasite, Green Book*). Note that in *Get Out*, the incident with the police officer takes place in the balance before Chris' character is embroiled in the weirdness of the Armitage family.

More subtle social rules also are important, such as the world's view of love and romance (*Mad Men, The Importance of Being Earnest, West Side Story, Sweet Magnolias, Shrek, Guys and Dolls, Friends*), family (*Our Town, Glass Menagerie, Modern Family, Zoe's Extraordinary Playlist, The Simpsons, Parasite*), or personal ethics (*Jojo Rabbit, All My Sons, The Harder They Fall, Wicked, Justified, Pushing Daisies, Knives Out, The Social Network*). The musical *Smoke on the Mountain* relies on the audience understanding that there is no swearing in this culture — so when a foul word is heard, the audience is just as shocked as the characters.[91]

The Balance is also the time to establish the style, genre, and tone. Let the audience know whether this is realism, absurdism, comedy, drama, etc. Viewers can be easily thrown out of a story by a type of humor that is out of place, or a scary sequence in a non-scary story, or a moment of absurdism that just doesn't belong. A good Balance informs the audience of style and tone.

This is why it is critical in a musical to have music in the opening. Imagine the middle of an episode of *This Is Us* where music comes from nowhere and the characters start singing. Off-putting at best. Therefore, shows that have a special "musical" episode are careful to introduce the concept. Among the best at doing this is "Once More with Feeling" from *Buffy the Vampire Slayer*. Not only was the anomaly set up, but the musical nature of the episode was also a major plot point.

For dramas, we show whether they are based in realism (*West Wing, 12 Angry Men*) or a hyper-realism (*The Curious Incident of the Dog in the Night-Time, Lost*). For comedy, are we talking wit (*The Importance of Being Earnest, Knives Out*) or more slapstick (*Fool Moon, The Simpsons*); is the comedy rooted in a down-to-earth reality (*Parks & Recreation, Troop Zero*) or farce (*One Man, Two Guvnors, Monty Python and the Holy Grail*)?

Even in a piece that mixes styles, the Balance (combined with the Hook) can go a long way toward preparing the audience for the shifts to come.

---

91. *Smoke on the Mountain* is a strong example of the positive, non-gratuitous use of a swear word. The instance is the set up for the most powerful Gospel moment in the piece. The word used is allowed these days on standard television — so the playwright works especially hard in creating an environment where the word becomes shocking. I remember a Taproot Theatre production so successful in establishing this, that in the lobby at intermission a gruff young man swore himself as he said, "I can't believe he f***** said that!" The audience was prepped and ready to see the fallout from the breach of this established social custom.

Up is a comedy with deep dramatic moments. When Carl chooses his house over Kevin near the end, the low point is not tinged with humor (as a Crisis would be in *The Simpsons* or *Some Like it Hot*). That dramatic, heart-crushing moment is not out of place because Bob Peterson and Pete Docter did their work. The Hook shows us the mix of humor and heartbreak while the Balance returns us to the main comedic tone of the piece. By the end of the Balance, the audience is ready for the range of emotions to come.

Normal for This World

One thing to keep in mind: the Balance is there to establish what is normal for the world of the story — not the world of the viewer. The separation of the two is important, whether letting us in on the fact that in this world balloons are capable of lifting heavy objects that can't be lifted in our universe, or that ogres, fairies, and talking donkeys are the norm.

The world might be typically at peace (*The Fellowship of the Ring*) or during world war (*Saving Private Ryan*). It could be "our" normal world (*Signs*) or a world of fantasy (*Toy Story*).

The "normal" of the Central Character is also going to be different from other people in the world of the story. Therefore, the Balance should focus in on the main character's story.

"The Jedi" episode of *The Mandalorian*'s season two is a wonderful example. The opening hook shows Ahsoka (a supporting character) fighting her way to the gates of Calodon and confronting the magistrate. This does what a hook should — promises the action to come, creates mystery, brings up questions. Note that our Central Character (the Mandalorian) doesn't even appear.

The Balance then is the arrival of the Mandalorian, his entry into town and discovery of the distrust of the people. We meet Governor Wing, who will become important later (planted clue), and lay groundwork for the Want (the search for a Jedi) and the likely conflict (the Jedi and the town are at odds). There are two different "normals" for this story — Ahsoka's and the Mandalorian's — our true Balance gives us the normal for our Central Character.

~

The Balance has a job to do (establish the normal world). It is also a place of opportunity, ways to enhance the experience of the story. Laying the groundwork of exposition is one — and I will leave that to a later section devoted to the problem of exposition. ("How do you catch a cloud and pin it down?")

Other opportunities presented in the Balance:

Foresight into Arc

The balance is a place to firmly establish the starting point of the Central Character.

Foresight into Want

The Want typically won't be established until the Unbalance; here we get a hint of what is to come. In some ways, we establish the importance of the Want prior to establishing the problem. *Hunger Games* gives us the moments outside of town, where the freedom from the politics of the day is yearned for. In *It's a Wonderful Life*, we hear George's dream of leaving Bedford Falls before he starts working towards that goal.

Foresight into Need

Unlike the Want, the Need usually exists before the action of the story gets into gear. Often the protagonist doesn't know or acknowledge their own Need; therefore, there is a chance to explore the Need without having to focus the audience's attention completely on it. The Orci/Kurtzman/Abrams relaunch of *Star Trek* shows us the wild child breaking the rules in the Balance. We see Kirk as a loner in need of community; a rebel in need of being a leader.

The Wizard of Oz shows us the runaway who needs to learn the value of home. *Romeo and Juliet* shows us Romeo desperate for romance, clearly a boy who doesn't understand love. *This Is Us* gives us a Kate (to pick one) at war with herself, who needs peace.

Planting Clues

The Balance is the time to set the audience up for all those things that come later that would otherwise make an audience say, "That would never happen."

Playwright William Mastrosimone[92] tells us that an audience wants to be surprised — but not fooled. The joy of a good surprise is when the audience says, "I never would have guessed; I should have known all along." Being fooled sounds more like, "I never would have guessed; and I'm not buying it."

There is a rule of thumb with coincidences in a dramatic work: audiences will buy one coincidence if it is in the first half of the show. Anything later — or a larger number of coincidences — and it feels like the author is manipulating the story rather than telling it.

Getting around that rule of thumb comes down to planting clues, giving the audience the inkling of what might happen (the "I should have known all along") while maintaining the surprise (the "I never would have guessed").

If your action hero is thrown into a pool of sharks and "just happens" to have a portable underwater breathing apparatus in his pocket, that is unbelievable. If Q gives James Bond an underwater breathing apparatus in the Balance, then he is later thrown into the pool, the reaction becomes, "Use your underwater breathing apparatus!"[93]

Even better if Bond mocks Q when getting the apparatus — "Why would I need to carry this old thing around?" There is a term in television called "hanging a lantern"[94] which refers to a character pointing

---

92. I was fortunate enough to attend a seminar that Mastrosimone gave at a local library in the Seattle area.

93. *Thunderball*, as if you didn't already know that.

94. Also known as "lampshading," "hanging a clock," "spotlighting" or "hanging a red flag." TV Tropes.org suggests this practice goes all the way back to Dante.

out a plot inconsistency. The (very useful) idea is that if a character notices a potential flaw in a story, the audience is more likely to forgive the flaw. As if to say, "Well, it can't be a mistake if the creators know about it, so how about I just stop thinking about it?"

If the audience is wondering, "Why would anyone need to carry a portable breathing apparatus around?", they are distracted. If Bond echoes their concern, they think, "Yeah, Bond and I think just alike." And no more worries.

The best of the mind-blowing stories work because of the setups — making the odd into an oddly ordered mess. *Eternal Sunshine of the Spotless Mind* is chockful of clues for what comes later: pages missing from the book, Joel commenting after seeing Clementine that he falls in love with every woman he sees, Clementine asking, "Do I know you?" at their first meeting, and on.

Common Mistakes

There are three common pitfalls for writers in approaching the start of their story and they are all about information: too little, too much, or unrelated to the plot.

1. Too Little Information

The audience must have enough knowledge of what's going on to hang their hat. Getting lost in a complicated plot is rarely a good thing, all the fans of James Joyce's *Ulysses* notwithstanding.[95] The goal of a good story is to get the audience to lean forward, looking to see what happens next; the failure of a story is when the audience is forced to look at their neighbor hoping they can explain what is going on.

2. Too Much Information

The solution to too little information is not the opposite. Goldilocks would have saved a lot of time if she understood that the solution to too hot wasn't too cold, or the solution to too big wasn't too little.

---

95. Let's be honest, most fans of Joyce's epic haven't actually read the thing. My book club (led by Jack Gilbert) decided to tackle it; anytime any one of us finished we went out to celebrate. And in reading it, we all became convinced that the idea of the book is much, much better than the actual book.

The audience should lean forward into a story; that's what gives them ownership of the tale ("I figured it out!"), that's what makes the story interesting to them. Give too much information, the audience sits back in their seat and become a passive observer.

3. Irrelevant Information

The beginning of the story is the time to establish what is needed for the story. It becomes important, therefore, to focus only on what is necessary for this journey. Audience members are looking for the fore-sights, the clues; they want to know which character they should follow, and what values are important. Flood them with irrelevant world-building, and you lose them.

C.S. Lewis puts it this way: "Whatever in a work of art is not used, is doing harm."[96]

Finding the balance of information in the Balance then becomes a balancing act. Okay, overused that metaphor.

A good Balance starts a story off right; it equips the audience for the journey ahead.[97]

The Eternal Story: Balance

Hook: In the beginning, God created...
BALANCE: The Garden of Eden

The Balance of history establishes our main characters (God and humanity), the critical relationships ("It is not good for man to be alone..."), sets the normal of the world that will be unbalanced ("then God blessed them..."), and the rules of the world are established (quite literally, the one rule, "...except the tree of the knowledge of good and evil...")

The stage is set; the story is ready to begin.

---

96. From the essay "On Science Fiction"
97. Just like a balanced breakfast sets one up for the journey of the day; but I'm not adding another "balance" metaphor, so forget I brought it up.

Catalyst

Catalyst

Also known as:
Unbalance
Call to Adventure
Call to Action

Now that the story is ready to get going, we encounter a triplet of events — Catalyst, Response to Catalyst, and Final Straw. These three combined make up our Unbalance. In a short script, the three may all be one action. For longer pieces, the three are distinct, each having their own function.

Catalyst defined: A scene/sequence giving the initial Unbalance of the normal world

The Catalyst is the first unbalancing of the world of the Central Character, triggering what will become the main action. We move from the known into the unknown; as David Ball puts it, there is an intrusion into the stasis.

Important for this stage is that while the world has changed, the Central Character is not yet on their journey. They may take some test steps in the reaction, but they won't commit to the quest until the Final Straw.

In some stories, the world has changed without the Central Character even fully realizing the change has happened. Chris in *Get Out* arrives at the house — everything is off, but he can't put his finger on what's happening. In *Hamlet*, the ghost has appeared to the guards; Hamlet's world has changed, but it won't be for another scene before he finds out about it. In *The Harder They Fall*, the world is unbalanced when Rufus Buck escapes from the prison train; it will be a while before Nat Love gets the news.

The keys for a good Catalyst are that the event affects the Central Character (or the ripples will!) and must have consequences. A common mistake is that the change to the world is too small — barely noticeable. The change must be a force big enough to push the Central Character through the story.

Here are examples — note how the quest is not yet defined. A problem may exist — the solution hasn't presented itself.

- *The Martian*: Mark is hit with the debris
- *Roman Holiday*: Joe Bradley finds the sleeping princess and takes her back to his place
- *MacBeth*: The witches make their predictions to Mackey and Banquo
- *The Wizard of Oz*: The tornado takes Dorothy to Oz
- *West Side Story*: Tony sees Maria at the dance
- "The Jedi," *The Mandalorian*: Mando is hired by the magistrate to hunt down Ahsoka
- TV Detective Shows (pick your favorite): a body is discovered

The Eternal Story: Catalyst

Hook: In the beginning, God created...
Balance: The Garden of Eden
CATALYST: Eve and Adam take the fruit

The world of, well — the world, is unbalanced, changed forever. Our characters aren't yet on a journey, there is no quest yet to fix things. The world has been broken; time to pause and react...

Response to Catalyst

Also known as:
Character Responds to Changed World
Debate

The Response allows space to orient the audience to the situation, to understand what is going on. *Star Wars: A New Hope* gives us time for Luke to meet Obi Wan and learn about the past. Miles in *Spider-Man: Into the Spider-Verse* discovers his new powers — and, to the audience's amusement, what a pain they are.

Hamlet finds out about the ghost after a meeting with the royal couple — his mother and new stepfather — orienting us to the state of Denmark. Before meeting up with the specter of his dead father, the audience is given more orientation: we interact with Polonius (whom Hamlet will later kill in the midpoint); Ophelia, Hamlet's love (who will trigger the Crisis for Hamlet through her suicide); and Laertes (responsible for the climatic duel). We don't know it yet, but the actions between Catalyst and Final Straw have outlined the trajectory of the second half of the play, including the cost and final tragedy that will result from Hamlet's meeting with the ghost.

This is also the space to test the options — what can be done? In *Gravity*, Kowalski orients Dr. Stone and outlines exactly what needs to be accomplished to survive. *Come From Away* shows the residents of Gander attempting to prepare for the arrival of the diverted 9/11 flights ("Blankets and Bedding"). The attempt to prepare for the arrival of the planes also lets us (and the residents of Gander) see the enormity of the unbalance, and sinks in the reality that there is no way to be prepared for what is about to happen.

The Response, therefore, gives shape to the Unbalance before the story becomes too busy with the action of the quest.

Character

The most powerful and interesting function of the Response (from a Story perspective) is a chance to take a moment and delve into character.

As we will see when we discuss character later, a character is defined by action. The more stress put on the character, the more the action reveals who they really are. This is one reason why the Response is important: in the peace of the Balance, we can't really know who our Central Character is. We add the pressure of the Catalyst, and we now have a clearer view.

The Catalyst has happened; the world has been upended. How will the character respond? What does that say about the character? What is revealed that we might not otherwise know?

Macbeth sends a letter off to his wife; in essence, he gives up power to her, having her take the action. The future king is not yet ready to take the reins; the driven powerhouse confronted by MacDuff in Act V has yet to take shape. Mando in "The Jedi" deceives the magistrate, making as if he is taking the contract on Ahsoka. We see a more fully formed character than in the prior example — one capable of seeing the episode through. Mando's character arc is more subtle here — a mark of the TV series. One should note that the Response ignores the plight of the town as learned in the Balance — Mando's action is to further his sole goal of getting the child to the Jedi; compassion for the others is a side-product of his mission.

Another thing that can come from this section is an exploration of what happens if the call to adventure is ignored. *Star Wars: A New Hope* has a Catalyst in the arrival of the droids. Luke, who in the Balance made clear his desire to be a hero like his pals, gets a distress message from a literal princess in peril. His response? Ignore the call. The result? The empire comes to him instead. Frodo — another character enamored with the stories of adventure that came before — also chooses to do nothing (*Fellowship of the Ring*). Both characters have a long journey ahead before they can claim the role of "hero."

Other characters flat out run away from the quest — Jonah heading away from Nineveh springs to mind. Both Biff and Willy pretend there is no Unbalance in *Death of a Salesman*. In the Crisis, both are confronted with the truth. Biff escapes the tragedy of the world by accepting the truth of the situation. Willy pays the price of continued denial through suicide.

Joe in *Soul* literally runs away from the great beyond, motivated by the belief that he is missing out on his reason for living — his passion. The movie is nearly a tragedy, until Joe realizes he was wrong in that belief and rejects the premise that made him flee to begin with.

As we see in these examples, the Response is a reverse engineering of the Crisis, giving shape to the character arc. This is where the character starts, which the audience needs to understand to feel the weight of where the character ends (for good, like Biff; or bad, like Willy).

Common Mistakes

There are two common mistakes made by creators in the Response to the Catalyst: too little space and too much space.

1. Too Little Space

If the Response is rushed or ignored, the character isn't fully explored, and this weakens the Crisis and final arc of the characters. *Toy Story* depends on the audience understanding what a jerk Woody is when his place as top toy is threatened. Woody doesn't grow if he goes from confident leader to savior. When he goes from insecure leader to reluctant savior to confident friend — now we have a journey.

Rushing the Response also loses the sense of scope of the Unbalance. Kowalski's orientation of Dr. Stone (*Gravity*) makes clear the impossible nature of the rest of the journey. Jean Valjean's (*Les Misérables*) attempts to survive in the world before receiving the candlesticks make clear his impossible situation — and the necessity for a new identity. Both examples show the importance of taking the time to respond.

2. Too Much Space

Indulging in the Response is also problematic. The audience is ready for the story to get moving and will bore easily if the story doesn't get in motion. There is a grace period at the start of storytelling given by the viewer; they understand that the story needs to be set up. Once the action starts rolling, that grace period has ended. The creators were given space to answer the audience's question created by the Catalyst: "Whoa! What just happened?" Now it is time to move the Central Character onto her journey.

The Eternal Story: Response to Catalyst

Hook: In the beginning, God created...
Balance: The Garden of Eden
Catalyst: Eve and Adam take the fruit
RESPONSE TO CATALYST: Adam and Eve hide from God — then blame others

The natural responses when caught in wrongdoing: hiding and blaming. Adam blames Eve; Eve blames the snake. The hiding is really an acknowledgment of wrongdoing — a confession of sorts. The blaming is a refusal to take ownership.

These characters have a long way to go before reaching salvation.

CHAPTER TWENTY

Final Straw

Final Straw

Also known as:
Big Event
Inciting Incident
Act One Turning Point
Break Into Two
Acceptance of the Call

Final Straw defined: the scene/sequence that sets the Central Character on the Quest

The Catalyst changes the world; the Final Straw pushes the protagonist into action to correct the change. The Quest is established (at least the first goals — which may alter at Midpoint) and the Central Character commits to action. Frodo is going to take the ring to Rivendell; Hamlet is going to figure out if his father was murdered; Zoey is going to find out if the person singing to her has a problem to be solved; Carl is going to fly his house to Paradise Falls.[98]

A quick note on terminology: David Trottier refers to this plot point as the Big Event; what happens is big enough to force the Central Character into action. I recently stopped using Trottier's term as students

---

98. *The Fellowship of the Ring, Hamlet, Zoey's Extraordinary Playlist, Up*

confused the Big Event with other big events – let's face it, most of the events that we name are, well, big. Andrea Nasfell (professor and prolific screenwriter) came to me with the wording "Final Straw," a nickname her students gave the plot point. To them it made sense: the Central Character isn't on their quest until that thing happens that finally pushes them into action. So, Final Straw it is.

As the Catalyst and Final Straw are inextricably linked, I find it best to think of both events together — the one/two punch helps understand each part. Hopefully you can see how the world is unbalanced in the Catalyst — however, the main action of the story hasn't started, and won't until the Central Character takes action propelled by the Final Straw.

Toy Story
- Catalyst: Buzz Lightyear arrives
- Final Straw: Buzz falls out the window, and Woody is accused of murder

Fellowship of the Ring
- Catalyst: The ring is discovered
- Final Straw: The Ringwraiths come to the Shire

Macbeth
- Catalyst: The witches make their predictions known
- Final Straw: Lady M persuades Mackie to take action to make the predictions come true

West Side Story
- Catalyst: Maria and Tony meet at the dance
- Final Straw: Maria and Tony swear their love on the fire escape[99]

(For Romeo and Juliet — substitute "party" for "dance," and "balcony" for "fire escape")

---

99. Note that the event that Unbalances the world need not be negative. While less common (less dramatic by nature), there are many solid precedents. For *West Side Story*, committing to love each other. *Ted Lasso* — getting a job in England. *Little Miss Sunshine* — being invited to a competition. *Hidden Figures* — having your talent discovered.

"The Jedi" *The Mandalorian*
- Catalyst: The magistrate hires the Mandalorian to kill the Jedi
- Final Straw: Ahsoka and Mando make a deal — he helps her get to the magistrate, then she will take the child

The Television Police Procedural (pick your favorite)
- Catalyst: The body is found
- Final Straw: A clue is discovered that suggests a suspect

The Glass Menagerie
- Catalyst: Amanda discovers Laura dropped out of secretarial school
- Final Straw: Amanda decides to get Laura married

Harriet
- Catalyst: Brodess rips up the letter from the lawyer, announcing that Harriet's (Minty's) mother and children will never be free.
- Final Straw: Gideon puts Harriet (Minty) up for auction

Knives Out
- Catalyst: The police reopen the investigation — Harlan may have been murdered
- Final Straw: Marta answers Blanc's questions — revealing to the audience that she is responsible for death of Harlan

Spider-Man: No Way Home
- Catalyst: The spell goes wrong
- Final Straw: Doc Ock attacks Spidey on the bridge

To everything there is a season, a time for every purpose under heaven.

—Ecclesiastes 3:1, NKJV

The writing gurus disagree about how to look at the Unbalance — many claiming that it is a single scene/sequence that changes the world. As you know, I side with those like Trottier who feel that the better approach is to break out the start into Catalyst, Response, and Final Straw. Certainly, shorts may have (indeed are likely to have) a single event that acts as Catalyst and Final Straw — think of the big bird's arrival in Pixar's "For the Birds," or the dad's discovery of his daughter's disastrous attempt at self-styling in "Hair Love."

However, fuller stories miss out by lumping the inciting incidents into one event. McKee (himself a proponent of lumping) says the inciting incident must wait for the timing to be ripe. The audience needs to be fully hooked emotionally for the break into two to work, for the audience to chase after the characters in the quest.

This is precisely the value of the three beats to Unbalance. The time between the Catalyst and the Final Straw gives the weight to the Final Straw. Luke may well go off to save the princess if the first thing that happens to him is the stormtroopers destroying his home and killing his aunt and uncle. Instead, we are wisely given the in-between — including Luke turning down the quest and telling Obi-wan that he is on his own.

The death of his aunt and uncle coming directly off Luke turning down the quest gives so much more power, nuance, and character growth than a jump into action.

Common Mistakes

In addition to the lumping of the inciting incident, other pitfalls include being too small, forgetting the Central Character, and not propelling.

1. Too Small

David Ball points out that the intrusion should change everything that can be changed; often the Central Character is left with no choice — doing nothing is an automatic loss. If the Final Straw doesn't have big stakes, the show must work all the harder to find the energy to drive into the Quest.

In *Toy Story*, Woody is left with no friends at all; in *A New Hope*, Luke is left with no home. Hamlet knows the kingdom (and his mother's bed) is ruled by a murderer. The residents of Gander have their small town tripling in size in a matter of hours (*Come From Away*). Mando has very few options among the Jedi — he loses this one if he doesn't help her, and likely won't ever complete his task ("The Jedi"). True love will never be found; a killer will get away; more people will die; she will have no means to live; they will lose their shot to break the curse; the police will catch her; the song will haunt her forever; he'll have to move to a retirement home; the troops will charge into a trap.

Big enough to change everything, and to drive the Central Character into the Quest.

2. Forgetting the Central Character

Some stories unbalance the world but forget to bring along the protagonist. Certainly, a murder, alien invasion, the arrival of a villain can all unbalance the normal of a world without touching on the hero. And that can work — but it weakens the story in the process. A Central Character who is not directly affected by the Final Straw is starting out in a position of passiveness — which may make the audience equally as passive.

Let's take stories done right for examples. Hamlet encounters the ghost of his father — setting him on the journey of discovering the truth about his uncle and his father's death. Imagine the same scene — but without Hamlet there. The ghost instead tells Horatio about his death; Horatio passes the information along to Hamlet.

That could work, I guess. The loss of energy is obvious — Hamlet needs a secondary kick-start to really get moving.

In *Toy Story*, Buzz could have been knocked out of the window while Woody was in another room. Imagine the toys begging Woody to go save their new friend. Okay, but just okay. Woody knocks Buzz out of the window? Irreplaceable energy.

3. Not Propelling

Which leads to the final pitfall — a Final Straw that doesn't drive the story forward. This event will set up the action of Act Two — the Want becomes clear (to save the daughter, to rescue the princess, to take care of the refugees, to discover the murderer, to get away with the crime). This is the beginning of a long drive; on average Act Two will be twice as long as Act One or Act Three. The story needs the caffeine to get the characters and the audience pumped for the ride.

The Final Straw comes with stakes, direction, a clear Want, and the energy to drive the story through the journey to come.

The Unbalance is now full, and it is time to enter Act Two.

The Eternal Story: Final Straw

Hook: In the beginning, God created...

Balance: The Garden of Eden

Catalyst: Eve and Adam take the fruit

Response to Catalyst: Adam and Eve hide from God — then blame others

FINAL STRAW: God kicks Adam and Eve out of the Garden

The Unbalance is complete — the consequence of the Catalyst has been played out. Adam and Eve have lost everything — as has God. Something must be done.

The Central Character must go on a Quest to restore Balance...

PART SIX

Events — Middle

CHAPTER TWENTY-ONE

Quest Part One

Quest Part One

Also known as:
First Half of Act Two
Fun & Games
Things Go Well
Departure
Crossing the Threshold
The Plan

We are now in Act Two of the story — the part where most stories fall apart. For creators, the opening and ending of a story are the easiest to envision. The middle often needs more work to shape and keep up the drive of the storytelling. This is really the meat of the story — the stuff that gets us from the setup to the glorious climax.

Act Two will have three major sections — Quest Part One, Midpoint (a redirection), and Quest Part Two.

Quest Part One defined: A series of events showing the steps of the Quest leading from the Final Straw up the Midpoint; will include subplots

Here we will see the first steps of the Central Character as they deal with the unbalance of the Final Straw. The Avengers will build a time machine, recruit team members, and set up their journey into the past. Woody and Buzz Lightyear will deal with the gas station and the pizza place. Tony and Maria will dream of their wedding, as Tony tries to bring peace to the gangs. In the horror film, the victims try to understand what is going on and go on the defensive.

In addition to moving the plot forward and upward, the scenes in this section have a job to do. Some of the elements we look for:

Delivering on the Final Straw

We just experienced the event that alters forever the life of the Central Character, forcing them on the journey that will be this story. What does this mean for the Central Character? What does this mean for the world? How will they respond — and with what attitude, frame of mind, level of purpose?

Luke, stunned by the death of his aunt and uncle, tags along more than leads the way to Mos Eisley. Bryan Mills is going to leap into action, immediately flying off to rescue his daughter. Jean Valjean fights off Javert to escape and find Cosette[100].

We also have an opportunity to show what the world is like in the wake of the Final Straw. It may be a brand-new world for the Central Character (and the audience) — so for Harry Potter (*Harry Potter and the Sorcerer's Stone*), a trip to Diagon Alley introduces him and us to the wonders of that new world. There might be a new normal for everyone, so in *Independence Day* we get a taste of the chaos of an America without a central government. For Zoey (*Zoey's Extraordinary Playlist*), she must explore the life of the person she is called to help. In *Les Misérables*, we will meet Cosette and be introduced to the world of the Thénardiers. In *The Importance of Being Earnest*, it's time to see what life is like in the country. For the airplanes landing in Gander (*Come From Away*), we venture from the known of the plane's interior to the unknown ("Darkness and Trees").

---

100. *Star Wars: A New Hope, Taken, Les Misérables*

Clarifying the Want

The Final Straw sends the Central Character on the journey to restore balance. Quest Part One is going to be the first attempts in getting us to the New Balance — which is also our opportunity to make clear just what the goal is for the character.

In *The Wizard of Oz*, the goal (first goal, at least) is made clear: Dorothy is to travel to the Emerald City to find a way home. Jean Valjean's meeting with the Thénardiers confirms his mission: he must take care of Cosette himself (*Les Misérables*). In *Knives Out*, Marta is told by Blanc that she will be his Watson, solving (for her, obscuring) the case. Many police procedurals find a way to state the obvious in this section — "we are going to find the killer and bring him to justice!"[101]

Building the Need and Theme

While the Goal for the main character is obvious by this point, the Need is (as it should be) more subtle. The balance for the creators here is tricky. The audience must be aware at least subconsciously of the Need, otherwise the viewers will not be engaged emotionally when the Need is met (or failed to be met). Yet if the Need is too much in the foreground, the story becomes contrived and cliché. So, we present Need and Theme in this section with a combination of clarity and obfuscation.

There are many tricks to handling this. Putting the Theme into the mouth of a minor character often lessens the blow. ("With great power comes great responsibility," says Uncle Ben, just before he is removed from the story never to be seen again.[102])

This can be an effective way to blatantly say what needs to be said while also allowing the audience (and Central Character) to dismiss

---

101. Often followed by the chastisement of the lead by a more experienced officer, "Never make promises to the victim's wife/husband/child/grandmother!"

102. None of the movie Bens moved me much; I gasped when May said the classic line — realizing what that meant for her future...

the information. *Jurassic Park* puts the Theme in the mouth of the Ian Malcolm. After he hits on Ellie in front of Alan Grant, well, he can say whatever he likes, and we aren't going to pay him no nevermind.

The Need is often seen in the actions of the characters without judging the character for the lack — maybe even masking the Need as a good thing. When Shrek abuses Donkey, trying to drive him away, we are a little bit on his side. Donkey is designed to be "too much" for this very effect.

Hamlet's quest for vengeance (that's a good thing, right?) comes with his plot to get away with it — convincing people he is insane. As an audience, we root for Hamlet to succeed, and at the same time are subconsciously uneasy as we see that the humor of his madness (tricking the goofy Polonius) is also painful to others (we can't quite bring ourselves to laugh at Ophelia's hurt).

Frozen plays with the audience by presenting Elsa's Need in opposition: "Let It Go," the beloved anthem, is the anti-theme. Elsa does not Need to let it go — the very thing that isolates her; rather she Needs to let others in. Her ice castle, as powerful and pretty as her ballad of self-empowerment may be, is just another prison, a re-locking of the bedroom door.

Deepening Audience Empathy

Also in this section is the opportunity to get to know the Central Character more, and through the revelations get to care about them more. John McClane chats with Officer Powell on the walkie talkies (*Die Hard*). Hamlet ponders "to be or not to be" — which gives us both an opportunity to enjoy his wit (assuming he knows he is being overheard) as well as to plunge a bit into his soul (as he starts to be too real in his playing of the part). Mendez in *Argo* interacts with his son, ensuring we see the agent as human and not simply a super spy.

Establishing Supporting Characters and Subplots

We may have already met our supporting players and kick-started the B and C plots; if not, here is the place to do so.

In *Les Misérables*, it is in Quest Part One that we first meet several major players: Cosette and the Thénardiers (as previously mentioned), Eponine, Marius, Enjoiras, and Gavroche. *Die Hard* introduces Powell here and establishes the parallel track of McClane working through the issues of his failing marriage while also working to save his wife from the terrorists.[103] *Star Wars: A New Hope* gives us an intro to Han Solo and Chewbacca, as well as kicks in the rivalry between Han and Luke; the subplot machinations of Darth Vader and Leia are also developed in this section.

Subplots have the same structure as the main plot — Balance, Unbalance, Quest, Crisis, New Balance. However, by definition of "sub" plot, less screen/stage time is devoted to the subplots. In fact, many of the beats may not ever be seen by the audience, but only inferred. Ophelia's romance with Hamlet has a rather full arc: the two in love (Balance); thrown off track by Hamlet's strange behavior (Unbalance); Ophelia pursues reconciliation (Quest); only to be rebuffed again (Crisis); resulting in Ophelia taking her life (New Balance). The Balance and New Balance are completely off stage, related to the audience via the dialogue of nonparticipants.

Ever Increasing Action

Lest we forget, the most important function of Quest Part One is to start the Quest. This may be focused on recruitment and training (*The Seven Samurai/Magnificent Seven*, *The Dirty Dozen*), first steps on the journey (Dorothy on the yellow brick road, Jean Valjean collecting Cosette, Schofield and Blake in *1917* heading through the trenches), investigating the situation (Zoey interrogating the person she is to help

---

103. Yeah, I know they aren't terrorists. But we don't know that at this point of the story.

in *Zoey's Extraordinary Playlist*, Hamlet setting up a play to find out if his uncle is a killer, Spider-Man brought up to speed by Doctor Strange[104]) and/or actual attempts to directly fix the problem (Marta covering up evidence in *Knives Out*, Joe in *Soul* testing sparks for 22, the people of Gander taking in strangers in *Come From Away*).

Common Mistakes

Act Two is notorious as the spot where scripts fall apart. It is easy to give too much weight to information over action, bogging down the script with exposition. Action tends to even out, rather than build. Or in opposition, there is so much action that character development is left behind, and plots move forward without also growing deeper. Writers (and directors) often feel compelled to race to the climax, forgetting that the story *is* the journey — not just the final result.

Good Quest Part Ones constantly move while taking time to get to know the characters and the subplots, feeling out the stakes and heart of the show. In the action of the first half, we are planting all the ingredients necessary to make the final act truly satisfying. Pacing combines with content to prepare the unwary audience for what is to come.

~

---

104. *Spider-Man: No Way Home*

The Eternal Story: Quest Part One

Hook: In the beginning, God created...

Balance: The Garden of Eden

Catalyst: Eve and Adam take the fruit

Response to Catalyst: Adam and Eve hide from God — then blame others

Final Straw: God sends Adam and Eve out of the Garden

QUEST PART ONE: God works through history to reconnect with lost man (aka the Old Testament)

Throughout Quest Part One, we meet our additional characters and run through multiple subplots. But the main action is always front and center: God trying to find ways to restore balance to our severed relationship.[105]

He tries a do-over, calls out a people, creates a nation, provides leaders and prophets and priests. He gently prods, forcibly scolds, and exasperatedly explains. He provides beauty and poetry, law and instruction, peace and conflict. Tactic after tactic, a long line of recruiting, first steps, explorations, and attempts at solutions.

All the while, Need bubbles underneath as the Wants of humanity interfere with the Goal of God.

---

105. One can look at this from two angles: either humanity is the Central Character seeking out God, or God is the Central Character. I initially focused on humanity (me) being the central character, but then realized that Copernicus was right. We are not the center of the universe.

CHAPTER TWENTY-TWO

Midpoint

Midpoint

Also known as:
Pinch
Supreme Ordeal
Intermission Cliffhanger
Halfway Point
Center Commercial Break

Midpoint defined: A major event at the center of the plot that alters the Quest of the Central Character either through a major amplification or redirection of the Want

This significant event takes place in the middle of the story. Our characters have been heading in a direction making progress, overcoming obstacles, and getting closer to their goal.

And then something happens that is more than just another obstacle, something that changes the picture of the world. Now they must redirect their goal. Or they realize that their goal was too small to restore balance. Everything is different again.

In our Five Part Story, this is the "but then this happens" in the middle of the Quest that forces a "so now the Central Character does this."

- In *The King's Speech*, Bertie has been trying to get over his stutter. But when King George dies the stakes have gone through the roof — now Bertie's voice is the voice of the nation.

- In *The Princess Bride*, Buttercup discovers that Westley is the Dread Pirate Roberts — and everything changes.

- T'Challa in *Black Panther* loses the fight for the right to be king.

- *Captain Philips* is put into the lifeboat, going from trying to save the entire crew to saving his own life.

- Logan goes a little cuckoo and tells Chris to *Get Out*.

- *The Wizard of Oz* won't help unless they kill the Wicked Witch of the West.

- Blake is sidelined in *1917* — turning Schofield from a supportive companion to the carrier of the mission.

- Biff finds the rubber tubing in *Death of a Salesman*, proving that Willy is suicidal — putting a new spin on everything his father has been telling him.

- In "Pilot" of *Breaking Bad*, Walt makes the offer to Pinkman to cook his meth, a change in trajectory that will establish the journey of the series.

- Macbeth is haunted by the ghost of Banquo, catalyzing the madness that will lead to the implosion of Macbeth's reign.

In a sense, whether from new information, new understanding, or a new force, the path is the same, yet everything is different.

Network television and two act theater acknowledges the Midpoint in a clear way. For theater, the midpoint is often marked by an intermission. The playwright designs the structure to peak at the midpoint, leaving us with a driving "what next?" question raging in our brains.

The commercial value of this positioning is obvious. An intermission isn't just a break, it is an opportunity for an audience to leave the theater and go do something more interesting. It behooves the playwright to make sure that the most interesting thing going on is the play itself. A good Midpoint does just that — everything is elevated for the characters, and for the audience. What will happen next?

Stick around to find out.

Television is the same, except that it is a lot easier to change channels during a commercial break than to leave a theater and drive home. So, the TV writers' room works to make sure that the mid-show commercial break is marked with a "dun-dun-dunnnn!" moment.

There is variation on the exact placement of the Midpoint in these situations. The Midpoint may happen right before the break, leaving the audience to wonder what the next steps may be. Or the Midpoint may be about to happen — making the audience wonder what is coming. Or the break happens in the middle of the Midpoint, raising the question of how the midpoint will turn out.

Shakespeare wrote in the era of the five-act play.[106] In that form, the Midpoint event happens smack dab in the middle of act three — allowing the act to ramp up to the change and see the first steps in the new direction (Quest Part Two) before breaking and giving the audience space to ponder the new world.

The five-act structure reminds us of the importance of the Midpoint. In Freytag's pyramid, the Midpoint is called "the Climax" — seen as the most important Event of the entire play. Vogler's explanation of the mythic structure agrees with this view.

While the final battle may feel more exciting than any prior scene or sequence, it is the Midpoint that does the real work. The Midpoint is the center of the story — the major event that will clarify the central question of the drama.

In a way, we are far enough into the story to be ready to know what the story is really about.

Star Wars: A New Hope is a good example. The first half of the movie is about saving a princess. Then the Death Star destroys Alderaan — an entire planet of people gone in an instant. The story stakes are much, much larger than the life of Leia.

And everything has changed.

---

106. Thanks again to John Yorke for his insights into Shakespeare's Five Act Play structure.

The Midpoint Triplet

Many scripts give more weight to the Midpoint by thinking of the event as a series of scenes/sequences rather than a singular plot point.

The Unbalance translates to Events as a three-part process: the Catalyst, Response to the Catalyst, and Final Straw. Midpoints often follow a similar pattern: the thing that happens that shifts the world; a chance to see the Central Character reflect on the shift; then the thing that sends us off in our new direction.

We will see this rhythm again in the Crisis — the Crisis, Reflection, and new direction.

Hamlet has a clean example of the Midpoint triplet in Act III.

First Hamlet gains the knowledge that changes everything — he proves that Claudius murdered his father and has illegally taken the throne.

The next scene, we see Hamlet deciding what to do with this information, as he approaches Claudius outside of the prayer chamber. Hamlet decides here that he is not after justice but vengeance; he will kill Claudius when he knows that Claudius will die in his sin.

Then in the following scene, in a confrontation with his mother, Hamlet kills Polonius (thinking he is killing Claudius). The new direction for Hamlet is cemented; the stakes raised; the character committed on the new path.

～

The Midpoint is often the place where the Central Character has a major win that shifts the plan to a different direction. In *The Shape of Water*, Elisa succeeds in getting the Amphibian Man out of the government facility; now she must keep him hidden in her apartment until she can get him out of town. In the original *Law & Order*, the Midpoint was typically the arrest of the villain; Quest Part Two was the attempt to convict the killer.

The win may come in the form of knowledge. In the police procedural, the detectives may discover the key clue that will lead to the perpetrator. In *Ghost*, Sam learns that it was his best friend Carl who arranged for his murder.

The Midpoint becomes a pivot point in stories about Central Characters on a positive character arc. The midpoint marks the first time they embrace the qualities needed to become their complete selves. Up to this point, the character has been trying to solve the problem using their old ways; now they try on the new information and see if it fits. This is the character learning about themselves.

In essence, the character puts on their new self, as described in Ephesians:

> *You were taught, with regard to your former way of life, to put off your old self, which is being corrupted by its deceitful desires; to be made new in the attitude of your minds; and to put on the new self, created to be like God in true righteousness and holiness.*[107]

The Midpoint then becomes the first test of the new self, or the thing that finally persuades the character to embrace real change.

In *Up*, Carl is completely self-centered at the start of his journey. He reluctantly takes Russell along but keeps him at a distance. At the midpoint, Carl starts to put Russell (and by extension Kevin) before his own self, going against his solo nature. In Quest Part Two, he will test himself as he goes against his best interests to keep Kevin out of Muntz's hands. The new self starts to work on Carl — until the Crisis, where the old self wins out once more.

In addition to the character reveal of the Midpoint, this event serves to reinvigorate the action of the story. The central scene becomes a shot of adrenaline for the plot. The stakes are often redefined. Hamlet has killed Polonius — now his own life is at risk. *Star Wars: A New Hope* sees that planets can be destroyed. *The Avengers* learn that it isn't just Loki they must battle, but a full-scale alien invasion.

For the cast of *Les Misérables*, the response to the Midpoint puts everything at risk. Jean Valjean may be captured by the authorities. Cosette may lose Marius; Marius may lose his life. Eponine is on the

---

107. Ephesians 4:22-24, NIV

brink of also losing Marius; Enjolas may lose the momentum of the revolution.

The Midpoint renews and redefines the quest for the Central Character. The event cements their path, pushing them forward. This new push requires a full commitment or recommitment from the Central Character — often a point of no return.

The Eternal Story: Midpoint

Hook: In the beginning, God created...

Balance: The Garden of Eden

Catalyst: Eve and Adam take the fruit

Response to Catalyst: Adam and Eve hide from God — then blame others

Final Straw: God sends Adam and Eve out of the Garden

Quest Part One: God works through history to reconnect with lost man (aka the Old Testament)

MIDPOINT: The Nativity — God becomes Man[108]

And everything changes. The quest of drawing humanity to Himself has not restored balance, so a new thing comes through — one that is the ultimate commitment of our Central Character, a

---

108. Let me offer a critique of my own take on the theology of history. As you will see, I play out the rest of history from Jesus' time on earth. There is an argument to be made that the entirety of Jesus' life is the midpoint, with the rest of the Act Two and Act Three points happening in our future, with the arrival of the anti-Christ and all the Revelation stuff filling out the Crisis, Climax, etc. I choose not to follow that more expansive look for two reasons. First, I strongly believe that the end times are by design a mystery (Matthew 24:36, Mark 13:32), and I will not pretend to understand a mystery the Bible claims that I can only see dimly. Second, I do believe the battle was won at the cross, so a perfect place to end our Act Two. The fractal nature of Story supports the idea that we would find the same story points whether viewing the life of Christ as the full second half of the Story, or just the midpoint of the larger narrative.

true point of no return. God will now embrace a new position, taking over the role of humanity.

So, the Word became human and made his home among us. He was full of unfailing love and faithfulness. And we have seen his glory, the glory of the Father's one and only Son.[109]

The stakes have changed; God Himself is now at risk. The goal has been redirected: God will offer Himself as the atoning sacrifice. The knowledge necessary for victory has been obtained.

For the wages of sin is death, but the free gift of God is eternal life through Christ Jesus our Lord.[110]

✝ CROSS FADE: Midpoints and Testimonies ✝

Act One: Writing for Hollywood, a training program for Christians seeking a career in screenwriting, was founded by Barbara Nicolosi, a former Catholic nun. The ministry itself was part of a larger Protestant organization sponsored by a Presbyterian church.

I remember Barbara talking about having to learn the Protestant lingo. The term "testimony" puzzled her for a bit until she heard enough people giving theirs to put the pieces together. She realized that for Protestants, when they tell their story, it typically ended with when they met God (or, in the parlance, when they were saved). As if to say, "Here is the life God has saved me from."

For her, she felt that Catholics in telling their story tend to start with the day they met God. As if to say, "Here's the life God has given me." It's as if these two sides of Christianity were telling half the story.

We see this in many movies targeted for the religious market. The standard evangelical movie ends when the wayward character is saved — the conversion moment is the Climax. The typical movie about the saints of the church uses the conversion moment as the Catalyst.

---

109. John 1:14, NLT
110. Romans 6:23, NLT

I find it helpful for me to think of my walk with God in story terms‘ — which would make the conversion from the old life to the new life the midpoint, rather than the kick-start or the climax.

It is the point where the Central Character gains the knowledge needed to complete the journey. It is a win that comes with a redirection of goal. Everything has changed. One goes from a life searching for God to a life living for God.

We often try to rush the salvation Midpoint, reducing it to a single moment and race into the second act. This might be a mistake — or at least a missed opportunity. As stated earlier, the weight of a Midpoint can be shown by telling the event in three points: the change event, the reflection, and then the event that pushes the character into the new life.

In Acts Chapter 9, we watch as God leads Paul through his conversion experience. The blinding light on the road to Damascus is the change event — the catalyst of Paul's midpoint unbalance. Paul, blinded, waits for three days in Damascus: a time of reflection, reorientation, and wonder. Then God brings Ananias to Paul, curing his blindness. Paul is now baptized as a new believer, ready for his new life, his new journey, his new quest.

Paul's journey wasn't completed at this time — this is not the climax to his story. Rather a new direction, the beginning of the new self.

And I am certain that God, who began the good work within you, will continue his work until it is finally finished on the day when Christ Jesus returns.[111]

---

111. Philippians 1:6, NLT

CHAPTER TWENTY-THREE

Midpoint Escape Offer

Midpoint Escape Offer

Also known as:
Offer of Grace
Way Out
Temptation

Brian Coley of ArtWithin put me onto the idea of a Midpoint Escape Offer — what he calls an Offer of Grace. It is an event near the center of the plot that tests the Central Character by offering a way out of the story.

The Wicked Witch tells Dorothy to turn over the silver slippers (for the play version of *The Wizard of Oz*, or the ruby red ones for the film). If Dorothy turns over the slippers, the story is over — no need to continue the journey, the antagonism departs.

There may well be several mini versions of the escape offer throughout a story. Such moments are good ways to remind the audience (and characters) of the goal and the forces of conflict. That's why the witch pops up multiple times as Dorothy winds her way along the yellow brick road. In *Serenity*, every exchange with the Operative includes the offer — give us the girl, and we will leave you alone.

What we are looking for with the capital "e" Escape Offer is a larger offer that is tied to the Midpoint. Here, the event either sets up the

Midpoint or comes shortly after (or during) the Midpoint. Hamlet's Escape Offer comes smack dab in the middle of the Midpoint — his chance to end the story by killing Claudius while the king prays. Valentin is given the offer to work in talking pictures just before he loses everything in the stock market crash (*The Artist*). Schofield has a chance to return to his unit rather than go forward with the mission shortly after the loss of Blake (*1917*). Peter Parker can return the villains to their own dimension — whether that action kills them or not (*Spider-Man: No Way Home*).

The Midpoint Escape Offer acts as a definer for the character — who they are before everything changes, or who they are to become.

Coley calls this a Point of Grace because for a protagonist who needs to overcome a weakness in their character, this event is typically a positive character choice.

- Charlie offers Willy a non-sales job (*Death of a Salesman*)
- Sky shares his favorite time of day with Sarah — experiencing an honest, intimate moment (*Guys and Dolls*)
- In *Blue Jasmine*, the titular character is offered happiness and a new start with Dwight — she only needs to be honest with him
- Lisa asks Steve Jobs to live with her before the NEXT launch (*Steve Jobs*)
- Marta can come clean to Blanc rather than follow Ransom's advice (*Knives Out*)

In each case, accepting the offer would avoid the tragedy that is to come (*Salesman, Jasmine, Jobs*) or the painful struggle they will have to endure to get to where they need to be (*Guys, Knives*).

I choose to call this event an Escape Offer, rather than Point of Grace, because the offer for a character of pure goals is a negative offer — yet still a way out of the story.

Harry Potter can join Voldemort; Dorothy can turn over the slippers; Peter can send the villains back. In essence, the hero is given an explicit offer to quit, allowing the villain to win[112]. For the character needing to grow (*Salesman*, *Jasmine*, *Jobs*, *Guys*, *Knives*), accepting the offer would be good for their soul. On the other hand, for the character with pure goals, the offer would be a regression.

- Thor can stay on Sakaar and fight alongside Hulk in the arena, living in luxury — and forgetting about the plight of Asgard (*Thor: Ragnorak*)

- Bryan Stevenson (*Just Mercy*) has lost his other case; now is the time to recognize that the McMillian case is impossible.

- Henrietta (*Silent Sky*) could stay home with her sister and have the life of a normal woman, rather than return to her unladylike work as an astronomer.

The Midpoint Escape Offer is always refused — for good or for ill.

The Eternal Story: Midpoint Escape Offer

Hook: In the beginning, God created...
Balance: The Garden of Eden
Catalyst: Eve and Adam take the fruit
Response to Catalyst: Adam and Eve hide from God — then
     blame others
Final Straw: God sends Adam and Eve out of the Garden
Quest Part One: God works through history to reconnect with
     lost man (aka the Old Testament)
Midpoint: The Nativity — God becomes Man
MIDPOINT ESCAPE OFFER: Jesus is tempted in the desert

Shortly after the Midpoint shift (in plot terms), God in the form of Jesus is offered a way out. The Devil meets Jesus in the desert, interrupting his preparations for his ministry. Three offers are made, offers

112. For Peter Parker, Dr. Strange isn't a villain — but is the force of antagonism in this one point — so the principle applies.

that would derail his purpose: two offers to use his power for selfish purposes (comfort and pride), the third a blatant call to give up the mission. Align with Lucifer, rule together — and Jesus doesn't have to face the tragedy to come.

Like all good Escape Offer moments, this is a testing of character. A reminder of the goal and the forces of conflict. A chance to make a stand for the right thing over the easy thing.

And, like all Escape Offers, the offer of a way out is refused.

Then Jesus said to him, "Away with you, Satan!"[113]

The Lesser Known Temptations

---

113. Matthew 4:10, NKJV

CHAPTER TWENTY-FOUR

Quest Part Two

Quest Part Two

Also known as:
Second Half of Act Two
Pursuit
Bad Guys Close In
Complications & Higher Stakes

Quest Part Two: A series of events in response to the Midpoint and the new goal, leading to the Crisis

In the second part of the Quest, more stuff happens. The characters need to respond to the new reality of the Midpoint, establish new alliances, set out on new tactics. Meanwhile, the forces of antagonism ramp up their game as well.

The scenes increase in rising action, building the story to its inevitable breaking point (Crisis) and resulting final confrontation (Climax).

As with the Quest Part One, the scenes throughout this section have functions to fulfill to keep the story moving forward.

Respond to the Midpoint

The first set of scenes is a chance for the characters to reset — the world has changed, so what does that mean? How are they to react?

- In *Serenity*, Mal and the team have found Haven destroyed and Shepherd Book dead (Midpoint). Running and hiding is no longer an option — every place they must hide is being destroyed. The first scene after Books' death is a conversation between Mal and the Operative — reinforcing the cost of the Midpoint and driving Mal to make his choice: give in and turn in River Tam or fight the unbeatable foe.

- *Come From Away* shows the town having succeeded in the first Quest — the passengers have all been settled in somewhere, even some bonds have been made ("I am Here," "Prayer"). But the settling in has created a whole new problem — the anxiety and powerlessness of being stuck threatens to spill over. The cast takes stock, re-evaluating the situation and potential problems ("On the Edge").

- In *Knives Out*, Marta has gone from the only person without a motive to the one with the greatest motive, with the reading of the will as our Midpoint. She takes stock, confiding in Ransom and relating her entire story.

Shifting or Altering the Want

Often the Want is not altered as much as amplified by the Midpoint. The Mandalorian in "The Jedi" still wants to pass baby Yoda[114] off to a Jedi; he just now must help the Jedi free the town first. Dorothy in *The Wizard of Oz* is still trying to get home; she now has to kill the Wicked Witch to do so. Schofield in *1917* continues with the primary mission; now he must figure out how to do it on his own. Hamlet has always planned on getting revenge — he couldn't move forward until he proved the king was guilty; now that the play pricked the conscience of the king, he is ready for the second half of his plan.

---

114. My apologies, but that character will always be baby Yoda, even though technically it is Grogu. I suppose I should compromise and refer to him as "the child." I'll try to be better.

In other stories, the Want shifts radically based on the Midpoint; the early scenes of Quest Part Two show that change of direction. Macbeth now has the kingdom, and pivots to keeping it by sending out murderers to take out his potential enemies, all while his enemies unite forces. Dave, in the eponymous movie, was working to cover for the president in the first half; now he realizes he can do more good by being president. Joel in *Eternal Sunshine of the Spotless Mind* at first is frantic to erase the girl from his brain; now he pivots to fight to remember her.

New Allies

Many stories have such a dynamic shift by the Midpoint that old enemies become new allies. Scenes will be devoted to the conversion of these contagonists.

Woody must convince Buzz to become an ally so they can escape Sid's house (*Toy Story*). Quill and the other Guardians win over the Ravagers to take on Ronan (*Guardians of the Galaxy*).

The Princess Bride has a lot of fun with this process as the team of good guys in the second half start out in opposition in the first: Westley battles the giant and the swordsman in his first quest; they become the team of heroes who save Westley and the princess in the second. Buttercup herself is resistant to the Dread Pirate Roberts before the Midpoint twist of discovering Roberts is Westley. We will explore contagonists more in our section on characters.

Increase Antagonism

Save the Cat!, Blake Snyder's screenwriting system, has a beat in this section called "Bad Guys Close In." This is a good reminder to not forget the forces of antagonism; the story is driving at this point to a final showdown, and that confrontation will only have power if it is set up.

There are a couple of ways this is addressed in stories. A common way is to cut away to see what the antagonists are up to. *Macbeth* shows Mackie's enemies at first on the run, then joining forces (Malcolm merging his army with Macduff). *Up* changes its format of only showing scenes with Carl and gives us some sessions with Muntz and his dogs. *Hamilton* gives the microphone to Burr not just as narrator, but burgeoning antagonist ("Room Where it Happened") as well as allowing Jefferson/Madison/Burr more than a few plotting sessions.

Challenge the Need

The forces of antagonism are not just external — often Central Characters are battling their old selves as well. The Need is truly challenged and tested throughout this act. Remember that the next point, the one that Quest Part Two is driving towards, is the Crisis, the low point for our Central Character.

In good stories, this isn't just a Crisis of plot, but a Crisis of character. Just as a final confrontation with an antagonist needs to be set up, so does a final confrontation of a character with herself.

- *Knives Out* shows a lovely progression of tests as Marta is forced to face who she is at every turn — standing up to Walt in the back hall; deciding to run from the police in a hilariously slow car chase; discovering her blackmailer is dying at her feet. The progression of Marta's struggle to decide who she is going to be — set in motion by Harlan on the night of his death — leads to her Crisis as she is arrested for choosing to be good. Note how beautifully this positions her with the strength to face the Climax.

- *Death of a Salesman* showcases Biff and Willy trying to change — Biff applying for a desk job, Willy looking for a position in the New York office. (This tactic won't go well for either, as it forces them to face who they really are.)

- *Hamlet*, a play that doesn't shy away from introspection, does not slow down in the Quest Part Two, as Hamlet gets to face his own impulsiveness and drive for vengeance outside his uncle's prayer chamber, while confronting his mother in her bedroom, and while pondering the fate of poor Yorick in the graveyard.

Empathy and Relationships

Another job in Quest Part Two is to buttress relationships for the final half. This is the chance to establish the stakes of the upcoming Act Three[115] — reminding us of what is potentially at risk. Relationships usually carry more heart than the plot, so losing the gold won't have nearly the effect of losing the girl.

It is in this part that Shrek unwittingly falls in love with Fiona. Luke creates a relationship with Leia and deepens his budding friendship with Han Solo (*Star Wars: A New Hope*). Hamilton's wife and her sister beg him to spend more time with family ("Take a Break").

The various groupings of Avengers in *Endgame* do deep character dives. Steve and Tony revisit their pasts — Tony connecting with his father and Steve seeing Peggy. Thor spends time with his mother, rediscovering his purpose. Clint and Natasha battle over which loved one will sacrifice themselves for the soul stone.

Common Mistakes

It is easy here for the action to flatline. We just had a big moment in the Midpoint, and we can see the big moments ahead — Crisis and Climax. These middle scenes, without the proper attention, can become filler — just passing time for the real drama.

As you can see from the examples above, that is not the case. Action needs to continue to rise and gain momentum. The Crisis will crash our story; the Wafer will be a moment of needed calm to reflect. So, Quest Part Two must counter-balance by increasing the tempo.

Another common pitfall is spending too much time on exposition. Since the Midpoint potentially changes a lot, a temptation for the creators is to wade into explanation. Enough needs to be given so the audience is not lost; yet if we stop the story to explain things, we lose the audience. The viewer gives plenty of grace at the start of the night to explain the world; and less grace as the night goes on.

---

115. In this case using "Acts" in terms of the classic three-act structure. Beginning (Act One), Middle (Act Two), and End (Act Three).

Act Two is a deadly spot for many stories. The key is to drive the story forward, all while deepening character and raising stakes.

The Eternal Story: Quest Part 2

Hook: In the beginning, God created...

Balance: The Garden of Eden

Catalyst: Eve and Adam take the fruit

Response to Catalyst: Adam and Eve hide from God — then blame others

Final Straw: God sends Adam and Eve out of the Garden

Quest Part One: God works through history to reconnect with lost man (aka the Old Testament)

Midpoint: The Nativity — God becomes Man

Midpoint Escape Offer: Jesus is tempted in the desert

QUEST PART TWO: Jesus' Ministry and Miracles

In the first part of the Quest, God uses history to try and reconcile humankind to Himself. In the second part, God uses His Son to make the connection. (To quote Thanos in the end credits for *Age of Ultron*, "Fine. I'll do it myself.")

Jesus' life and ministry is the response to the Midpoint twist of God becoming human. The new rules are established ("Not everyone who says to me, 'Lord, Lord,' will enter the kingdom of heaven." — Matthew 7:21, NLT) and an attempt is made to get people to understand ("Hear another parable." — Matthew 21:33).

The Goal is the same, but completely redefined. Religion is upended ("But woe to you, scribes and Pharisees, hypocrites! For you shut the kingdom of heaven in people's faces." — Matthew 23:13-15, NLT) and old ways of thinking uprooted ("How difficult it will be for those who have wealth to enter the kingdom of God!" — Mark 10:23, NLT).

New allies are gained — including former enemies to the message, like tax collectors, prostitutes, zealots, and the occasional churchman. The forces of antagonism are also on the rise, as we check in with Pharisees, Romans, and betrayers.

Emphasis is put on relationships, as empathy is established and the cost of the coming Crisis is made clear. Jesus doesn't just preach, he parties, he heals, he cajoles, he breaks bread, he ministers, he loves.

The Gospel drives forward, all while deepening the character of Christ, giving us a full picture of the man. The stakes are raised — God Himself is at risk.

And our hearts are ready to break.

PART SEVEN

Events — End

CHAPTER TWENTY-FIVE

Crisis

Crisis

Also known as:
All is Lost
Worst Point
Death
Hitting the Wall

Crisis defined: An event (scene or sequence) where the Central Character has reached the lowest point; an "all is lost" moment

In the Crisis, the worst has happened. We are at the bottom of the barrel; all is lost. There is a truism in story: the hero must die. This is rarely literal (although sometimes it is — Harry Potter in *The Deathly Hallows*, for example) and typically refers to a loss so great as to feel as permanent as death for the story.

- In *Gravity*, the Soyuz is out of fuel — Stone's last chance is a bust, she will die in space.
- In *Bridesmaids*, Annie ruins Lillian's shower so thoroughly that there is no going back; the friendship is permanently broken.
- In *Knives Out*, Blanc knows the truth, and Marta will be arrested for murder.

- Biff barges in on Willy in the hotel room, discovering that his cheating father is a complete fraud (*Death of a Salesman*).
- In *Get Out*, Chris has been hypnotized again, and is helpless before the family.
- In *Saving Mr. Banks*, Travers has returned to London and given up on the enterprise.
- In *Fences*, Cory has been kicked out of the house — Troy has lost his son.

A crisis point always embodies the worst possible consequence of the decision taken when the initial dramatic explosion occurred.

—John Yorke, *Into the Woods*

The Crisis is directly linked to the decision made at the Final Straw at the end of Act One. The character sets out to make fast money by manufacturing meth; what's the worst that could happen? (*Breaking Bad*) The character sets out to become king by any means possible; what's the worst that could happen? (*Macbeth*) Two characters from opposing races/houses decide to defy tradition and family and start a relationship; what's the worst that could happen? (*West Side Story, Romeo and Juliet*)

Crisis in Events versus Crisis in Climax

There is often confusion about the placement of Crisis. Robert McKee says that the Crisis is often inside the Climax; and here I depart with the guru.

In a well-made story, the Crisis is a separate scene/sequence before the Climax begins, with space in the plot for a response to the Crisis. The Crisis is there to set up the Climax, and therefore will be distinct.

The confusion comes in because of a mirroring within the Climax that often takes place. Good scenes/sequences have a structure of their own — the same as the structure for the whole piece. Balance, Unbalance, Quest, Crisis, New Balance. A good Climax, therefore, is going to be a mini story with a start, an unbalance, a quest, and so on. A good number of stories have a very full Climax (see discussion of Climaxes below), and will often include a crisis and a climax within the Climactic scene/sequence.

In *West Side Story*, the Crisis for the play is Tony learning that Maria is dead — all is lost, there is nothing left worth living for. This scene sets up the Climax — the final rumble.

Within the Climax, there is a crisis for the scene — Tony's death. This sets up the climax of the Climax — Maria holding Tony, bringing her hellfire condemnation on both houses.

So, a capital "C" Crisis that sets up the Climax, and a lower-case crisis of the Climax. The second is powerful; the first is essential to set up the end of the play.

Character Test — Need Revealed

> *Our English word "crisis" comes from the Greek "krisis" meaning "judgment" or "moment of distinguishing.*
>
> —Earl Palmer, *The Communicator's Commentary*

The Crisis is the ultimate moment of truth for the Central Character. Will the protagonist quit? Have they been defeated? Or will they stand up and try again?

The Crisis lays the groundwork for a choice — the essential choice that will drive us to the Climax and the end of the plot — for good or for ill.

In dramas with three-dimensional characters, the Quest has been a trial of the new self against the old self. The Crisis point forces the Central Character to make the choice — which self will they embrace?

Carl in *Up* is in the process of being that new self, doing all that he can to save Kevin. But then his house is set on fire — the object that represents Ellie, his past, all that he defines himself by. In the Crisis he chooses the house, losing Russell, Kevin, and Dug along with his redeemed self. He will now be forced to make the final decision: keep the house and his old self or choose Russell and his new self.

Shrek's lowest point is when he gets what he wants: to be left alone. Will he stay that way, ignoring all he learned in his travels with Fiona and Donkey?

In the Crisis, the Need is exposed and the full price of the Want is shown. We now clearly see what the real missing piece of the character is as well as the clear cost of achieving Want over Need.

- Rick in *Casablanca* has a low point that could feel like a victory. He has persuaded Ilsa to choose him over her husband (truthfully, for the sake of her husband). The choice coming out will be completely a choice between Want and Need — a choice between earthly pleasure and the soul.

- Woody starts out selfish, acting for himself (*Toy Story*). Will he overcome his flaw?

- Caroline (*I and You*) rejects all around her; will she completely reject Anthony? (A rejection with a much deeper consequence than she knows...)

- Jojo (*Jojo Rabbit*) dreams of being like his hero, Hitler; will his complete loss cement that Want, or will he be redeemed?

The testing is true in character tragedies as well, with the characters embracing their worst selves. After the Crisis, Macbeth follows his new self to the very end, facing off against the man who skirts the prophecy of Mackie being invulnerable against any man of woman born. Walter White ("Pilot," *Breaking Bad*) goes full-on bad guy; Michael (*The Godfather*) eliminates his rivals; Hamlet goes forward seeking revenge.

The "moment of distinguishing" is often the key to whether the story will be one of hope or one of despair.

The Visceral Hit

The Crisis is a chance to grab the audience by the gut, a visceral moment that speaks straight to the heart. The audience should hate the creators for letting this happen.

Spielberg's take on *War Horse* sets up the visceral nature of the Crisis. Violence in this film is very carefully put off screen. Soldiers charge on their horses; we cut to the Germans opening fire; the horses pass by riderless. A spoke in a windmill crosses the screen, blocking a shot to the head. Violence is shown, but with a buffer between audience and action. Until the Crisis.

Joey (the horse) races through No Man's Land and becomes entangled in the barbed wire. And we see the violence for the first time, the barbs cutting into our hero as he hopelessly, helplessly thrashes against the metal. In a movie about masses of death, the Crisis of one horse in peril is completely devastating — and completely visceral.

Come From Away is a musical about an ensemble of dozens of characters facing a devastating situation. The creators brilliantly make the Crisis stand out by reducing us from the myriad of stories to one: Beverly walks us through her love affair with flight and how that love has been permanently shattered ("Me and the Sky"). The chaos is silenced for one very real scar coming from the situation. Visceral.

My wife often mocks me for talking back at the screen. Usually, it is in the moment of Crisis, and my monologue is often just one word: "No!" Or an extended, "No, no, no, no, no!"

- The people turn against Jefferson Smith (*Mr. Smith Goes to Washington*)
- Anita's anger gets the better of her, and she tells Tony that Maria is dead (*West Side Story*)
- Schofield gets swept over the waterfall, and away from his objective (*1917*)
- Aunt May just needs to catch her breath... (*Spider-Man: No Way Home*)

Note that the "no!" response comes from a well-set-up Crisis. The lowest point must come from the natural progression of the story — in some cases, the inevitable outcome of the Quest. What enhances the visceral power isn't that the audience is fooled by an out-of-the-blue event, rather from our worst fear crossing our hopes. The natural consequences of daring to try, of choosing to fight, of taking the steps out of the comfort zone of the Balance.

A good Crisis makes the audience wonder how this whole thing is going to turn out. Despite our history with movies/television/theater, this one might end bad; our hero might lose. Harry Potter is dead; he's our hero, for goodness' sake! Obi Wan lost against Darth Vader — Obi Wan, our only hope! Marta has been caught, and Blanc is taking her in; it's over, right? Clementine has been completely erased from Joel's memory — and the memories cannot be brought back[116].

The complete nature of the Crisis allows a chance for the Central Character to prove herself beyond the limits of the story. Coming back from a minor loss — anyone can do that.

Coming back from death requires serious depth of character.

Common Mistakes

As writers, we often fall in love with our characters. We know them better than anyone, and we wish them well. And no decent human being asks for a friend to suffer. We mess up our Crises in a misguided attempt to save our hero some pain.

And as they say, "No pain, no good story." Or something like that.

Many movies go too soft on the character, delivering a paper cut instead of a killing stroke. Without the cost, the value of the victory is also diminished; a ho-hum Climax is often traced straight back to an easy Crisis — or no Crisis at all.

Allow me to go on a rabbit trail for a moment. A visit to a Protestant church and then a Catholic church, and an outsider will notice one obvious difference between the two sects: the cross. Protestants have an empty cross; Jesus sits actively crucified on the Catholic cross.

I grew up with a foot in several denominations. My Protestant brethren explained to me that they aren't as crass as to show such violence; the cross is empty because Jesus conquered death. Focusing on the death of Jesus is morbid; we don't celebrate a God who died, but one who rose from death!

---

116. *Deathly Hallows: Part 2, A New Hope, Knives Out, Eternal Sunshine of the Spotless Mind*

Let me defend my Catholic siblings for a moment. The crucifixion in no way negates the resurrection; rather, it is the very thing that gives power to the resurrection. Skipping over the unpleasantness of Friday is not a step of power, but rather something that undercuts the effects of Sunday.

Don't misunderstand me — I have no problem with empty crosses. Just as long as we understand that the power of the empty cross is dependent on the fact that the cross was not originally empty.

> *For I resolved to know nothing while I was with you except Jesus Christ and him crucified.*
>
> —1 Corinthians 2:2, NIV

The Eternal Story: Crisis

Hook: In the beginning, God created...

Balance: The Garden of Eden

Catalyst: Eve and Adam take the fruit

Response to Catalyst: Adam and Eve hide from God — then blame others

Final Straw: God sends Adam and Eve out of the Garden

Quest Part One: God works through history to reconnect with lost man (aka the Old Testament)

Midpoint: The Nativity — God becomes Man

Midpoint Escape Offer: Jesus is tempted in the desert

Quest Part Two: Jesus' Ministry and Miracles

CRISIS: Jesus dies on the cross

No one saw this coming, despite Jesus repeatedly attempting to warn them. The cross is the inevitable consequence of God becoming man, the event that all of Quest Part Two leads towards. And yet we scream our "no!" along with the women at the foot of the cross. We wait for the angels to come and save him; we are ready for the miracle that stops this from happening.

We are not ready for the miracle of God allowing this to happen.

Bottom of the barrel; complete loss. The disciples could only think the ministry of Jesus is over. There is no coming back from this.

If we take our time, the modern viewer should feel the same. Living through the events rather than jumping ahead, we must wonder: what now?

From a Story point of view, the Bible uses the same technique Frank Darabont so brilliantly puts in play in *The Shawshank Redemption*. We see the events unfold from the point of view of humanity, not from our Central Character (Christ); just as *Shawshank* is viewed from Red's point of view, rather than Andy's. This story-telling technique allows a greater emphasis on theme.

Thus, the Bible puts us in the thematic position, and the questions of the Crisis become our questions: how will we respond? Will we allow the loss to be the end, or will we keep going? Will we use this opportunity to embrace the new self, or revert to our old selves?

Is the story over, or will we have the strength of character to rise back up?

CHAPTER TWENTY-SIX

Wafer and Post Crisis

Wafer

Also known as:

Dark Night of the Soul

Wafer defined: A brief event immediately following the Crisis, showing the emotional cost of the Crisis

I am indebted to Christopher Riley (author of *The Hollywood Standard*) for pointing out the Wafer to me. I was walking him through my take on structure, and he asked, "Where's your wafer?"

I nodded sagely and gave him my complete answer.

"What's a wafer?"

The Wafer is a small but critical scene/sequence in the story immediately following the action of the Crisis. This is the chance for the Central Character to feel the weight of the loss they just suffered. The action during the loss is often too busy to really feel the cost.

The Rileys (Chris and Kathy) call this a "wafer" because it is designed to be thin; this is a time to feel, not to wallow.

> *"A voice was heard in Ramah, weeping and loud lamentation, Rachel weeping for her children; she refused to be comforted, because they were no more."*
>
> —Matthew 2:18, NASB

The Wafer is less about action and more about emotion. A chance to live in the moment, to make the loss real. So real that moving on becomes a bigger deal.

Chris in *Get Out* listens to the tape that explains exactly what is going to happen to him. Harry Potter meets Dumbledore on the train station platform between here and there (*Deathly Hallows: Part 2*). Ryan Stone talks to an Inuit fisherman (*Gravity*). Hamilton walks with his wife through the streets ("It's Quiet Uptown"). Schofield listens to a soldier pray out "I am a Poor Wayfaring Stranger" (*1917*).

Macbeth is rattled having learned of his wife's death; the first time he is truly thrown off since the re-assurance of the witches. He cannot die; but has to wonder if living should be the goal.

Life's but a walking shadow, a poor player,

That struts and frets his hour upon the stage,

And then is heard no more. It is a tale

Told by an idiot, full of sound and fury,

Signifying nothing.

—Macbeth, Act V, Scene 5

The Eternal Story: Wafer

Hook: In the beginning, God created...

Balance: The Garden of Eden

Catalyst: Eve and Adam take the fruit

Response to Catalyst: Adam and Eve hide from God — then blame others

Final Straw: God sends Adam and Eve out of the Garden

Quest Part One: God works through history to reconnect with lost man (aka The Old Testament)

Midpoint: The Nativity — God becomes Man

Midpoint Escape Offer: Jesus is tempted in the desert

Quest Part Two: Jesus' Ministry and Miracles

Crisis: Jesus dies on the cross

WAFER: Saturday

We can only contemplate the questions of the Crisis if we take the time to feel the Crisis. God put this very clearly in the design of history; the death of His Son is not brushed over. Jesus does not rise from the cross.

Instead, we have three days of contemplation, of feeling the weight, of understanding the reality of the loss. The disciples lock themselves away; no more action, just feeling.

Jesus stopped in front of Lazarus' tomb, after Lazarus' death and before his resurrection, and Jesus wept. Jesus knew what was coming; but that he took the time to feel. It is not much of a leap to assume that Saturday isn't just for us; it is for God as well. He looked down and watched His Son die; and he took the time to weep the loss.

Surely He has borne our griefs,

And carried our sorrows...

—Isaiah 53:4, ESV

Post Crisis

Response to the Crisis

Between the Crisis and the Climax we have some space to transition from all is lost to final confrontation — steps from response to redirection. Every story is going to find its own rhythm to make this shift. Some of the possible types of scenes here include:

The Wafer

Technically part of this response section.

The Decision

The Central character makes their final decision about how they will respond. Sometimes this comes with a visit with mentoring characters, such as Harry and Dumbledore (*Harry Potter and the Deathly Hallows: Part 2*) or Miles listening his dad apologize outside the door of his room (*Spider-Man: Into the Spider-Verse*). Or another version of Spider-Man listening to two other versions of himself (*Spider-Man: No Way Home*).

Regrouping, Healing, Re-arming

Having decided to go forward, the Central Character takes the time to heal from the earlier defeat. There may be a montage of getting better, training or restocking of weapons (for action stories, at least).

A new plan may be developed, like in *Star Wars: A New Hope*, as Leia shares the Death Star plans, and the group gathers for instructions.

Final Goodbyes

We have one more shot at reminding the audience of the stakes should the Climax fail. For example, *Independence Day* gives us a wedding between Hiller and Jasmine. *Argo* has a scene of goodbyes at the house. Hamilton doesn't say goodbye, but we are given the equivalent as Eliza tries to get him to go to bed as he writes the last letter of his life ("Best of Wives, Best of Women").

Harry Potter in *Deathly Hallows: Part 2* finds space for this before the Crisis, as the dead walk with him to his fate with Voldemort.

Premature Rejoicing

In a similar vein, we often visit the opposition to see them prematurely rejoicing. The rejoicing of the bad guys buttresses the audiences desire for a reversal in the Climax. Voldemort displaying the body of Harry for all those at Hogwarts to see (*Deathly Hallows: Part 2*).

Subplots Resolved

Depending on the pacing of the final actions of the story, some subplots are best resolved here rather than left hanging. In *Come From Away*, we find out what happened with the animals that were on the grounded flights. In *Hidden Figures*, Dorothy's plot line of training to take over programming the computers is resolved before reaching Katherine's climax.

~

The key to this response section is a combination of pause and ramping up. The audience needs a chance to gather strength for the climax as much as the protagonist does. The pause here allows that break.

At the same time, the response allows us to build up to the Climax. This includes setting up plot points that will pay off in the final battle, which can be doubled up with other functions. Luke parts ways with Han in *A New Hope*, setting up the rapscallion's surprising return at the critical moment. Marta wraps up the story line of the missing medical examiner's report, laying out a crucial piece of evidence for Blanc (*Knives Out*).

We've experienced the Crisis, felt its weight, made the critical decision, and regathered our strength. Now on to the final battle.

CHAPTER TWENTY-SEVEN

Climax

Climax

Also known as:
Final Showdown
Finale
Matter Resolved
Catastrophe

Climax defined: A sequence of scenes showing the final action of the plot, resolving the conflict; the final showdown

We have arrived at the moment that everything from the Catalyst on has led to: the moment of truth, the showdown, the last attempt to achieve the quest. David Ball (*Backwards & Forwards*) says, "Stasis comes about at the close of the play when the major forces of the play either get what they want or are forced to stop trying." Freytag's Pyramid calls the Climax "Catastrophe": "The conflict is resolved, whether through a catastrophe, the downfall of the hero, or through his victory and transfiguration."[117]

---

117. Quoted from John Yorke's *Into the Woods: How Stories Work and Why We Tell Them*

The Avengers battle for New York, or battle for the capital of Sokovia, or battle against Thanos (*The Avengers*, *Age of Ultron*, *Infinity War*, *Endgame*). Harry Potter takes on Voldemort (*Deathly Hallows: Part 2*). Biff confronts Willy one last time (*Death of a Salesman*). Macduff's forces invade Macbeth's castle. Hamlet fights Laertes and takes his revenge on Claudius. The Mandalorian and Ahsoka fight Lang and Elsbeth ("The Jedi"). The passengers in *Come From Away* fly back home and confront the changes to their world ("Something's Missing").

The Climax is going to determine the resolution — what the New Balance might look like. "[The Climax]...is not necessarily full of noise and violence. Rather, it must be full of meaning." (Robert McKee, *Story*)

We often think of the Climax as the moment of biggest action and explosions, yet the best Climaxes hold the moments with the most meaning.

In *West Side Story*, the Climax's power isn't in the fight, or the death of Tony: it is Maria learning to hate. Arthur Laurents (along with Sondheim and Bernstein) chose to alter the ending from the source material (*Romeo and Juliet*); rather than Maria dying, we have the potentially worse tragedy of Maria losing her faith.

The Princess Bride plays delightfully with expectations in its Climax. Leading up to the final confrontation, we are given a whiz-bang sword fight between Inigo and Rugen. How can we possibly come up with a more satisfying battle?

By making it a battle of character rather than brawn. The biggest physical action in Westley's face-off with Humperdinck is Westley standing up. But the psychological battle is massive, and Westley's victory over (and humiliation of) the prince is so much more satisfying than discovering that the dread pirate was better at swordplay.

Meaning trumps explosions any day.

Functions of the Climax

Obviously, the Climax is there to finish off our story. Yet to finish well, the sequence should achieve the following four goals.

Fulfill the Want/Need

The Climax answers the questions of Want and Need — either in achieving, completely losing, or redefining the Want.

Shrek, in going after Fiona, changes his Want from being alone and embraces his Need to engage in community. Hamlet rejects his Need to go for his Want — vengeance. Joy (*Inside Out*) embraces her need to let go, allowing her charge to experience all emotions, at the same time changing her Want from keeping her charge happy to giving her charge a full life. Willy in *Death of a Salesman* rejects the Need to live in reality, choosing the fantasy, dying thinking he is a hero.

Fulfill the Promise of the Unbalance

The Climax completes the pattern by answering the questions raised in the Catalyst/Final Straw. The antagonist is faced; a chance is made to restore Balance.

Harry Potter faces Voldemort — the catalyst to his whole life of problems starting with the moment that gave Harry his scar. T'Challa faces off against Killmonger, the manipulator behind Klaue's original museum heist. Hamlet takes on the man the ghost fingered for his dad's murder all the way back in Act One[118].

Note that the outcome of the Climax doesn't matter — just that the pattern is complete. In the section on New Balance, we will discuss more the idea of failed final battles.

Final Test of Character

A decision was made coming out of the Crisis to keep fighting; the Climax is the keeping of that decision, the proof that the character was sincere in their choice. Without the action, the choice isn't real — any more than a child saying they will clean their room is real. Until the room is cleaned...

---

118. *Deathly Hallows: Part 2, Black Panther, Hamlet*

- Tony (*West Side Story*) seeks out Chino, not for vengeance but to end the cycle (by ending his own life)
- Shrek — and every other guy/gal in a romance — takes the risk to go and get the girl (or guy, as the case may be)
- Schofield in *1917* could easily quit — he is too late to stop the advance, and it isn't his brother in harm's way; and still he chooses to keep going

Adaptations of *A Christmas Carol* (and there are a lot of them[119]) often misunderstand the Climax, and therefore miss this point. Typically, the big final act scene is Scrooge showing up at his clerks' home, providing a goose for Mrs. Cratchitt and hope for Tiny Tim. Dickens' original (which indeed gets this right) doesn't play to the maudlin, and Scrooge does not go to Bob's house — his Climax is more personal, and far more dangerous. Christmas Present earlier takes Scrooge to his nephew's house, and Ebenezer sees how they have fun — by mocking Scrooge. He is not loved in the home of his last living relative, a fate he earned. And in the original story, that is where Scrooge goes on Christmas Day — not a Climax of joy that Scrooge brings to others, but a Climax of humility and truly changed character, as Scrooge makes himself vulnerable to others.

Catharsis for the Audience

Lastly, the Climax needs to pay attention to the hearers of the story: the audience. There should be a dramatic payoff for the journey in the hearts of the viewers. Aristotle (in his *Poetics*) speaks in terms of "catharsis" or purging of the emotions built up over the course of the story.

Screenwriter Michael Arndt, in his brilliant video essay "On Endings,"[120] breaks down *Star Wars: A New Hope*, giving especial atten-

---

119. *The Muppet Christmas Carol* is the best movie version. Patrick Stewart's one man show the best stage version. Change my mind.

120. Available at http://www.pandemoniuminc.com/endings-video. I first heard Arndt's take at the 2015 Austin Film Festival — another fantastic source

tion to the last two minutes of the Climax. Arndt advises that there are really three types of stakes — external, internal, and philosophical (thematic). For *Star Wars*, the Death Star's approach to the rebel base represents the external stakes; Luke's dream of destiny, the internal; and the theme of selfishness against altruism the philosophical.

Arndt's suggestion for a great ending is to reverse the stakes in each area from failure to success — and to do so as close to each other as possible. *A New Hope* gets the audience cheering not just by having Han return (philosophical), or Luke trust the force (internal), or blowing up the Death Star (external) — but by having all three happen within 43 seconds of each other. This is what Arndt calls an insanely great ending.

Common Mistakes

A good story can be completely ruined by a bad ending. Series television knows this well: series that were beloved for an entire run become tainted as "bad" by a lousy closing season. *Game of Thrones* serves as a prime example. Rotten Tomatoes, a website that tracks scores for reviews and audience reactions, records a critical score of 93% in the penultimate season, which plummets to 54% in the last season.

A couple of decades after it became the highest grossing film in America, the most talked about moment in *Titanic* is when Rose clearly had enough room on her block of wood to save Jack. I doubt the film-makers were hoping that would be the scene that defined their epic.[121]

More common mistakes that can tank a Climax — and thus tank a story, include:

1. Stakes Too Low

The final showdown should be for higher stakes than the previous parts of the story. *A New Hope* starts with an attempt to save a princess and ends with an attempt to save the galaxy.

2. No Danger of Losing

---

for all things screenwriting.

121. On the flip side, a good ending can elevate a story. Lauren Gunderson's *I and You* is a good play, until the climax. Then the show is revealed to be a great play.

If the conclusion is a foregone, well, conclusion, then audience investment will drop to zero. Zack Snyder's *Justice League* falls into this trap; once Superman arrives, Steppenwolf has no chance of success. The movie's ending is pretty, but empty.

Often stories will remind the audience of the very real possibility that their heroes can lose just before or in the early parts of the Climax such as the deaths of Obi Wan in the Crisis of *A New Hope*, Wash in *Serenity*, Bouc in *Death on the Nile*.

Other stories require a loss to win. The Iron Giant (of *The Iron Giant*) must sacrifice his own life to save the village. The entire cast of heroes in *Star Wars: Rogue One* faces a similar choice. The beauty of the mournful yet hopeful ending of *West Side Story* is that the leads do indeed lose.

3. Victory Not Earned

If the prize is too easily won, all that comes before is overshadowed. Sometimes this is a case of poorly used coincidence, so the ending seems easy. In romances, we often see the final decision to choose each other motivated by the fact that the two-hour time slot for our TV movie is coming to an end.

As stated above, the Climax is a chance for us to see who the character has become. We long to see growth in our Central Characters, and we know that ease is an enemy of growth.

> *Not only so, but we also glory in our sufferings, because we know that suffering produces perseverance; perseverance, character; and character, hope.*[122]

---

122. Romans 3:3-4, NIV

CLOSE UP: Climax Structure
Serenity

We discussed in the section on Crisis that each event/scene/sequence has its own full structure, so you can see a crisis in the Climax, separate from the main Crisis of the whole plot.

Some stories take a deep dive into their Climaxes, and really build out the story within a story that these sequences create. The battle for New York in *The Avengers* is a good example — a large chunk of the movie is devoted to that battle. Or, on the battle theme, the battle for Hogwarts in *Harry Potter and the Deathly Hallows: Part 2.*

Many creators in trying to mimic the power of the massive climaxes in the prior movies simply make long Climaxes. Bigger explosions, bigger action, sure; but ultimately more boring and less fulfilling. A good Climax isn't just whiz-bang action (as we said before); rather, it reflects the whole journey.

Joss Whedon's *Serenity* is a great example for us. The show follows a standard, full structure. The Climax also has a full structure, and the actions in the finale mimic and comment on the whole.

Here is the breakdown (numbers denote page numbers in the script):

EVENT	THE WHOLE STORY	THE CLIMAX
CATALYST	26* The Reavers attack the crew!	100 Mal attacks the Reavers
FINAL STRAW	45-46 River battles everyone	100 Mal and the crew attack everyone!
MIDPOINT	82-84 Book dies	105 Wash dies

RESULT OF MIDPOINT	Crew unites to go to Miranda	Crew divides – the group to defend, Mal to take the Miranda message to the universe
CRISIS	94-96 The crew hears Caron's message; realize the Alliance is too big to defeat	108 Mal hears Mr. Universe's message – the Alliance destroyed the equipment; the Operative is too powerful to defeat 112-115 The crew fights the Reavers – the Reavers are too relentless to defeat
WAFER	96-97 Mal goes off alone to mourn, they have survived, but there is no hope for the universe	116 The crew lie together without Mal, they are going to die, but there is hope for the universe**
CLIMAX	100-120 Mal and the crew go to battle together	118 Mal alone finishes the fight against the Alliance 118-119 River alone finishes the fight against the Reavers
NEW BALANCE	120-126 They have won the battle at great loss; Mal and the crew are warned that the Alliance isn't done with them	119-120 They have won the skirmishes at great cost; Mal and the crew realize the Alliance still might kill them

*Arguably, this happens just before the Catalyst — Simon and River opting to leave the crew. The Reavers could be just one of the six things that need to be changed.

**Zoe: (almost convincingly) "He got through. I know he got through."

~

Note how Whedon plays with the times of alignment (someone dies) and reversals (uniting, splitting up). This plays into character development as well. For example, River finishing the battle against the Reavers alone is a cap to her character throughout the series and the movie: from being the one putting all into danger, to being the one who saves everyone.

Not every story is going to have such an intertwined Climax; and not every story calls for one. Certainly, if the creators are going to give a lengthy Climax, one would hope they would honor the whole in the peak moments and pay attention to how structure can give deeper meanings to the sequence.

The Eternal Story: Climax

Hook: In the beginning, God created...

Balance: The Garden of Eden

Catalyst: Eve and Adam take the fruit

Response to Catalyst: Adam and Eve hide from God — then blame others

Final Straw: God sends Adam and Eve out of the Garden

Quest Part One: God works through history to reconnect with lost man (aka the Old Testament)

Midpoint: The Nativity — God becomes Man

Midpoint Escape Offer: Jesus is tempted in the desert

Quest Part Two: Jesus' Ministry and Miracles

Crisis: Jesus dies on the cross

Wafer: Saturday

CLIMAX: The resurrection; Jesus defeats death

J.R.R. Tolkien tells us that true fairy tales (true myths) contain happy endings — they are the opposite of tragedies. He refers to the "Eucatastrophe" — described as a swift, joyous turn, a sudden and miraculous grace. No matter how hard and ugly the journey, the end is a salvation brighter even than the start.

The resurrection is that swift, joyous turn, from the darkness of death to the grace of everlasting life.

Remember Freytag's Pyramid's definition of the Climax: "The conflict is resolved, whether through a catastrophe, the downfall of the hero, or through his victory and transfiguration."[123]

We all face battles. Some we win, some we lose. Jesus took on the ultimate battle, reaching victory and transfiguration.

---

123. Again, quoted from John Yorke's *Into the Woods: How Stories Work and Why We Tell Them*

CHAPTER TWENTY-EIGHT

New Balance

New Balance

Also known as:
Resolution
Denouement
Return with the Elixir
Aftermath

New Balance defined: A series of events showing the new world of the Central Character

We have reached our resolution, and now we show the result of the journey. The key for this Event is the same as in the Five Part Story — the Balance must be new. The situation, the characters and/or the audience must have significantly changed to justify the journey. Too many poorly told stories end back at the beginning — losing out in their potential of truly affecting audiences. Even "mere entertainments" have more lasting impact — more lasting joy and laughter — when told as a proper story.

The New Balance is typically a series of scenes, a chance to rest in the new world. As with every section, the length depends on how much time is needed. *North by Northwest* has a brilliantly short New Balance. We see a literal cliffhanger at the end of the Climax, as Kendall hangs by her fingertips off Mount Rushmore. Thornhill reaches for her, trying to pull her up — and pulls her straight out of the Climax into the upper berth of a sleeper car: they are celebrating their honeymoon. The movie ends moments later, with the audience filling in all the blanks themselves.

West Side Story also has a short resolution — a procession as both gangs join to carry Tony's body out of the park. It is again up to the audience to decide if this moment of truce — and the sacrifices to get there — will last.

Scenes here will often mirror moments from the Balance, showing just how much the world has changed. We see the hero punished or rewarded for their journey.

- *Frozen*: the kingdom is thawed out, and the bad guys deported
- *Guardians of the Galaxy*: the guardians honored, and records are cleared
- *Toy Story*: celebration of Christmas at Andy's new house
- *Macbeth*: the new king is established, and Mackie's head is put on display
- *Glass Menagerie*: Tom takes off to find himself
- Numerous episodes of *Law & Order*: everyone gathers for drinks in McCoy's office and discuss their reactions to the way the trial ended

The pattern has been completed; the promise of the opening fulfilled.

Note that the ending does not need to be tidy. Everyone doesn't have to be happy, and all questions answered, just the pattern is completed.

The Fellowship of the Ring does not in any way end in a tidy knot. Frodo and Sam are off on their own; Merry and Pippin are captives; Aragorn, Legolas, and Gimli are in pursuit; and Boromir and Gandalf are dead. The story is not over — but the pattern is complete. The movie/book is about the Fellowship; now that the Fellowship is ended, so is this part of the story.

Most people forget that Rocky (in the first of the franchise) does not win. He technically loses the final fight — yet the goal wasn't to win, but to prove himself. He went the distance; we can save the idea of winning the title for another chapter.

- Mad Max (*Fury Road, The Road Warrior, Beyond Thunderdome*) still has not found a home; he still wanders.

- Billy Beane (*Moneyball*) did not win the World Series; but he did prove his system works.

- We don't know what will happen next for Chris and Ann (*All My Sons*); we do know the saga of Joe and his lies has concluded.

Functions of the New Balance

A major function of the New Balance is to show the growth (or lack thereof) of the Central Character. They have learned or changed, and it is in action that such change is cemented as real and lasting. In *Toy Story*, we see Woody working alongside Buzz, celebrating (and then fearing) Christmas morning and the arrival of new presents. In *A Christmas Carol*, Scrooge gives Cratchitt a (gasp!) raise. In *Up*, Carl shows up to Russell's badge ceremony, and then sits with the boy eating ice cream and watching cars.

Often the New Balance will show the response of the world to the result of the Climax. It may include scenes of celebrations (*Star Wars: A New Hope/Return of the Jedi*), weddings or funerals (*Shrek*/Shakespeare's comedies/*Death of a Salesman/Avengers: Endgame/Fences*), news spreading (*Glass/Serenity*), commentary on the future (*Hidden Figures/Modern Family/Hamilton*), returning home (*The Return of the King/The Wizard of Oz*), or death/transition of the Central Character (*Les Misérables/The Return of the King*).

The cost of the journey can be reinforced here. A common pitfall is to ignore the sacrifices made to arrive at this point. The most obvious transgressors are the movies with high death tolls, and all we see after the Climax is rejoicing that the Central Character made it out okay. The flip side are the movies that acknowledge what it took out of the characters: *Serenity*'s tribute to its fallen, *Endgame*'s funeral for Tony, Linda demanding that attention must be paid to her dead husband in *Death of a Salesman*.

A good ending deepens the victory (or loss) by reminding us of the journey. Consider how the audience is meant to leave *Romeo and Juliet*, as the Prince admonishes:

> *A glooming peace this morning with it brings;*
> *The sun, for sorrow, will not show his head:*
> *Go hence, to have more talk of these said things:*
> *Some shall be pardon'd, and some punished:*
> *For never was a story of more woe*
> *Than this of Juliet and her Romeo.*

The New Balance is also a chance to tie up minor loose ends. Bond defeats the forgotten henchman (pick any early Bond film); Thornburg gets his well-deserved punch in the face by Holly in *Die Hard*; we discover what happened to Malvolio in *Twelfth Night*.

Audience closure and/or audience food for thought is another function of the New Balance. As stated above, it may not be closure for the characters, but a completion of the pattern for the audience. *Star Wars: The Empire Strikes Back* ends with the team's missions in failure — Han is in carbonite; Luke has lost his hand and the honor of his father. Yet with the pattern complete, the audience can wait for answers in the next story.

Argo revisits the players in Hollywood, and we see Mendez with his son. Joe in *Soul* starts his new life, committed to enjoying it. In *Come From Away*, the crew and passengers reunite in Gander, and we get our updates (Nick and Diane get together; Kevin T moves on; Beulah, aided by Hannah, is recovering). Audiences have enough answers, enough information, enough closure.

However, we should keep in mind that closure does not mean the audience leaving the story behind. The best of stories have the audience taking the story with them, giving food for thought.

X-Men ends with Charles playing chess with Magneto — is forgiveness possible? *Cabin in the Woods* and *Snowpiercer* both leave the audience reeling, wondering if we would make the same choice — and is the choice possibly justified? *Come From Away* inspires; *Hamlet* warns;

Just Mercy challenges; *Get Out* unsettles; *Les Misérables* moves; *Knives Out* models; *Up* encourages. All are stories continuing to work after the storytelling is done.

This is part of the strength of teaching in parables. Jesus would often leave the audience to ponder the stories, to carry them away. Whether perplexed over their place in the story ("The Sower"), or if they could ever live up to the actions of the characters ("The Lost Son"), or how to answer the question left hanging ("The Good Samaritan — who is your neighbor?"), the New Balance has power in fulfilling the story yet still living on.

The Eternal Story: New Balance

Hook: In the beginning, God created...

Balance: The Garden of Eden

Catalyst: Eve and Adam take the fruit

Response to Catalyst: Adam and Eve hide from God — then blame others

Final Straw: God sends Adam and Eve out of the Garden

Quest Part One: God works through history to reconnect with lost man (aka the Old Testament)

Midpoint: The Nativity — God becomes Man

Midpoint Escape Offer: Jesus is tempted in the desert

Quest Part Two: Jesus' Ministry and Miracles

Crisis: Jesus dies on the cross

Wafer: Saturday

Climax: The resurrection; Jesus defeats death

NEW BALANCE: God restores creation with New Jerusalem

Balance is restored; the journey set upon when Eve and Adam first sinned is finally at an end. Note that we start in a garden and we end in a city. This is not a restoration or return to Eden; we have gone on a journey and ended someplace new.

I saw the Holy City, the new Jerusalem, coming down out of heaven from God, prepared as a bride beautifully dressed for her husband. And I heard a loud voice from the throne saying, "Look! God's dwelling place is now among the people, and he will dwell with them. They will be his people, and God himself will be with them and be their God. He will wipe every tear from their eyes. There will be no more death or mourning or crying or pain, for the old order of things has passed away."

—Revelation 21:2-5, NIV

CHAPTER TWENTY-NINE

Tag

Tag

Also known as:
Epilogue
Stinger
Post Credits
Mid Credits

Tag defined: An event outside of the concluded plot that teases to something beyond this story

This final Event, like the Hook, is not required for a well-rounded story. In fact, most stories do not have a Tag. Yet it has been used to great effect recently in franchise movies to build buzz between films.

Marvel movies have become notorious for their mid- and post-credit scenes; and for the first time in modern film history, audiences regularly stick around for the credits. Tags aren't new, although many people may have missed them in the past.

The first film Tag I remember was *Young Sherlock Holmes*; as the credits rolled, a sleigh wound its way through the mountains. As a film geek, I would stay for the credits anyway (to the annoyance of my siblings); but this time it paid off as we discovered that Sherlock's math teacher not only lived, but now had a new identity: Professor Moriarty.

If I was a tad older, I would have been the right age to see *Carrie* at the theaters. At the very end of the story, Sue has a dream of visiting Carrie's final resting place and is shocked as a hand jumps out of the dirt to grab her. Carrie may (or may not) be gone, but the effects of her story live on.

Tags are standard for television sitcoms. After the main story is resolved, we come back for one more short scene: often a funny wrap-up of a forgotten subplot. It is as if to say, "You thought the funny was over? The funny goes on! Come back next week for more."

The musical play *Into the Woods* has a marvelous Tag. The story starts with characters all wishing for things; Act One is what they do to get their wishes; and Act Two is how they pay the consequences of wishing. When balance is finally restored (at a goodly body count), the chorus sings of what has been learned ("Wishes come true, not free," "Careful the tale you tell, that is the spell — children will listen!"). Then they break into a rousing reprise of "Into the Woods" — crescendoing into a final: "And happy ever after!"

Ah, but it does not end there. The New Balance does — but not the musical. It has a two-word tag, as Cinderella quickly steps forward, and between the final lyrics and the final note, says, "I wish." After everything, we still foolishly wish.

Queen of Katwe has a very simple, and incredibly moving Tag. During the film's closing credits, each main actor steps into the frame and is joined by the real person they just portrayed in the movie. The reality of the story, the Truth it had to tell, cascades over the viewer. Yeah, I cried at this simple moment of Truth.

The idea is that the story is bigger than the telling; it goes on past this particular plot. The characters have a life beyond this; and even for those who don't (Hamlet, for instance), there is a life beyond for the characters who replace them. The end is never the end; what happened in this story is just there to prepare us for the next story.

Instead train yourself to be godly. Physical training is good, but training for godliness is much better, promising benefits in this life and in the life to come.

—1 Timothy 4:7-8, NLT

The story has been fulfilled, not finished. There is a life to come; our trials and tribulations are the workouts for that life.

CHAPTER THIRTY

The Eternal Story Summary

Hook: In the beginning, God created...

Balance: The Garden of Eden

Catalyst: Eve and Adam take the fruit

Response to Catalyst: Adam and Eve hide from God — then blame others

Final Straw: God sends Adam and Eve out of the Garden

Quest Part One: God works through history to reconnect with lost man (aka the Old Testament)

Midpoint: The Nativity — God becomes Man

Midpoint Escape Offer: Jesus is tempted in the desert

Quest Part Two: Jesus' Ministry and Miracles

Crisis: Jesus dies on the cross

Wafer: Saturday

Climax: The resurrection; Jesus defeats death

New Balance: God restores creation with New Jerusalem

Why do we look for this structure in every book, film, play, and show? Why is Story structure hardwired within us? Because it is The Story. We are hardwired to seek out the story of God's redemption in every tale we hear.

Let me be clear: I am not saying that the Gospel happens to fit the hardwiring inside of us; I believe we are hardwired because it is the shape of the Gospel. God wishes for us to seek him — so we look for His salvation at every turn.

J.R.R. Tolkien argues that fantasy/stories help us to see reality clearer, to help us to see as we were meant to see. That is why for him "true" stories are marked by the eucatastrophe — to mirror the Great Eucatastrophe we know to be the Truth and the Life. Our stories are reminders of the Way.

> *He has made everything beautiful in its time. He has also set eternity in the human heart; yet no one can fathom what God has done from beginning to end.*
>
> —Ecclesiastes 3:11, NIV

We have been given a promise; and we wait for the fulfillment of that promise.

We know we are not worthy, but only with God's grace can we succeed.

We seek out our goals; but we know the truth is that we have a Need greater than our goals.

And the story of how that need is fulfilled, even though it requires death, is the only story that will ever satisfy.

CHAPTER THIRTY-ONE

Five Part and Events

For clarity, here is how the typical acts, Five Part Story, and Events nestle into each other.

ACTS	5 PART STORY	EVENTS
		Hook
	Balance	Balance
Act One		Catalyst
	Unbalance	Response to Catalyst
		Final Straw
		Quest Part One
	Quest	Midpoint / Escape Offer
Act Two		Quest Part Two
	Crisis	Crisis
	Crisis (continued)	Wafer
		Post Crisis
Act Three		Climax
	New Balance	New Balance
		Tag

CLOSE UP: Event Points
Hamilton

Let's integrate all the steps and events using one example. For our case study, I've chosen Lin Manuel Miranda's work of genius, *Hamilton*. The musical play comes from Miranda's extreme talent wedded to his work ethic — going through countless drafts, workshops, and test runs before landing on the Broadway stage.

Structure in theater tends to be less obvious than in films — and this is for a very good reason. Linda Seger in *The Art of Adaptation* outlines the difference between novels and films in terms of language. In sum:

In literature, the language is "words," which are used to build "detail," to create "theme." In film, the language is "images," which build "action," to create "story." Story is king of the moving pictures — not that film doesn't have theme, but the theme is there to support story. In a novel, plot is there to support theme.

Yes, this is a generalization, but a useful one. What film does best is story.

Linda doesn't cover theater in her book, so I've devised my own take. Theater relies on two distinctives: its ephemeral nature — it happens, then disappears; and the live aspect. Theater is designed to be experienced by a live audience in a room with live performers — it happens in the space, with all involved undergoing the same experience.

So, in theater, the language is "dialogue," which builds "relationships," to create a "human connection."[124] As compared to film and

---

124. One play perfectly modeling this view of theater as human connection is *In & Of Itself* by Derek DelGaudio. The play (which I will not give any plot or explanation of — as it is best experienced knowing absolutely nothing about what is going to happen) strips away all other elements, giving a very clear view of the visceral connection between actor and audience. A version shows on Hulu — were you to watch, imagine how it must have felt to be in the audience. You will start to understand the power that theater has that we can assume in watching film/TV but must be experienced to be fully appreciated.

television, plays are much more visceral. The audience experiences theater in their gut just as much as in their senses.

The audience is a witness to the event, inexorably inseparable from the performance.

Plot, then, is subservient to the experience, and thus more subtle in a play than in a film. The character dramas of Horton Foote rely on minimal plotting, which in no way lessens their impact and power.

Plot is subservient — but still present. The bones are still the platform on which the characters say their dialogue and form their relationships. *Hamilton* is the perfect example — a play that spans a man's lifetime. At first glance, the skeleton may not be obvious — and yet Lin Manuel Miranda, like Shakespeare, shows himself to be a master of plotting.

The Core

To help get our minds around the structure, let's first look at its core, the two-part Quest[125]: Hamilton fights for independence for America, and when America wins, he fights to create the new nation, thus creating his legacy.

In this simplified view of the musical, we have room for all the main plot points as well as the intertwined subplots of Aaron Burr and Eliza.

Scene List

Here is a list of the scenes/songs of Hamilton:

ACT I

1. "Alexander Hamilton"
2. "Aaron Burr, Sir"
3. "My Shot"
4. "The Story of Tonight"
5. "The Schuyler Sisters"
6. "Farmer Refuted"
7. "You'll Be Back"

125. Per our Five Part Story for Features

8. "Right Hand Man"
9. "A Winter's Ball"
10. "Helpless"
11. "Satisfied"
12. "The Story of Tonight (Reprise)"
13. "Wait For It"
14. "Stay Alive"
15. "Ten Duel Commandments"
16. "Meet Me Inside"
17. "That Would Be Enough"
18. "Guns and Ships"
19. "History Has Its Eyes on You"
20. "Yorktown (The World Turned Upside Down)"
21. "What Comes Next"
22. "Dear Theodosia"
23. "Non-Stop"

ACT II

1. "What'd I Miss"
2. "Cabinet Battle #1"
3. "Take A Break"
4. "Say No To This"
5. "The Room Where It Happens"
6. "Schuyler Defeated"
7. "Cabinet Battle #2"
8. "Washington on Your Side"
9. "One Last Time"
10. "I Know Him"
11. "The Adams Administration"
12. "We Know"
13. "Hurricane"
14. "The Reynolds Pamphlet"
15. "Burn"
16. "Blow Us All Away"

17. "Stay Alive (Reprise)"
18. "It's Quiet Uptown"
19. "Election of 1800"
20. "Your Obedient Servant"
21. "Best of Wives and Best of Women"
22. "The World Was Wide Enough"
23. "Who Lives, Who Dies, Who Tells Your Story"

Hook

Coming in as an audience for the show, most people would know little about the title character, other than he is on US money (which bill was that again?) and he died shooting in the air as Aaron Burr shot true. Truth be told, we also mostly assume that he was a dry and dusty historical figure, a founding father nowhere as interesting as those more colorful establishing parents — Washington, Jefferson, and Franklin.

The opening song, "Alexander Hamilton," provides our hook — pulling us into the drama, including establishing the expectation of style. This will not be a dry, dusty history; rather, we will be surprised, electrified, moved. This will be history done modern — or as creator Lin Manuel Miranda says, "Hamilton is the story of America then, told by America now."

Our Central Character Hamilton is introduced, yet the plot has not begun. Note that this isn't a play about how Hamilton got to America, but how he freed and formed America. The immigrant backstory lays critical character work, just as the Hook of *Up* does; yet the plot has not started.

All the main characters are teased, setting up the questions that the show must answer — starting with "how does a bastard, orphan...grow up to be a hero and a scholar?" continuing through to "When America sings for you, will they know what you overcame?"

As a hook, this opener is brilliant, drawing you into the main character, and making the audience thirsty to find out about those who fought with him, died for him, trusted him, loved him — and yes, what would bring us to the point where that damn fool shot him.

Balance

Much like *Up*, with a significant hook in place, there isn't much required to establish our Balance.

Hamilton, a poor young man in New York, sets out to get an education and find his place in the tumultuous, prewar New World.

This normal world is established in the exchange "Aaron Burr, Sir" with Hamilton's inner desire played out in "My Shot."

Catalyst to Final Straw

The Catalyst — the world changing for the Central Character, even if they don't yet know it — is when Hamilton falls in with the revolutionaries ("My Shot" and "The Story of Tonight").

If you don't believe me that Hamilton's world has changed, the revolutionaries themselves pause to make it clear that this is the start of it:

> And when our children tell our story,
> they'll tell the story of tonight.

Hamilton's world has changed, but he isn't full out on his journey yet. The show takes a few side steps — introducing "The Schuyler Sisters," seeing Hamilton step tentatively (at first) into the debate ("A Farmer Refuted"), and crossing the pond for King George's thoughts on the possible revolution ("You'll Be Back").

The Final Straw, forcing our Central Character fully onto his journey, comes in "Right Hand Man." The British send their forces into New York Harbor, and Hamilton takes action alongside the revolutionaries. By the end of the scene/song, Hamilton is now full-time on the cause of war as George Washington's right hand.

Quest Part One

Now that Hamilton is full on his journey, his tactics drive the story — divided into three types of actions: personal, parallel, and direct.

Personal includes Eliza entering Hamilton's story ("A Winter's Ball," "Helpless," and "Satisfied"). Hamilton's pursuit of Eliza is not just a love story — but part of his work to establish his place in the world. As Angelica puts it,

> He's after me cuz I'm a Schuyler sister;
> That elevates his status;
> I'd have to be naive to set that aside.

The seeming deviation into Hamilton's love life (it is anything but a deviation) also allows us to observe two mirrors (parallels) to Hamilton: Angelica ("Satisfied") and Burr ("Wait For It"). Angelica mirrors Hamilton's drive to advance — she herself passes on courting Hamilton in part because he cannot help her in her social climb.

Burr, a constant mirror for Hamilton, shows his opposing style of ambition — waiting for the right moment, rather than grabbing at every opportunity. Burr himself makes the connection to his rival:

> Hamilton's pace is relentless...
> Hamilton doesn't hesitate.
> He exhibits no restraint.
> He takes and he takes and he takes...

The direct scenes are Hamilton's straightforward actions towards (or away) from the battle against the British, starting with "Stay Alive" — where he outlines the political actions in support of Washington and his battle with Charles Lee — culminating in "Ten Duel Commandments."

Hamilton then tries to get his own command (again), only to be sidelined ("Meet Me Inside"). This sets us up for the Escape Offer and Midpoint.

Escape Offers

There are two main offers of escape for Hamilton, one leading into the Midpoint, the other at the start of his progress in Quest Part Two.

"That Would Be Enough" comes just as Hamilton is sidelined from the war. Eliza makes the argument that Hamilton can make his legacy through his soon-to-be-born son rather than through war. His escape from the show's plot is simple: stay home with family.

> If you could let me inside your heart

Oh, let me be a part of the narrative
In the story they will write someday
Let this moment be the first chapter
Where you decide to stay
And I could be enough
And we could be enough
That would be enough.

Per the rules of the Escape Offer, Hamilton does not stay home.

The second Escape Offer also comes from Eliza, joined with Angelica — "Take a Break."

Take a break
Run away with us for the summer, let's go upstate
We can all go stay with my father
There's a lake I know
In a nearby park
You and I can go when the night gets dark

Again, Hamilton refuses and he does not take a break.

Writer Miranda uses these two offers brilliantly to reflect the changing nature of the show. The first half ends in triumphant victory over the British — in essence an uplifting story. The second half chronicles the demise of Hamilton's career, the loss of family through death and near dissolution of his marriage, and his senseless death at the hands of Burr.

In essence, a tragedy. Note that Hamilton foreshadows this in "Take a Break," comparing himself to Macbeth.

My dearest, Angelica, tomorrow and tomorrow and tomorrow
Creeps in this petty pace from day to day
I trust you'll understand the reference to another Scottish trag-
edy without my having to name the play
They think me Macbeth, and ambition is my folly
I'm a polymath, a pain in the ass, a massive pain
Madison is Banquo, Jefferson's Macduff
And Birnam Wood is Congress on its way to Dunsinane

The Escape Offer before the Midpoint reflects the typical Offer for a heroic Central Character: asking the good character to step out of the plot, like Voldemort asking Harry to join the villain's side. The refusal seals Hamilton's status as "hero."

The Escape Offer at the start of the second act is typical of Escapes for Central Characters who need to grow: asking the Central Character to deviate from their tragic course and join in the "good." If Hamilton were to take Eliza's offer, the Reynold's situation would have been avoided, and along with it the dominoes of Philip's death, Eliza's estrangement, and the collapse of Hamilton's political career.[126]

Hamilton's refusal of Eliza's second offer seals the character's tragic ending.

Midpoint

The event that changes everything, completely redirecting Hamilton's Quest is the winning of the Revolutionary War — now Hamilton goes from trying to win the war to trying to win the peace. Note that while the Quest moves in a very different direction, it is a continuation of the first half. Miranda does not make the mistake of "this happens, then this happens," but stays with the strong storytelling technique of "this happens, and because of that, this next thing happens."

The Midpoint for *Hamilton* has a full structure of its own.

Balance: Hamilton is sidelined at home with his wife ("That Would be Enough")

Unbalance: Lafayette convinces Washington that they need Hamilton in the field to win the war ("Guns and Ships")

Miranda gives a reminder of the stakes and a refresher on theme ("History Has Its Eyes On You").

Quest: To win the battle of Yorktown ("Yorktown (The World Turned Upside Down)")

Crisis: The thought of death and loss creeps in ("I imagine death so much it feels like more a memory — this is where it gets me...")

---

126. Some may argue that a consequence of taking a break would mean the fall of the defense of Hamilton's national banking plan. I'm not so sure — Alexander would still have written from upstate, and he would have the added benefit of Angelica's brain to bounce his ideas off. With her instant feedback (rather than the months between trans-Atlantic mail), who knows? Maybe the national bank plans would have been won even quicker.

Climax and New Balance: With their inside man, they defeat the British, and the world has turned upside down

---

Intermission

In classic Five Act theater (with four intermissions), the Midpoint would take place in the middle of act three.[127] The move to two act plays shifted the placement of the Midpoint. With the desire to keep the audience from wandering away during intermission, the writers would give the peak of the production at the break. We see this reflected in commercial TV with the half-hour/midpoint break a cliffhanger or highly dramatic moment.

The Midpoint of *Hamilton* wraps up a storyline — the winning of freedom. If Miranda chose to break at that seemingly natural point, the audience may have been left wondering, "Is there anything next?"

I witnessed this confusion with audiences of Stephen Sondheim's *Into the Woods* — a brilliant show with a brilliant first and second act. Act one retells several classic and new fairy tales, ending the act with the conclusion of the original stories — Cinderella has her prince, Little Red has been saved from the wolf, Jack has killed the giant, and on.

Act two wonderfully takes on the consequences of each character getting their wish, and the cost of their actions to do so. Cinderella and Rapunzel are now married to men who are more in love with the pursuit of romance than the wives they left at home (princes "charming, not sincere"), and the giant's wife has come down the beanstalk for revenge.

The problem arose at intermission when some audiences were confused as to whether the show was over. Ushers would stand at the doors to remind departing viewers to return for the second half.

Hamilton avoids this confusion by having the King of England ask the question the audience has, "What Comes Next" — a Hook for the second half of the show. The king points out how fraught with drama the future will be — and how unlikely this experiment will succeed.

---

127. For an excellent breakdown of Five Act play structure, see John Yorke's *Into the Woods*

What comes next?
You've been freed
Do you know how hard it is to lead?
You're on your own
Awesome, wow!
Do you have a clue what happens now?
Oceans rise
Empires fall
It's much harder when it's all your call
All alone, across the sea
When your people say they hate you
Don't come crawling back to me

Miranda then gives a new "I want" type song to Burr and Hamilton ("Dear Theodosia") and launches into the Quest Part Two with "Non-Stop."

Note the pause in action between the asking of the "what comes next" and the answer in "Non-Stop." The "Dear Theodosia" scene serves several purposes. First, it slows down the action — the respite between the battle and the non-stop drive of Hamilton that will make up the second half.

Second, the scene clarifies the quest in Quest Part Two, and the reason for that quest.

You will come of age with our young nation
We'll bleed and fight for you, we'll make it right for you
If we lay a strong enough foundation
We'll pass it on to you, we'll give the world to you

The audience likely doesn't need an explanation of why fighting for freedom is important. However, the machinations of politics may seem less critical — is it really that significant to the lay person if the states have credit or not? By tying the results to the next generation — to the baby children of Hamilton and Burr — the stakes are set. We do not need to understand the intricacies of the policies — we only need to know that if Hamilton fails, it's his children who will suffer.

Third, the play re-establishes and updates us on the mirroring of Burr and Hamilton. At this point, they become nearly one in purpose and drive — fathers marveling over the miracle of their children, and coming to grips with the responsibility that comes with those little miracles.

Note that at the first meeting, Hamilton comments that he and Burr are the same. We soon see they are very different, as Burr refuses to ruffle the feathers that Hamilton is more than happy to upset. Here at the Midpoint, they are together again. Later in the second half, they will swap positions — Burr setting out to ruffle feathers, and Hamilton (broken) fading back into "Wait for It" mode.

Miranda gives us a physical action that reflects this interior switch — in act one, Burr is defined by his affair with the wife of a British general while Hamilton is seen as the faithful spouse of Eliza; in act two, Hamilton is defined by his affair with Mrs. Reynolds, as Burr legitimizes his relationship with Theodosia.

Quest Part Two

The tactics of governing take off in Quest Part Two, starting with the Constitution battle ("Non-Stop") and the tussle with Jefferson over state debt and the national bank ("What'd I Miss," "Cabinet Battle #1").

After an escape offer, we see the cost of Hamilton's tactics ("Say No to This"), and his choice to use Burr's advice to win his battle ("The Room Where It Happens").

Opposition builds up, reflected in Burr's rise ("Schuyler's Defeated"), and the bitterness of the next battle: neutrality ("Cabinet Battle #2"). Just as Hamilton seems poised for full success — Jefferson resigning from the cabinet ("Washington on Your Side") — he hits another crisis: the loss of Washington as his ally/protector ("One Last Time").

Hamilton's actions become more frantic (mirroring Macbeth, as he predicted) with his tiffs with the new president ("I Know Him," "The Adams Administration"), taking Hamilton's station even lower. He loses his cabinet position and burns bridges on the way out.

His political rivals hope to put Hamilton out of the way completely with an accusation of speculation; Hamilton's tactic is to show he had an affair rather than cheated with money ("We Know," "Hurricane," "The Reynolds Pamphlet").

This tactic completely backfires, leaving Hamilton out of politics ("He's never gon' be President now...") and estranged from his wife ("Burn" — again mirroring Macbeth and the loss of his wife).

Crisis

Hamilton is in a deep dive, and about to hit rock bottom. His son, in an attempt to defend his father's honor, gets into a duel. Using his father's pistols and advice, Philip goes to his doom ("Blow Us All Away").

As Philip dies in the arms of his parents ("Stay Alive Reprise"), it is clear that choosing Hamilton's path ("I did exactly as you said, Pa...") over Eliza's path ("Mom, I'm so sorry for forgetting what you taught me...") led to his destruction. This final blow is a consequence of our Central Character's own choices.

Wafer

The musical provides one of the most heart-wrenching and beautiful Wafer scenes in dramatic literature ("It's Quiet Uptown"). The moment to feel the pain of the loss is given full weight and space.

> *There are moments that the words don't reach*
> *There is suffering too terrible to name*
> *You hold your child as tight as you can*
> *And push away the unimaginable*
> *The moments when you're in so deep*
> *It feels easier to just swim down*

Miranda doesn't just give us the feeling, then move on. Instead, he marches us through it, like a Psalm of Lament.

> *I take the children to church on Sunday*
> *A sign of the cross at the door*
> *And I pray*
> *That never used to happen before*

Hamilton is broken; his priorities completely rearranged. He banked his legacy on his policies — even as that tact was undermined, the audience had a hope given in "That Would Be Enough." Eliza said his child would be their future, their legacy.

And that hope is now gone as well.
If I could spare his life
If I could trade his life for mine
He'd be standing here right now
And you would smile, and that would be enough

And like the psalms, the pain is not healed, but grows into something else. The loss is not covered up, but the scars allow for a new thing to be at work. Hamilton is not restored to his old self, but finds a new self — one that maybe is more mature, and more worthy of legacy.

There are moments that the words don't reach
There is a grace too powerful to name
We push away what we can never understand
We push away the unimaginable
They are standing in the garden
Alexander by Eliza's side
She takes his hand
It's quiet uptown

Note how perfect this scene is as Wafer — it is about emotion, not action. No steps are taken by Hamilton to get back to his Quest; the scene rests completely in feeling our way through the consequence of the Crisis.

It is a beautiful pain.

Climax

Hamilton, at rock bottom, is now ready to finish his story. He is pulled back into politics and restores his goal of leaving a legacy ("Election of 1800"). This time it is in helping choose the next president, and thereby the next direction of the new nation.

This is the action of the new Hamilton; not self-serving, and not to secure his own name, he backs a former, bitter rival. This action sets in motion the final confrontation with Burr, setting up the duel ("Your Obedient Servant").

With a pause before the final storm ("Best of Wives and Best of Women"), Hamilton goes to face the climactic battle, choosing who he will be in death by throwing away his shot ("The World Was Wide Enough").

New Balance

Hamilton is dead, no longer able to resurrect his reputation and legacy. Burr is now a pariah — his legacy whittled down to his last, dishonorable act.

> *History obliterates, in every picture it paints*
> *It paints me and all my mistakes*
> *When Alexander aimed at the sky*
> *He may have been the first one to die*
> *But I'm the one who paid for it*
> *I survived, but I paid for it*
> *Now I'm the villain in your history*

Burr kicks off the show as our narrator — ostensibly the show will be his point of view, explaining how he got to this ending. However, throughout the show, Hamilton himself hijacks the narrative, choosing to tell his own story. This play is a battle — which man gets to tell the story?

The verdict comes in at the duel: neither man has earned the right to tell the story. Instead, it is Eliza who takes up the narrative ("Who Lives, Who Dies, Who Tells Your Story").

> *I ask myself, what would you do if you had more time*
> *The Lord, in his kindness*
> *He gives me what you always wanted*
> *He gives me more time*
> *...And when my time is up, have I done enough?*
> *Will they tell your story?*

Tag

After Eliza tells us the rest of the story, ending on the question, "Who lives, who dies, who tells your story?" — she comes to the edge of the stage, eyes brightening, and her final line is...

A gasp.

What does that gasp mean? The script does not tell us. The lights go to black before the characters can expound.

The actress will tell you, that for her, the gasp is not defined — and changes night to night[128]. Sometimes it is the gasp of meeting her husband in heaven (she does say in the lyrics that she looks forward to seeing him soon).

Often, for her, it is seeing the audience — gasping at their presence.

And wondering — will they tell the story?

---

128. The ephemeral nature of theater; each night, Eliza and the audience share a different meaning to this moment.

PART EIGHT

Structure Variations

Story Structure for Series

Story structure is more than just the structure of a show; it is also the structure of the micro. Scenes themselves follow the structure — with a Balance, Unbalance, Quest, Crisis/Climax, and New Balance.

The same can be a tool for the macro — for stories told longer than one plot at a time. This would include seasons of a TV series, book/ movie series, trilogies, and the like. Clearly not all movie franchises consider how the different movies dovetail together; the early James Bond movies were simply further adventures of the spy.

Yet franchises can be deepened by applying Story structure principles across the arc of the series.

J.K. Rowling does this with the *Harry Potter* series (and thus the movie franchise follows closely along). Each book has a complete, standalone structure from Balance to New Balance. Also, the series follows the emotional arc of our structure.

- *Harry Potter and the Sorcerer's Stone* (Balance) establishes the normal world for series.

- *Harry Potter and the Chamber of Secrets* (Unbalance) throws the balance out of whack, as the long arm of Voldemort keeps coming for Harry.

- *Harry Potter and the Prisoner of Azkaban* (Quest Part One) sees Harry on his Quest to defeat the agents of Voldemort (mistaking the prisoner of Azkaban as the threat).

- *Harry Potter and the Goblet of Fire* (Midpoint) is the midpoint twist that changes everything. The stakes are raised (there is a murder of a fellow student), and the goal is no longer to keep Voldemort from rising — he has risen. We will no longer be just fighting Voldemort's minions.

- *Harry Potter and the Order of the Phoenix* (Quest Part Two) shows Harry in his new goal of convincing others of Voldemort's rise as well as creating an army of peers ready to fight.

- *Harry Potter and the Half-Blood Prince* (Crisis) gives us our "all is lost" moment — the death of Dumbledore, and the loss of hope in fighting against the rising Voldemort.

- *Harry Potter and the Deathly Hallows* (Climax, New Balance) contains the final showdown, and establishes the new normal for the wizarding world.

~

The television series *The Chosen* uses this arc for their series. Writer Ryan Swanson explains: "So it's a three-act story. We've got Seasons 1 and 2, they were Act 1. Seasons 3, 4, and 5 will be Act 2, and then we will be in the home stretch for Seasons 6 and 7."[129]

Television will often map out individual season arcs the same way. Hinting at the conflict of the season in early episodes; the action takes a major turn in the middle of the season; near the end of the season, the hero(es) suffer a major setback; the final episodes of the season contain a final showdown and result.

Game of Thrones arced their seasons (ignoring the final seasons) this way — most clearly seen in the last three episodes of each season. The third show from the end of the season had some major setback (Crisis); the penultimate show was a big battle/fight that the season had been building up (Climax); and the final episode of the season would be character-driven, showing the results of the journey (New Balance).

---

129. From the interview in Deseret News, "'We come in peace': What the writers of 'The Chosen' want you to know about the show." Deseret.com, September 7, 2022

Limited television series also use this structure to great effect. *Mare of Easttown, Broadchurch, Ted Lasso, The Morning Show, The Flight Attendant* — all have this natural flow across the season-long stories of setup, midpoint reversal, crisis, and climax.

While it is easy to think of this in terms of action, it applies to romantic or other arcs as well. Think of your favorite soapy show: the desire is established at the start of the season (she really likes this guy!); in the middle, a new conflict gets in the way (his ex-wife moves back to town!); towards the end of the season all is lost (he got back together with his ex-wife!); and in the season finale, the issue is resolved (she goes to the airport — and he doesn't get on the plane — big kiss!).

Movie series use this model as well — when the movies are planned out. *Star Wars: A New Hope* establishes a Balance and start of the Quest to go against the Empire. *Star Wars: The Empire Strikes Back* continues the Quest and ends in Crisis. *Star Wars: Return of the Jedi* gives the final Climax and New Balance.

The Godfather and *Godfather Part II* can be seen as one continuing story with *The Godfather* ending at the Midpoint. The final three movies of the Marvel Infinity Saga are clearly meant to work as a Crisis (*Avengers: Infinity War*) and Climax (*Avengers: Endgame*) and New Balance (*Spider-Man: Far From Home*). Doesn't that finally explain the reason for *Far From Home* being included in the saga?

Again, series of stories need not try to fit this form, and most don't. Yet planning ahead can pay off marvelously with satisfying dividends.

CHAPTER THIRTY-THREE

Bending the Form

For writers:

According to our form, in general the first act will be about 25% of a script; act two will be about 50%; act three will be about 25%.

In general, the Midpoint will have more weight than the scenes around it.

In general, the wafer will be a very short scene.

In general...

In general...

In general...

HOWEVER, you are not writing a general screenplay/teleplay/play. You are writing a specific story; and the needs of the specific outweigh the peer pressure of gurus telling you the general "rules" of writing.

This is a good time to remind ourselves: Story structure is not about rules, but a guide. Not about a formula, but form. Not a recipe to follow, but a way of understanding what is and is not working.

Let's follow the recipe analogy: What I have done in outlining structure is to say, "Look at all these great cakes. Let's examine what they all have in common." It would be a mistake to take the list of commonalities, and say, "If I follow this recipe, I will have a great cake."

This is what lousy producers do; and what lousy writers think is the road to success. They forget that art is inspiration and skill and ability and knowledge; they forget that variety is as natural an ingredient as structure, dialogue, or theme.

Some cakes are moist, some are thick and creamy. Some are chocolate, or vanilla, or marble, or lemon, or poppyseed, or even carrot. Some are airy like angels, or devilishly fudge-like. Some have cream frosting, some sugar ice, some are too good to be topped without distracting from the whole. And to play with homonyms, some even have a hole in the middle!

The form of structure still has great value — claiming a variety is not the same as claiming that any variation is a good variation. You might decide, as the recipe is not locked in stone, that you will substitute salt for sugar in your cake mix. And you will end up with a pretty crappy cake.

Those who substitute do so successfully because they understand the function of the original ingredient. They know the purpose of the sugar — so may substitute with honey, or brown sugar, or fruit juice. And are thereby more likely to have success.

Neil Gaiman on *David Tennant Does a Podcast With...* (season two wrap up) talks about rules, using the metaphor of a door marked "no exit." According to the rules, you cannot go out that way. The guy who doesn't know the rules discovers you can indeed go out through that door. So, the world is open to those who don't follow the rules.

Gaiman is right in that if we hold on to the guidelines as rules, we miss the marvelous "no exit" exits — along with going out the window, the fire escape, the dumb waiter, the mouse hole in the wall — and even the occasional Platform 9 3/4. Yet what would happen if we put a sign on a load-bearing wall that said, "No exit"? Are we still happy that the guy who doesn't know the rules kicked out the wall to make an egress?

When people don't know (and have no interest in learning) what went before them, they usually spend all day running into walls, bragging about how they are innovative while creating pure crap. My mentor, Howard Stein, would grouse all the time about uninformed rule breakers, saying you can't break the rules unless you first know the rules.

And if you know the rules, then you can create all kinds of cool effects by breaking them!

For example, typically if a story completely skipped a major event, we would not enjoy the show. I can think of a major movie that did not have a Climax[130]; instead, the characters talked about the final fight that the two leads had off screen. The movie was a dud.

But what if the creators denied us a major event in order to make a point? *If Beale Street Could Talk* does this very thing with the Climax — and it works in their favor. Actually, we are given two Climaxes in the film, but neither is the main character confronting the "big bad" of the movie; this is a movie about a trial, and we never get our day in court. Instead, we have a supporting character battle a potential witness (a physical climax of sorts) and we see our main character give birth (an emotional climax of sorts).

So, we "feel" a climax without the satisfaction of an actual final showdown. And this works because the characters in the movie — the black man falsely arrested and imprisoned, and his wife who fights to get him out — are denied their climax as well. The audience walks out of the theater unsatisfied, which completely aligns with the film-makers' theme.

Mare of Easttown (looking at the whole series) does a lovely job of understanding audience expectations and fulfilling those expectations while at the same time subverting them. The first season follows two police investigations that may be linked — a recent murder and a pair of abductions (one a year old, one recent).

Traditionally (or "in general"), the climax of a police series would include a major action sequence. *Easttown* chooses to have the biggest action sequence of the season be in the Crisis episode, where Mare (the character) faces her biggest loss. At the same time, that loss (or Crisis) solves one of the cases; what should be a moment of story elation becomes a mixed bag — a moment of mourning rather than celebration.

---

130. I'm not mentioning the title in part because I adore the lead actress, and don't want to diminish her light!

The next episode ends on a cliffhanger in the middle of a traditional Climax — as Mare faces the murderer about to commit another murder. The climactic scene completes itself at the start of the next episode, and Mare's cases are solved. Or so Mare (and the audience) thinks. The confrontation with the murderer is a false Climax; the one we were expecting, but not the one the series had been leading up to.

The real Climax has barely any action at all as Mare slowly (ever so slowly) tracks down the true "big bad"; the final arrest is literally a slow walk up to a house as the villain turns themselves in.

We get our action and tension, our adrenaline rush; and then we get the true Climax — a pure emotional/character moment.

As a side note, the Climax for the series is the arrest of the true villain; the Climax for the episode comes later. The arrest is the Midpoint of the episode; the Crisis, a confrontation with Mare's best friend; the Climax is the reconciliation scene. It is a lovely interlacing of Season Structure and Episode Structure.

~

Structure should bend towards the good of the whole. The overall effect trumps the individual parts. (Imagine the individual events are Spock and the whole story is Kirk. "The needs of the many outweigh the needs of the few," our brave, sacrificial events say, hand on the glass with fingers spread in a "V."[131])

Thor: Ragnorak has a very thin Quest Part Two (arrival in Asgard and short battle) and Crisis. The story is leading to the choice to destroy Asgard — the movie (and Thor's character arc) depends on a full understanding of the gravity of the decision. The plot gives us what appears to be three goals: finding Odin, getting off Sakaar, the battle for Asgard. However, the search for Odin is really part of the Balance; Hela's arrival is our Catalyst. Time and weight are given to the opening search to solidify the importance of Asgard to Thor.

So, we have an extended Balance. By giving this extension a quest, the change to structure is masked. As an audience, we don't ever feel

---

131. *Star Trek II: The Wrath of Khan*, as if you didn't already know.

like the plot has stalled, or that the symmetry is skewed. A perfect understanding of structure leading to a perfect bending of structure.

Up is another fantastic example.[132] The Hook, typically a single scene, takes up almost one sixth of the entire film. *Up* is about an old man flying his house to South America, and we don't even meet the old man until page 14 of a 101-page script. Without this setup, the movie doesn't have nearly as much of an impact: we stick with Carl because of Ellie, because of who he used to be, because we are in love with the Carl whom Ellie inspired. The audience just spent an entire lifetime with him; we are vested. To make up for the time, the Balance is a bit short, and Quest Part Two is very quick; both sacrifices that are worth the cost.

The Avengers has a very short Balance before the story is kick-started with the arrival of Loki (Catalyst). The functions of the Balance are transferred to the Response to Catalyst section, as each member of the Avengers is recruited. We get the normal of each character and establish the foresight into Want and Need for this ensemble.

This is the technique for many movies that include the recruiting of the team as a major part of the story. *The Magnificent Seven* (the magnificent 1960 version) employs this process to perfection. We don't meet our leads until after the story is set in motion. The recruiting section doubles as Balance and Response to Catalyst — giving a mini-story in Chris' process of finding the team. All the character setups are there: Vin just seeks the next job; Harry only wants money and will learn there are greater treasures; Lee is paralyzed by his nightmares; Britt is driven by challenging his skills; Bernardo denies his heritage; Chico is focused on fame. All will face their Balance-selves and come out changed in the New Balance.

Like *Thor: Ragnorak*, the movie keeps the action goal-oriented, so the story doesn't slow down for character work, and the audience stays within the story.

---

132. Pixar is the expert at story — just about any of their projects will be great case studies.

Christopher Nolan is another master of structure and has a lot of fun playing with the form. He knows how to mess with time without messing up structure. He also knows that there is no limit to how many stories are told — as long as each story is given a full structure.

Dunkirk (case study below) is really three shorter movies told at the same time. Each of the three stands alone, with a complete structure. *Batman Begins* is two movies — original movie and sequel — played out together (Bruce Wayne vs Ra's al Ghul; Batman vs Scarecrow). The tie-in with the villain (Ra's is the force behind Scarecrow) allows the stories to dovetail nicely.

The Dark Knight is also two movies (Batman vs Joker; Batman vs Two-Face). This iteration is more complicated, as the Balance/Catalyst/Final Straw of the Two-Face movie is intertwined with the ending of the Joker movie.

Multiple stories are used in anthology movies (*The Ballad of Buster Scruggs, Paris Je T'Aime, Sin City*) or plays that collect one acts (*All in the Timing, The Dining Room*) that tell a series of short stories.

Scripts that include a story-within-story often elevate the bookends to full stories (*Big Fish, Fried Green Tomatoes*). *The Usual Suspects* plays with this idea as Verbal's telling of Keyser Soze is its own story with a hero-goal-obstacle. The true goal is hidden until the end — and that ending is satisfying in part due to the completeness of the tale-telling portion.

Structure is a form that if used improperly can sink a story; however, the hands of a master can bend and reform structure in ways that sparkle and elevate far beyond standard or formulaic story telling.

⁜ CROSS FADE: The Parable of the Lost Son ⁜

At first glance, the Parable of the Lost Son[133] is an odd duck. It seems pretty traditional; a Balance of two sons and a Dad; an Unbalance of the younger son taking his share of the inheritance; a Quest of finding

---

133. Luke 15:11-32

happiness — with a Midpoint twist and a Quest Part Two of survival; a Crisis in a pigsty; a Climax as father runs to son; and a New Balance of a party with a son outside watching and wondering, who calls a servant, and gets upset and refuses to go in, and his dad comes out to him and they have a fight and... And no more story.

We were going so well until that New Balance. Then Jesus messed it all up!

Okay, Jesus didn't mess up. One of my personal laws: whenever I find what seems to be bad storytelling in the Bible, chances are I'm missing something — and usually that something has significant ramifications.

Let's back up and put on our Story critical lenses: the ending doesn't make sense. In fact, it feels like a whole other story. And that is exactly what it is.

Jesus tells the Parable of the Lost Younger Son. Then in a very Nolanesque move, he dovetails the end of one story into the next: the Parable of the Lost Older Son.

Balance: Son is out in the field working

Unbalance: He comes home to see a party for his disgraceful brother

Quest: Show his disapproval to his father

Crisis: Dad is confronted, and the old man rather than seeing reason, calls his older son to change his view of both his life on the farm and his younger brother

Jesus does not give us the Climax or the New Balance to this second story, which is very awkward. As pointed out earlier, we are hardwired for story, and we are not satisfied with an incomplete story. Jesus is very aware of this — and this is where the significant ramifications come in.

The burden of what's next — of what the older son is going to do — is put on the listener, the audience. As we answer for ourselves what the older son will do next, we also explore the question, "What would *we* do?"

The brilliance of this choice by Jesus is seen in his audience. We are told that he is surrounded by tax collectors and sinners, listening to his stories. And the Pharisees and the teachers of the law are also there and making their displeasure with Jesus' audience clear.

Jesus tells two stories. The first reflects the tax collectors and sinners — the story of a lost one like them. The audience, at the start of the telling, know they are lost. That story is complete with a surprising happy ending, a reversal of expectations. The sinners in the audience are affirmed.

The second story reflects the Pharisees and law givers — the story of a judgmental older brother like them. The audience, at the start of the telling, believe they are securely not lost. That story is incomplete — rather than a reassurance, it becomes a challenge.

Your ending, Jesus is saying to the religious people, is up to you. You are just as lost as the younger son; you've just been blind to your lostness. Now that I've opened your eyes, and you are without excuse, what will you do?

The father waits: are you willing to let your character complete an arc? Are you ready to truly come home?

CHAPTER THIRTY-FOUR

Structure and Time

I often hear people say that a story does not follow traditional structure because the scenes are being told out of time order (non-linear). However, I have yet to be given an example of a successful movie/play/TV show told out of time order that doesn't follow the order of the traditional structure.

The reason people get this wrong is because of people like me. We talk about structure and we use linear stories to do so — focusing on how the hero experiences the events (which happens to be the same order in which the audience experiences the events).

Here's a reminder of the truth:

Plot is how the audience experiences the story.

Messing with time does not change that. When an audience sits in the theater and the show begins, what they see happens in this order:

1. Balance
2. Unbalance
3. Quest
4. Crisis/Climax
5. New Balance

Memento follows this pattern. *Eternal Sunshine of the Spotless Mind* follows this pattern. Pinter's *Betrayal* follows this pattern. *Lost* follows this pattern.

This means that in a character's timeline they may experience Unbalance before the Balance. The Crisis may happen in the past — for the character.

Despite linking each step to the Central Character, a deeper view sees that it is the audience's perception that defines each Event. Which is why we can be manipulated by the creators of *Mare of Easttown*, or how *Modern Family* can get away with switching Central Characters throughout an episode.

This concept can be a little trippy and may be more easily understood with stories about time travel.

Arrival seems pretty straightforward. It opens with Louise Banks' twelve-year-old daughter dying. This is great Balance material — fueling Bank's work through the rest of the movie. Flashbacks throughout show us more of the death of her daughter and dissolution of her marriage.

Only they aren't flashbacks, rather they happen in Banks' future; her daughter has not yet been born when Banks is called on to interpret the language of the aliens.

The Balance for the audience — Banks as a divorced mother with a child who has passed on — won't be part of Banks' life until years after the movie is over. We, the audience, experience the Balance right where it belongs, at the start of the movie.

Flashbacks

Writing teachers often discourage young writers from using flashbacks. This isn't because flashbacks are bad writing (flashbacks are awesome!), rather because they are so often used poorly. Partly because of this common misconception that altering a timeline somehow messes up structure.

To the young writer, a flashback is a convenient way of giving exposition without having to work too hard to make the flashback integrate with the flow of the plot.

However, for a flashback to work well, the story needs to move forward through and during the flashback; on return to the present, the plot/char-

acter/theme should be more developed. This only works when we understand that flashbacks are part of the line of the story — not a departure from the line of the story.

The Paris flashback in *Casablanca* happens right after the Final Straw — Ilsa's arrival in town. Rick's Quest Part One is to win Ilsa's love; we see Rick moping at the bar, and Sam prompts the flashback. We are now years in the past, where we see Rick winning Ilsa's love.

This flashback is not an explanation of Rick and Ilsa's past (well, it is, but that is only a minor function of the flashback), rather it is the Quest Part One. The action of winning Ilsa is playing out — in the past for Rick, in the proper order of structure for the viewer. The plot doesn't stop for the flashback; the flashback IS the plot.[134]

Screenwriter Todd Komarnicki speaks of the "eternal now" in storytelling.[135] Flashbacks in this view are happening "now" — not "then" — in good storytelling. *The proper use of a dive into the past is to change the character's present.* They recall a memory in a key moment and come out of the memory changed. This is true for the audience as well; the story has changed for the audience because of the trip to the past.

Lost built its wonderful first season on flashbacks, and you can see how effective they were, especially in changing the story from an audience's point of view. We see Locke as this enigmatic survivalist, clearly a man with combat training, probably a Navy Seal or Army Ranger who now works for the CIA. In the episode "Walkabout," we see Locke hunt and kill a boar with just a knife and face down the mysterious smoke

---

134. An interesting study in flashbacks can be done by comparing two Star Wars TV shows on Disney+: *The Book of Boba Fett* and *Obi-Wan Kenobi*. Fett tells two stories side by side by using flashbacks. However, the flashbacks in no way correlate to the actions in the present — making the storytelling feel listless; the flashbacks become interruptions rather than additions. *Kenobi* uses flashbacks to show the emotional states of the characters in the present and become a "compare and contrast" device to show growth in the main storyline. This enhances the present-day story, an obvious difference to its cousin show, *Boba Fett*.

135. You can hear Komarnicki talk of this on the July 1, 2020 Act One Podcast, episode 2. https://actoneprogram.com/podcast/

creature. We also flashback to Locke planning his trip, where we find out he was an office drone in a box company and — in the most major of twists — paralyzed from the waist down.

The whole story has changed.

CLOSE UP: Structure
Dunkirk

We'll look at two examples of messing with time while keeping a traditional structure. First, we'll look at one that tells the story in time order, but with three different speeds (*Dunkirk*); then we'll look at a story that is not told in time order at all (*Eternal Sunshine of the Spotless Mind*).

Dunkirk from writer/director Christopher Nolan is a marvelous example of playing with time while keeping structure. The story of the World War II evacuation is three separate stories that intersect towards the end of the movie: the story of the men on the beach (land); the story of the men on the boats who come to help (sea); and the story of the pilots who provide overhead support (air).

Where the telling gets all Nolan-y is how time is presented. Each of the three stories is told from the start of the movie to the end; yet the amount of time that passes in each story is different. The story of the men on the beach takes place over a week; the story of the boats takes place over one day; the story of the pilots takes place over one hour.

Rather than tell each tale individually in order, Nolan jumps back and forth between the three adventures, pacing each so they reach their critical event points in proximity to each other. Each story gets its own Catalyst, Final Straw, Midpoint, etc. (The air story gets two Crisis moments — one for each major pilot. Collins' Crisis happens as he transitions from being part of the air story and into the sea line.)

To make the three stories work, Nolan uses the form to his advantage. He cuts the Balance short — 2 pages total (combined with the Hook) to set up the beach. The world is explained within the action, and we forgo character introduction. The plots of the sea and the air each begin in Catalyst; Quest scenes are reduced to single sequences.

There isn't much breathing space from the opening moments until the finale; and then Nolan gives us 9 pages of New Balance (out of 81 pages of script). This puts the emotional weight on the reflections on the efforts — a chance to finally breathe.

THE MOLE *One Week* **Land**	THE MOONSTONE *One Day* **Sea**	THE SPITFIRE *One Hour* **Air**
BALANCE P1-2 Tommy runs thru streets to the beach		
CATALYST/ FINAL STRAW 3-4 Tries the line of men; the beach is bombed	CATALYST 4-5 Moonstone is requisitioned	CATALYST 5-6 Planes head out (first fuel check)
6-8 Try to use the stretchers to get on the boat – stopped by airplane fire	9 Peter and George load vests; see the other boats being "crewed"	9 Spitfires look to the skies for the enemy
10-11 Tommy and Gibson get the stretcher to the boat	FINAL STRAW 11-12 Dawson, Peter, and George (jumping on) opt to crew their own boat and take off	FINAL STRAW 12-13 Attacked by squadron of ME 109s
13-14 Kicked off the medical boat	14 Pass destroyer heading home	14-16 Defeat the 109s; squad leader is missing

16-19	19-20	20-22
Overhear command describing the situation (Exposition appears!)	Rescue Shivering Soldier from the water	See the downed leader; fuel gauge is broken
22-23 Hospital ship is sunk; Tommy and Gibson save some soldiers, including Alex	23-24 SS won't go below	24-25 Spitfires head higher to prep for the next engagement
25-27 Blend in with the hospital ship survivors; taken to the Destroyer; Gibson won't go below	27-28 SS doesn't want to go back to Dunkirk; Dawson sends him below	MIDPOINT SEQUENCE (1) 28-30 Engage the bomber taking on the minesweeper; Collins is hit
MIDPOINT SEQUENCE (1) 30-32 Destroyer is torpedoed; Gibson saves Tommy and Alex	MIDPOINT SEQUENCE (1) 32-34 Hear spitfires go by (now RAF planes); SS breaks out and confronts Dawson	MIDPOINT SEQUENCE (2) 34-35 Farrier chases off 109 as Collins crash lands into the ocean
MIDPOINT SEQUENCE (2) 36-37 Gibson drops a line from a long boat, towing Tommy and Alex ashore; Shivering Soldier is in the boat	MIDPOINT SEQUENCE (2) 37-38 SS fights Dawson, knocks George off the top deck – George is seriously injured	MIDPOINT SEQUENCE (3) 39 Takes out the 109; sees the swamped Blue Trawler ESCAPE OFFER Checks his fuel, should go back, thinks...

39-41 *The engineers making a pier in low tide;* Tommy, Gibson, and Alex head to a swamped boat	ESCAPE OFFER 41-43 George is dying – should we go back? (repeat "thinking") They keep going; bombers come in	43 Farrier refused to go home; heads back into the fight (to take on bomber over the Blue Trawler and Destroyer)
43-45 *News that the French are losing ground; explain that small ships are being sent (the plot of Moonstone)*	45-46 Head away from the minesweeper as a bomber heads towards	
46-47 Opt to hide in the trawler	47-48 See Collins get shot down	
48 Tide is coming in too slow	CRISIS 49-50 Collins crashes, is stuck in the cockpit	50 Farrier goes to take on the Heinkel
50-51 Dutch seaman returns to the Trawler; a gunshot pierces the hull	51 Moonstone didn't see a parachute; Dawson won't give up	51 Farrier dives for the Heinkel
52 More bullet holes	CRISIS 52-53 Moonstone approaches the plane; Collins can't get out and the water is rising	52-53 The 109 banks to counter Farrier

53 Seaman shot; the holes are leaking water	53 Collins using flare gun against the canopy	CRISIS 53-54 Tries to take out the bomber while rolling away from the wingman; the bomber drops its load
CRISIS 54-55 Need to lose weight on ship; turn on Gibson, who won't speak	55 Collins drops the flare gun	55 Sees the Destroyer was hit
55-59 Decide to sacrifice Gibson, Tommy fights for Gibson; the firing continues to make sure the boat will sink; the tide is in and the boat rises!	59 The boathook breaks through – Collins is saved!	WAFER 59-60 Sees the Destroyer leaking oil
CLIMAX 60-61 The Destroyer casts off; the Trawler is moving, but must plug the holes	61-62 WAFER George is dying; they see the Destroyer being bombed – there are men in the water!	62 Loses his reserve fighting the 109

62-63 *See the armada of small ships coming in;* Trawler heads towards the Destroyer as they plug the holes below	CLIMAX 63 Head into leaking oil, as they pull men out	CLIMAX 64 Goes after the Henkel, trying to bomb the leaking Destroyer again
64 The Trawler is sinking; they abandon ship; Gibson is the last to leave plugging the holes and is sucked down with the Trawler	64-65 Dawson sends the men below to make room for more survivors; George is dead	
65-66 *Officers and Destroyer deck see the coming small boat armada and cheer*	66 Peter lies to SS, telling him George is okay; Collins looks up to Farrier's dogfight	67 Farrier fires on the bomber, dives out of fire himself, the 109 zeroing in
67 Swim toward the Destroyer, but it gets bombed	67-68 The armada is pulling people off the beach (from the makeshift pier); the Destroyer is listing	68 Farrier takes out the bomber – which catches fire
	68-69 Moonstone pulls away as the ocean catches on fire; Tommy is pulled on board	69 Farrier runs out of gas

69-70 *Commanders watch the evac; realize a Stuka is heading toward the Mole and the men trapped on it*	70-71 Moonstone heads home – sees the 109 bearing down on them	
71 *Stuka goes into its dive*	71 Dawson gives orders as Peter steers; the Stuka dives	
71 *Bolton prays as – a Spitfire glides by!*		72 Farrier takes out the Stuka before it can fire; he nods, feeling the silence of his engineless plane
	72-72 Moonstone evades the 109 at the last moment	NEW BALANCE 72 Farrier glides down the beach
NEW BALANCE	NEW BALANCE 73-74 Head to Weymouth; Alex feels they are failures	74 Farrier continues his glide
	74 Moonstone lands; Collins is accosted; Dawson assures him that he knows Collins did his part	

75 Tommy and Alex board a train 75-76 *Commanders take the last men out – 300,000 saved; Bolton staying to help the French* 76-77 Tommy gets the paper; Alex hides his face in shame	77 Peter takes a picture of George to the paper	77 Farrier preps for his crash landing
78 Tommy reads; they are being received as heroes		78-79 Farrier lands the plane
	79 Dawson gives Peter the Herald; the article is on the hero George	79 Farrier destroys his plane
80 Continues to read Churchill's inspiring words as we see the beach littered with abandoned vehicles, and piles of bodies		80-81 Farrier surrenders to the Germans and is led away from his burning plane
81 Tommy continues reading as we push into-		81 The burning Spitfire.

CLOSE UP: Order
Eternal Sunshine of the Spotless Mind

Eternal Sunshine of the Spotless Mind is a memory film told out of time, and in time as the memories are experienced backwards. Okay, that's a bit confusing — so let me try again.

It is the story of a man named Joel who is in the breakup stages with his girlfriend, Clementine. He runs into her and realizes she has no memory of him. There is a company, Lacuna (run by Mierzwiak, staffed by Patrick, Stan, and Mary), that will erase a bad relationship from your life. Joel, in deep pain, decides that he is going to have Clementine erased from his memory as well.

As the memories are being erased backwards through time, Joel changes his mind. However, being in a dream state, he is limited in what he can do. Eventually his memories are erased. However, he meets Clementine again, and although they don't remember each other, they start dating again. That is the order of events for the characters — but not the way the audience experiences the plot.

So — all wibbly wobbly timey wimey.

However, despite all that the creators give us our story in a conventional order. Here are the main plot points, in the order in which they are experienced by the audience:

- **Balance:** Joel meets Clementine on a deserted Montauk beach, and rides home with her on the train, hitting it off. (7) Also, Joel prepares for his memory wipe. (6)
- **Catalyst:** Joel finds out that Clementine has her memory wiped of him — their relationship is over! (4)
- **Final Straw:** Joel demands to get a memory wipe as well. (5)
- **Midpoint:** Joel experiences a memory that reminds him of why he loved Clementine in the first place. He decides he does not want her memory erased, and fights to stop it. (3)

- **Crisis:** Joel meets Clementine for the first time at a bonfire party; they connect — but the memory fades as they say goodbye. The wipe has been successful. (1)
- **Wafer:** Final flashes of Clementine's memories as they wisp away (2)
- **Climax:** Joel and Clementine are back together — but confront their past as first they hear Clementine's session tapes (where she says why she wants Joel wiped from her memory), and then hear Joel's tapes. They now know that they were not good together. (8)
- **New Balance:** Joel catches Clementine before she leaves; they decide that maybe they will try again, even knowing how painful being together may turn out. (9)

That is the order in which the audience experiences the story. You can see the flow of the story fits the traditional model.

However, the order of the memories (and reality) for Joel went in this order:

- **Crisis:** Joel meets Clementine for the first time at a bonfire party; they connect — but the memory fades as they say goodbye. The wipe has been successful. (1)
- **Wafer:** Final flashes of Clementines memories as they wisp away (2)
- **Midpoint:** Joel experiences a memory that reminds him of why he loved Clementine in the first place. He decides he does not want her memory erased, and fights to stop it. (3)
- **Catalyst:** Joel finds out that Clementine has memory-wiped him — their relationship is over! (4)
- **Final Straw:** Joel demands to get a memory wipe as well. (5)
- **Balance:** Also, Joel prepares for his memory wipe. (6)
- **Balance:** Joel meets Clementine on a deserted Montauk beach, and rides home with her on the train, hitting it off. (7)

- **Climax:** Joel and Clementine are back together — but confront their past as first they hear Clementines session tapes (where she says why she wants Joel wiped from her memory), and then hear Joel's tapes. They now know that they were not good together. (8)

- **New Balance:** Joel catches Clementine before she leaves; they decide that maybe they will try again, even knowing how painful being together may turn out. (9)

Screenwriter Charlie Kaufman wrote an amazing, mind-bending story, keeping multiple memories and flashbacks coming at us in a beautifully timed parade. The reveals that come (to those who haven't had the story spoiled by reading things like this book) create a lovely and compelling mystery.

And still, it all feels right to our hard-wired-for-story brains. It's twisty telling that is properly structured.

PART NINE

Character

CHAPTER THIRTY-FIVE

Character and Plot

Character and structure then are indivisible;
one is the manifestation of the other.

—John Yorke, *Into the Woods*

A character is who they are in action. We tend to get caught up in lists of traits, backstory, ethnicity, occupations, and schoolings — all of which play into how a character may think and present themselves; however, lists of attributes are not at the core of who those characters are.

Jesus — not a slouch when it comes to storytelling — makes this clear to us numerous times. In Matthew 25, he tells the story of how in the days of judgment people will be separated in two groups the way a shepherd separates out the sheep and the goats. One group he invites into the kingdom, much to their surprise. The second group is equally surprised when they are denied the kingdom. Jesus' rationale for the division isn't about who said they believed, or who thought they were good; it was based on their actions.

The Biblical book of James does a deep dive into this, pointing out in chapter 2 that a faith without action is not a faith at all. In essence, we are told that what we think/believe cannot be trusted on its own — it only is proven to be true in action.

The same is accurate with our characters — who we think they are is irrelevant until we see that thought played out in action.

Jesus again affirmed this truism in the parable of the two sons, told in Matthew 21. A father asks his older son to go work the vineyard and the boy agrees to go. But he doesn't go. The younger son is also asked and tells his father he won't go. But he does go. Jesus then asks his listeners, "Which kid did his father's bidding?"

Jesus' lesson to the leading priests and elders is a warning about their own actions.

Jesus' lesson to writers is — "don't tell the audience who your characters are; show them."

Goal + Obstacle + Response

David Ball points out that action for dramatic purposes isn't just a character doing something. Rather action is a triplet of a goal, an obstacle, and a response to the obstacle. That triplet is what reveals character and separates one individual from another.

Let's walk through this using three highbrow dramas: *Macbeth*, *The Avengers*, and *The Brady Bunch*.[136]

- Macbeth is hosting the king
- Tony is having a drink
- Bobby is washing his clothes[137]

What do we know about these folk? Not much, really. So, let's add a goal and an obstacle to their action.

- Macbeth wants to be the king, but the actual king has the throne
- Tony wants to defeat Loki, but Loki corners Tony in his penthouse
- Bobby wants to keep his parents from learning he went into the abandoned building, but his clothes are covered in soot

Now we know their dramatic circumstances, yet still not much about who these people are, what makes them tick. What comes next will tell us about character. Each one has many options open to them, many

---

136. "Law and Disorder" episode

137. Passive tone is intentional here, to subtly make you think that the examples aren't quite right yet. See what I did there?

ways to respond to the obstacle. Mackie could wait until the throne opens up; Tony could rush Loki and try to overpower him; Bobby could confess to his parents. What do they do?

- Macbeth wants to be the king, but the actual king has the throne; Macbeth murders the king

- Tony wants to defeat Loki, but Loki corners Tony in his penthouse; Tony distracts Loki with clever conversation until he can get his suit on and escape

- Bobby wants to keep his parents from learning that he went into the abandoned building, but his clothes are covered in soot; Bobby washes his clothes (even though he doesn't know how the machine works)

Now we know more about who each of these people are, what they are capable of. John Yorke says, "It's a standard definition of character, but it's a good one: everyone surmounts the same obstacle uniquely and in doing so leaves their fingerprints behind."

Banquo is told his kids will become king; he chooses to wait rather than try to force his destiny to happen. The Hulk finds himself facing Loki in the very penthouse that Tony faced their foe — and the Hulk bashes Loki's skull into the floor. When older brother Greg gets into trouble, he sweet talks Alice into helping him out of his dilemma.

Each has a unique fingerprint.

Stakes

The level of stakes or pressure on a character reveals the character in deeper ways. Pressure on a character pushes out more of the real self.

This is why the apostle Peter weeps so bitterly after the cock crows and he realizes that Jesus' prediction of his denial was true. Sure, Peter is upset that his Christ was denied, but for more than that Peter is mourning for himself. He was sure that he was a brave man, ready to fight to the death for his Lord (how brave to cut off the ear of the servant just hours before!).

That night, under incredible pressure, Peter found out who he really was — someone who couldn't fight even the words of a maid around the fire.

Character cannot be developed in ease and quiet. Only through experience of trial and suffering can the soul be strengthened, ambition inspired, and success achieved.

—Helen Keller

A common writer's adage is: "Put your characters through hell." This isn't just for compelling action, but for compelling characters. One of the reasons that every story demands a Crisis is because the Central Character can never be fully revealed without one.

CLOSE UP: Character
Olympus Has Fallen & *White House Down*

In 2013, two films came out about a group of terrorists who takeover the White House: *Olympus Has Fallen* and *White House Down*. The two have a set of common roles, including the president of the United States, facing very similar circumstances, so the comparison becomes an interesting character study.

Let's start with *Olympus Has Fallen's* President Asher (played by Aaron Eckhart). The terrorists hold the president and several of his team hostage and demand the codes to America's nuclear weapons system. The code is in three parts, one each held by Asher, his Secretary of Defense, and the Chairman of the Joint Chiefs.

The terrorists start to torture the Secretary, and Asher immediately orders her to give up the codes rather than risk Asher having to watch the Secretary in pain. They then threaten the Chairman, and Asher again orders him to give up the codes rather than face watching his Chairman in pain. President Asher uses as his rationale for giving in that he will never give up his codes, so why risk any unnecessary pain of his coworkers?

Of course, the terrorists don't need Asher's code — they already had a work around, and thanks to the President's actions, the US is nearly turned into a nuclear wasteland.

White House Down's President James Sawyer (played by Jamie Foxx) finds himself in a similar position, only with greater emotional stakes. The terrorists demand of him access to the nuclear codes — he is the only one with them, so no need for the Secretary or Chairman. Sawyer has his out just as Asher did; for Asher, he thought that maybe he could withstand torture and not give up his codes, so it wouldn't matter to give the terrorists two thirds of what they wanted. For Sawyer, he believes that the system would have automatically reset, so his codes would not work.

So, giving up the codes — giving the terrorists what they want — probably wouldn't matter so much.

And the emotional stakes — rather than threatening to torture the Secretary of Defense or Chairman of the Joint Chiefs, the terrorists in this movie threaten to kill a child in front of President Sawyer.

With the threat of being forced to watch a child die, and knowing that the information likely can't be used, Sawyer makes a choice that shows him as a remarkably different character than the other President.

He explains to the young girl that he hopes she can understand why he has to let her die.

> *We must all face the choice between what is right and what is easy.*
>
> —Albus Dumbledore, *Harry Potter and the Goblet of Fire*

Linda J. Cowgill in *Writing Short Films* reminds us that the best moral choices or decisions have consequences; the choice is strong because it costs something to make that choice. One of the presidents made a choice to avoid consequences; the other president made a choice fully aware of the awful consequence. And those choices show which was a character of greater strength.

CROSS FADE: The Two Character Tests

Tim Keller tells us that there are two ways that God tests our character: suffering and prosperity. We can use those two ways to test our fictional characters as well.

Suffering is easy to see in Story — we discussed this in the last section. Who are we when we are at our lowest? In the book of Job, Satan argues that it is easy to love God when things are going well, but what happens if someone suffers instead? Job passed the test; the assumption by the Accuser is not all people would pass.

Yet for those who do, suffering not only tests but builds character.

We can rejoice, too, when we run into problems and trials, for we know that they help us develop endurance. And endurance develops strength of character, and character strengthens our confident hope of salvation.

—Romans 5:3-4, NLT

The second form of testing is a bit counter-intuitive yet is equally as compelling — the test of prosperity. True temptation can lie in who we are when we have everything.

Then Jesus said to his disciples, "I tell you the truth, it is very hard for a rich person to enter the Kingdom of Heaven. I'll say it again — it is easier for a camel to go through the eye of a needle than for a rich person to enter the Kingdom of God!"

—Matthew 19:23-24, NLT

When, as a writer, one is trying to think outside the box, consider testing a character by giving them the desires of their heart. Shrek gets what he wants, and that signals the Crisis of his film. Bruce of *Bruce Almighty* wishes that he could be God — and the story is based off God granting that wish.

One Man, Two Guvnors shows Francis getting his wish — two jobs! The farce is built on how he attempts to keep up with what he wished for. In *All My Sons*, Joe Keller gets his wish before the play begins — to be successful. The drama deals with the consequence of such success.

The question for a character receiving abundance is simple: what do you do with that abundance? In *Parasite*, Ki-woo Kim and his family get what they want — all the trimmings of living in a nice house without a care. Their story spirals in part because they mistakenly believed that such a life would remove their problems — instead their worries are compounded by the success of their machinations.

These stories aren't always tragedies — although many tragedies are all about the Central Character being blessed with abundance (*Macbeth*, *Citizen Kane*). A subplot of the film *In the Heights* is the announcement that someone from their community won the lottery — $96,000. The characters talk about what they would do with that money; mostly it involves fulfilling selfish desires. Usnavi ends up with the winnings, which he could sorely use in his dream of restoring his father's business in the Dominican Republic. Apparently without thought, he instead gives the money to his cousin Sonny to cover the legal fees of getting a green card.

Tim in *About Time* is given a great gift — the ability to time travel. He spends much of the movie using the gift to "fix" anything that doesn't go his way. He slowly begins to understand that the hardships of life are part of what makes life worthwhile. The give and take, the tragedies and successes — all go into what makes life precious. By movie's end, he opts to give up the gift, realizing that prosperity is not the goal of a well-lived life.

CHAPTER THIRTY-SIX

Character Paradox

Paradox

Also known as:
Mirror Traits
Character Conflict
Character Complexity

A mistake often made by writers in their attempt to create interesting characters is to beef up their lists, piling on additional character traits (gets mad a lot), histories (lost his tricycle), and hobbies (likes long walks on the beach). This ends up making the characters wider, not deeper.

To make a character deeper, to make them feel more real, instead of piling on random traits, an author integrates what at first glance may seem to be contradictory characteristics. A hero known for courage is given moments of fear; a headstrong person shows caution; a peaceful individual has moments of mania.

John Yorke refers to this as paradox; Robert McKee discusses this as the part of the Character Wheel.

A close examination of any well-drawn character is likely to reveal an opposition trait for every major trait. When Blanc first meets Marta (*Knives Out*), despite having a dominant trait of honesty, she attempts to fib to keep from throwing dirt at the family. Hamlet shows remarkable patience in his planning to prove the guilt of the king, and then goes and stabs Polonius without a thought in a fit of pique. Fred Rogers (*A Beautiful Day in the Neighborhood*), while showing remarkable care and attention to anyone who crosses his vision, at the very same time disregards the needs of the crew of his television show.

The two most common mistakes made in attempting to create paradox are 1) confusing paradox with growth, and 2) creating contradiction rather than complexity.

1) Character growth is the essence of Balance to New Balance storytelling; a character starts out one way and ends another. Scrooge (*A Christmas Carol*) starts out greedy and changes to be generous. Joy (*Inside Out*) starts out controlling and learns to share authority. Jojo (*Jojo Rabbit*) starts out intolerant, and by movie's end is more like his open-minded mother.

This is character growth — not paradox. True character paradox is not how a character changes, but how a person holds seemingly opposing traits within themselves at the same time. Hamlet does not learn to be impulsive; he is just at times plodding and at times impulsive. Marta does not learn to be dishonest — her fib (that proves that she cannot lie) happens in act one of the movie.

2) The second mistake is an easy one to do: creating contradiction rather than complexity. The cry of "that was out of character" is a valid one — if a character acts against their nature in an unbelievable way, the audience is thrown from the story. *Game of Thrones* has been accused of crossing that line in their rushed final season, as Daenerys switches from protector of the common people to destroyer of the common people for apparently no reason other than plot needs. Television's *24* ended the first season with a major plot twist — a discovery of a traitor close to home. Many fans felt tricked — the actions of the traitor in the first half of the season did not align with this revelation; and it turns out that the writers did not decide that character was a traitor until after the midseason break, showing the audience to be correct in their feelings.

The subtle work of the writer is to find believable conflicts within a character. This is based on how people really work: none of us are purely one thing. We get angry and show patience, we are selfish and selfless, we are prideful and full of self-doubt. It all depends on the circumstance we are in and the people we are around. We may act one way to our friends, another to our parents; one way in peace, another way in a fight. And that is true for believable characters as well.

Hamlet is thoughtful and patient — except when around his mother. Marta constantly tries to be good but attempts to lie to save hurting others. Fred Rogers is people first: fully considerate when in a person's presence, uncaring when the harm is to his business.

Think of the glorious main-trait paradoxes that define these characters:

- *The Shawshank Redemption*: Red is hopeless, yet constantly finding moments of temporary hope
- *Casablanca*: Rick looks out for number one, yet is constantly finding circumstances to look out for others (especially his staff)
- *I and You*: Caroline wants to be left alone, yet is desperate for companionship
- *Doubt*: Sister Aloysius is certain; Sister Aloysius is wracked with doubt
- *Spider-Man: Far From Home*: Peter Parker is cocky in front of crooks, and weak-kneed in front of Mary Jane

Great characters are often at war within themselves; paradox is part of that war. Paradox is about opposing traits, but for these characters they also have opposing wants, needs, and desires.

Luke Skywalker (*Star Wars: A New Hope*) wants to make his mark in the galaxy, and he wants to stay home and be responsible.

Luke wants to be treated as an adult, and wants to be young and play with his friends.

Luke wants to learn about his father, and he wants to ignore that urge.

But there is another power within me that is at war with my mind.

—Romans 7:23, NLT

This is the battle of Want versus Need, of self versus selflessness, of safety versus risk. The internal conflict that clashes out into the external — into the plot and the action.

Because, as we know, character is defined in action.

✞ CROSS FADE: Paradox and Christ ✞

Jesus is the epitome of character paradox, and a great showcase of consistent complexity. He never acts out of character, yet his character is a lot harder to pin down than maybe we would like. A quick survey of major traits makes this point all too clear.

Loving

John declares to us, "God is love."[138] Jesus proved this time and again, as he reached out to touch lepers, took time out of his day for the tax collector, wept over the suffering at the death of Lazarus.

Yet Jesus did not show love to everything, and certainly acted less than lovingly at times. He absolutely showed no love to the legion of demons possessing the Gadarene man, sending them into the pigs and then over a cliff. His words to the hypocritical religious leaders did not have that hippy-dippy quality of love to them — calling them blind fools and whitewashed tombs. The Matthew 23 rant is just that — a rant; not a gentle chiding, or a loving correction, but a full out tirade and call for judgment.

Forgiving

Forgiveness is the raison d'être of Jesus coming to earth, right? This is the man who forgave the sins of the paralyzed man in Mark 2. He forgave those who were in the process of crucifying him ("Father, forgive them, for they don't know what they are doing." Luke 23:34, NLT).

---

138. 1 John 4:8

Yet he warns that not all will receive forgiveness — some will end in eternal punishment. The parable of the sheep and the goats (Matthew 25), for example. Even those who think they are shoo-ins (in fact, *especially* those who think they are shoo-ins).

> *"Not everyone who says to Me, 'Lord, Lord,' shall enter the kingdom of heaven, but he who does the will of My Father in heaven. Many will say to Me in that day, 'Lord, Lord, have we not prophesied in Your name, cast out demons in Your name, and done many wonders in Your name?' And then I will declare to them, 'I never knew you; depart from Me, you who practice lawlessness!'"*
>
> —Matthew 7:21-23, NKJV

Gentle

Especially in comparing Jesus to his cousin, John the Baptizer, our Lord comes off as quite meek. Paul attempted to emulate the gentleness of Christ (2 Corinthians 10:1); Jesus gathered children up in his arms (Matthew 19). And still he drove men out of the Temple with knotted cords (John 2), overturning tables and creating quite a scene. And the aforementioned treatment of the religious leaders He saw as hypocritical was less than gentle.

Obedient

> *...he humbled himself in obedience to God and died a criminal's death on a cross.*
>
> —Philippians 2:8, NLT

Here is a clear example of situation and person defining a trait. Jesus was obedient, all the way to death. The desires of his Father outweighed his own ("...nevertheless not My will, but Yours, be done."[139]). For God, Jesus is unrelenting in his obedience.

Yet he challenged his earthly parents by disappearing to the temple at age twelve (Luke 2) and constantly messed up the orders being given

---

139. Luke 22:42, NKJV

out by the religious leaders. He healed on the Sabbath, touched lepers, talked with women (without a chaperone present!), and ate with sinners. He even forgave sins — in front of the religious leaders who forbade such actions!

Jesus was obedient to God, and obedient to love. Which meant he sometimes was disobedient to religion.

God and Man

Jesus is the perfect example of Paradox because he was not an "either/or" character. This is shown in this final example: Jesus was fully and without a doubt God (John 1:1, John 10:30). And yet:

> *Though he was God, he did not think of equality with God as something to cling to. Instead, he gave up his divine privileges, he took the humble position of a slave and was born as a human being.*

> —Philippians 2:6-7, NLT

Jesus was fully and without a doubt human (John 1:14, Matthew 1:23). Human and God; not at war, but in blended co-existence.

The perfect paradox.

CHAPTER THIRTY-SEVEN

Character and Dialogue

There is a big gap in every character (and every real-life human, come to think of it). We all have a facade — the way that we want to be seen; and then there is reality — who we truly are.

Macbeth spends the second half of the play trying desperately to show that he is in charge, when in reality he is a hot, lunatic mess. As Tony Stark becomes more of a hero, he still clings to his outward persona of the carefree playboy; yet he is driven by a messiah complex, thinking that he is the only one who can save the world (*Avengers: Age of Ultron, Captain America: Civil War*). Tyrion Lannister (*Game of Thrones*) plays into his image as drunkard and fool — and much of the time he believes in that facade; still, he is a brilliant strategist and natural leader.

Dialogue is one of the areas where this character gap is most evident. All dialogue is driven by intent: characters speak because they want something. At the same time, good dialogue is not controlled completely by the character.

Good dialogue does two things at the same time. First, it reflects how a character wishes to be seen — the conscious part of the character's words. And while those words are spilling out, the dialogue also reveals what a character is truly like — the unconscious mind at work on the tongue.

John Yorke refers to this in terms of betrayal: "Good dialogue conveys how a character wants to be seen while betraying the flaws they want to hide."

We see this in an exchange between Angelica and Hamilton at their meeting ("Satisfied," *Hamilton*).

> *Angelica: Where's your family from?*
>
> *Hamilton: Unimportant, there's a million things I haven't done. Just you wait, just you wait!*

We can see the struggle for Hamilton here. He is desperate to impress, to show his importance. At the same time, he has a deep insecurity in his heritage, coming from a disreputable family situation. Angelica sees right through his attempts at bravado:

> *Angelica: I asked about his family, did you see his answer? His hands started fidgeting, he looked askance. He's penniless, he's flying by the seat of his pants.*

Hamilton was making a conscious attempt to control the conversation; his reality betrayed him.

Let's look at an example Jesus gave to us:

> *Two men went into the temple to pray. One was a Pharisee and the other a tax collector. The Pharisee stood over by himself and prayed, "God, I thank you that I am not greedy, dishonest, and unfaithful in marriage like other people. And I am really glad that I am not like that tax collector over there. I go without eating for two days a week, and I give you one-tenth of all I earn."*
>
> *The tax collector stood off at a distance and did not think he was good enough even to look up toward heaven. He was so sorry for what he had done that he pounded his chest and prayed, "God, have pity on me! I am such a sinner."*
>
> —Luke 18:10-13, CEV

The Pharisee in this parable has a very blatant agenda. His words are designed to give the impression of himself he hopes God and all other hearers believe — he is a holy, upright man of impeccable character and nary a flaw.

Yet we don't walk away from his monologue thinking any of that — the unconscious is betraying the dickens out of this guy. We see him as proud, arrogant, self-righteous; he is a man without pity or love for his fellow man, especially the less fortunate.

The tax collector is much more in tune with himself; he knows himself better than the Pharisee. And look at how much we get from what he doesn't say — there is no list of actions, no excuses, no explanations. He comes out as humble, self-aware, and repentant.

Dialogue is a mix of character intent and reality; if properly crafted, the audience is given a double dose of character to play with.

CHAPTER THIRTY-EIGHT

Character and Theme

The Need of the Central Character is often directly linked to the theme of the Story. As they work through their Need (selfishness, separation, greed, pride), the story works through the questions it is imposing on the audience. This plays out through the interaction of Need and Want.

We've discussed quite a bit the stories where Need conflicts with Want. *Shrek* and *I and You* (wants to be alone, needs community), *Inside Out* (Joy wants her person to be happy all the time, needs to learn the value of all emotions), or *Death of a Salesman* (the want of fantasy over the need of reality).

In stories where Need and Want are in conflict, the Central Character cannot have a satisfying ending unless they learn to put aside the Want for the sake of the Need. Tragedies are often tragic because the Central Character's Want overpowers the Need. Mark holds onto pride (*The Social Network*), Mackie won't let go of power (*Macbeth*), Willie would rather die wrapped in fantasy than live in reality (*Death of a Salesman*).

There are also many stories where Need is parallel to Want, with the two running side by side. In these stories, once the Central Character is able to fulfill their Need, they have the tools necessary to also gain their Want.

Marta (*Knives Out*) wants justice and peace of mind; she needs to be able to stand up for herself and her own values. Once she can do that, justice and peace follow. Bertie (*The King's Speech*) wants to get through his speeches; he is only able to do that after fulfilling his Need of finding his own voice.

Both journeys — Need vs Want and Need parallel to Want — mark a sort of character plotting that runs alongside the physical plot of the story. The character's inner journey is forced by the exterior pressures. Yorke's Roadmap of Change is a good illustration of this. Trottier talks about this in terms of the "emotional story" of a character leading to a Realization.

Billy Mernit (in his chapter in *Cut to the Chase*)[140] aligns the character arc with the three-act structure. Here are the points alongside Event Structure's labels:

- **Balance**: Character Defined
- **Catalyst**: Character Questioned
- **Final Straw**: Growth Opportunity
- **Midpoint**: Change Acquired
- **Crisis**: Change Tested
- **Climax**: Epiphany and Its Result
- **New Balance**: New Awareness

The arc of Jean Valjean (*Les Misérables*) may look like this from the character's interior point of view:

- **Balance**: Character Defined ~ I live for me
- **Catalyst** (the candle sticks): Character Questioned ~ Do I live just for me?
- **Final Straw** (death of Fantine): Growth Opportunity ~ I will live for Cosette
- **Midpoint** ("One Day More"): Change Acquired ~ I will build a life for Cosette
- **Crisis**: Change Tested ~ I will die for Cosette so she can have that life

---

140. "Deepening Characters and Defining their Arcs" by Billy Mernit, in *Cut to the Chase*, edited by Linda Venis

- **Climax**: Epiphany and Its Result: I will always choose others (Marius and Javert)
- **New Balance**: New Awareness: I can now join the saints

Each step is not only a testing and exploration of character, but also of theme. We learn as the character learns.

CHAPTER THIRTY-NINE

Character Counts:
The MCU versus DCEU

Ginger or Mary Ann?
Kirk or Picard?
Team Edward or Team Jacob?[141]

The culture wars, especially among us nerds, often come down to these dual preferences. This section, on a personal level, becomes painful. In the DC or Marvel question, I'm typically DC. In the comics, I liked Daredevil and Captain America; Black Panther has always been my favorite Avenger; and I collected X-Men. However, DC was my preference. I'd rather read the Legion of Superheroes than any Marvel team; more of a Batman guy than Spiderman; and would prefer to spend an afternoon arguing over who would win in a fight — Batman or Superman[142] — than wonder who could best the Hulk in a throw down.

But that is comic books — when it comes to the movies, the question becomes: DCEU or MCU? For purposes of this discussion, I'm looking at the DC Extended Universe as the Warner Bros./DC Comics run directed or produced by Zack Snyder (from *Man of Steel* through *Birds*

---

141. Mary Ann, Picard, and not interested.
142. Batman. End of discussion.

of Prey).[143] For the Marvel Cinematic Universe under the producing eye of Kevin Feige (*Iron Man* to *Spider-Man: Far From Home*).

From a box office point of view, both franchises have made gobs of money. Marvel more so, not just because of their greater quantity (23 MCU movies, compared to 7 DCEU movies), but also one on one. MCU's highest grosser was *Avengers: Endgame* ($858 million domestic/nearly $2.8 billion worldwide).[144] DCEU's top grosser was *Wonder Woman*, at well under half that ($412 million domestic/nearly $822 million worldwide).

From the critics and populace, MCU also wins. Here are the comparison scores from Rotten Tomatoes:

	Rotten Tomato Scores		Critic	Audience
1	*Black Panther*	MCU	96	79
2	*Iron Man*	MCU	94	91
3	*Avengers: Endgame*	MCU	94	90
4	*Thor: Ragnorak*	MCU	93	87
5	*Wonder Woman*	DCEU	93	87
6	*Marvel's The Avengers (2012)*	MCU	92	91
7	*Spider-Man: Homecoming*	MCU	92	87
8	*Spider-Man: Far from Home*	MCU	91	95
9	*Guardians of the Galaxy*	MCU	91	92
10	*Captain America: Civil War*	MCU	91	89
11	*Captain America: The Winter Soldier*	MCU	90	92
12	*Doctor Strange*	MCU	89	86

143. The DCEU does not include the Christopher Nolan *Dark Knight* movies. I am also excluding *Shazam*, as Snyder was not involved in that movie, and will have to address any additions later. (Although *Suicide Squad* vs *The Suicide Squad* is an interesting comparison within this debate — with "The" going against the Snyder philosophy. Ditto on *The Batman*. Oh, what a difference an article makes!)

144. Box Office numbers from Boxofficemojo.com

13	*Ant-Man and the Wasp*	MCU	87	75
14	*Avengers: Infinity War*	MCU	85	91
15	*Guardians of the Galaxy Vol. 2*	MCU	85	87
16	*Ant-Man*	MCU	83	86
17	*Captain America: The First Avenger*	MCU	80	74
18	*Iron Man 3*	MCU	79	78
19	*Birds of Prey*	DCEU	78	78
20	*Captain Marvel*	MCU	78	48
21	*Thor*	MCU	77	76
22	*Avengers: Age of Ultron*	MCU	76	83
23	*Iron Man 2*	MCU	73	71
24	*The Incredible Hulk*	MCU	67	70
25	*Thor: The Dark World*	MCU	66	76
26	*Aquaman*	DCEU	65	74
27	*Man of Steel*	DCEU	56	75
28	*Justice League*	DCEU	40	71
29	*Batman v Superman: Dawn of Justice*	DCEU	28	62
30	*Suicide Squad*	DCEU	27	59

From the critical side, the DCEU boasts one of their movies in the top 10, *Wonder Woman* at #5. A second one in the top 20, with *Birds of Prey* at #19. It may be interesting to note that both movies were directed by women.

The remaining five DCEU movies fill the last five slots on the scale.

Using the audience rankings, *Wonder Woman* hits #10, *Birds of Prey* at #18, with the bottom five rearranging spots with some of the Marvel movies at #22 and under.

There are many theories trying to explain the discrepancy, from hero fatigue (which doesn't explain why MCU's box office numbers keep going up) to tone (DCEU is noted for being much darker than the MCU).

I have my own theory.

I think it boils down to character and worldview.

DCEU Philosophy

Quite simply, in the world view of Zack Snyder's DCEU, physical strength determines victory.

The hero must either be physically stronger than the enemy or find a weapon that is stronger than the enemy's weapon.

In *Man of Steel*, Superman is able to defeat General Zod because he is strong enough to break Zod's neck. *Batman v Superman* — Superman summons the strength to beat down Doomsday (Doomsday is just as strong, so it ends in a tie). *Justice League* — the only strategy of the team is to find a fighter stronger than Steppenwolf; once that weapon shows up on screen, the battle is over.

Wonder Woman (directed by Patty Jenkins, screenplay by Allan Heinberg) is an outlier for the DCEU — in tone, reception, and refreshing emphasis on character. Yet even this movie falls into a disappointingly typical DCEU ending — a special effects laden beat-down to determine who wins. Wonder Woman is physically stronger than Mars, and therefore wins.

Marvel Philosophy

Kevin Feige's Marvel Universe, on the other hand, believes that strength of character is what wins the day.

In virtually every movie, it is made crystal clear that the enemy is much, much stronger than the hero. The hero must win, not because they are stronger, but despite the fact they are outgunned. Because that's what heroes do[145] — at least in this universe.

Instead of focusing on bombastic battles (don't get me wrong, Marvel movies do indeed have bombastic battles), the films focus on

---

145. Thank you, Thor.

character and character development. And lest you misunderstand me, they focus on developing Biblical character.

Due to his pride, Thor, the eponymous character in his franchise, loses his superpowers and is no longer worthy to hold his hammer. He must learn humility and show it in action — sacrificing his life for his friends — before he can regain his powers and defeat the Destroyer and Loki (Proverbs 11:2; 18:12; James 4:10).

Thor, through his time on earth, literally lives out Romans 12:16:

> Live in harmony with each other. Don't be too proud to enjoy the company of ordinary people. And don't think you know it all![146]

Doctor Strange, in his movie, is clearly no match for Dormammu; it takes the lord of the Dark Dimension only a few seconds to kill Strange. We know this, because he does it many, many times. The good doctor creates a time loop, dying countlessly, yet keeping Dormammu trapped in the loop with each death. Strange does not defeat Dormammu, he just has greater perseverance: he outlasts Dormammu (James 1:12).

The entire movie shows Strange's move from conceited self-interest to willing self-sacrifice and does so through how he deals with his suffering. In essence, Roman 5:3-5a:[147]

> But that's not all! We gladly suffer, because we know that suffering helps us to endure. And endurance builds character, which gives us a hope that will never disappoint us...

In Marvel's *The Avengers*, Tony (Iron Man) spends quite a bit of time teasing Steve's (Captain America) belief in being a soldier. The idea of sacrificing for others, of living for something greater, is not a natural place for Tony.

> Steve: The only thing you really fight for is yourself. You're not the guy to make the sacrifice play, to lay down on a wire and let the other guy crawl over you.

> Tony: I think I would just cut the wire.

---

146. NLT
147. CEV

Steve: Always a way out — You know, you may not be a threat, but you better stop pretending to be a hero.

Tony: A hero? Like you? You're a lab rat, Rogers. Everything special about you came out of a bottle!

In the Battle of New York, the team cannot win against Loki's army. Tony, who has started to see Captain America's worldview, makes the sacrifice play — giving his life to push away the Chitauri forces. "Greater love has no one than this, than to lay down one's life for his friends."[148]

Peter Parker goes one better in *Spider-Man: Homecoming*, when he saves Toomes (The Vulture) after their final fight. I realize that Iron Man saved all of New York, so saving a single person might not seem like "goes one better." However, in a world where strength of character is more important than physical strength, Peter's sacrifice may be a harder choice.

Tony Stark saved his own people; Peter saved an enemy. And not just an enemy, but one who knows his secret identity — saving Toomes means an end to his web-slinging career, as well as a threat to everyone Peter loves. Tony sacrificed his own life; Peter's principles extend past his own life[149] (1 Peter 3:9, Luke 6:27, Matthew 5:43-48). Peter's superhero verse might be Romans 12:21: "Don't let evil defeat you, but defeat evil with good."[150]

If a character in a Marvel movie does not grow, or hold the right moral outlook, then the movie ends as a tragedy. *Captain America: Civil War* is a great example. The story centers on Captain America's old friend, Bucky Barnes — who has been brainwashed into being an assassin. (For those who are not fans of comic books, I apologize for our overblown plots!)

Steve Rogers represents forgiveness and redemption, holding out hope for Bucky. Tony Stark represents blind justice (the Javert to Steve's Jean Valjean). Tony starts to come to Steve's way of thinking, then reverses into revenge (when finding out Bucky assassinated his

---

148. John 15:13, NKJV
149. A theme played out again in *No Way Home*.
150. CEV

parents). The movie ends with the two trying to kill each other — and the collapse of the Avengers (Matthew 26:52: Romans 12:19).

Tony's journey is mirrored in this movie by T'Challa (The Black Panther), who is also after vengeance for the murder of his father. However, he is able to see the cost of vengeance. He confronts his father's murderer as Iron Man and Captain America fight:

> Vengeance has consumed you. It's consuming them. I am done letting it consume me. Justice will come soon enough.

He refuses to kill Zemo; he also refuses to allow Zemo to kill himself — the villain still must pay for his crimes. T'Challa now understands the difference between justice and vengeance.

Physical Strength versus Strength of Character

Perhaps a better way to look at this is in direct comparison of DCEU movies with the MCU.

Let's go back to Black Panther, and the movie named after him. The world of Wakanda has a tradition right in line with their DCEU cousins — the king of Wakanda proves himself in physical combat. The winner of the ritual combat is then crowned king. The movie is a test of that tradition, as Killmonger briefly becomes king. Yes, he has physical strength, but the kingdom comes to realize that physical prowess is not enough. The warrior Okoye puts it this way when confronting Killmonger: "You! Your heart is so full of hatred you are not fit to be a King."

Aquaman also has a ritual combat contest. In this DCEU movie, Arthur (Aquaman) challenges Orm to a duel. Orm handily beats Arthur, until Arthur cheats (yes, Aquaman cheats) to escape the consequences of losing. Arthur then seeks out a weapon that is more powerful than Orm. When he returns with the weapon, Arthur agrees to resume their fight, but on the condition that it take place in a location that favors Arthur and if he can use a weapon stronger than Orm's weapon.

In Marvel's Wakanda, T'Challa also fights against his antagonist — Killmonger — and nearly loses in the first go around. However, T'Challa doesn't cheat — his opponent ends the fight too soon. Later, T'Challa will return to continue the fight (decreed within the rules). Both men fight on equal terms, with only Killmonger having an extra weapon. T'Challa wins and proves he is worthy of kingship in the mercy and care (Matthew 5:44) he shows the defeated and dying Killmonger. Here, T'Challa completes the journey of character growth started in *Captain America: Civil War*.

As mentioned above, a big part of the *Aquaman* movie is Arthur searching for a weapon that is more powerful than his opponent. The weapon is what wins the day in the movie. This is very similar to the main quest of *Justice League* (also DCEU): Batman and company race to bring back a weapon stronger than Steppenwolf (the weapon is Superman). Once they find the weapon, the battle is over.

This is a storyline also used in *Avengers: Infinity War* (MCU). Just as in *Justice League*, the heroes are confronting a villain with godlike powers — Thanos. Thor, whose character has been tested to its limits, takes the same tactic as Aquaman and Batman, and sets out to find a weapon stronger than Thanos. He is clear on his motivation, as Thor tells Rocket:

> *I'm only alive because Fate wants me alive. Thanos is just the latest in a long line of bastards, and he'll be the latest to feel my vengeance. Fate wills it so.*

Not exactly in line with Biblical values, so it should come as no surprise that it doesn't end well. Thor gets his weapon (Stormbreaker), and the weapon is stronger than Thanos. Despite that, this being a movie universe where character is more important than brawn, Thor loses, and Thanos destroys half of the universe.

Which is how the movie ends. It is a tragedy, where the heroes lose — not because they aren't strong enough, but because they don't have the necessary strength of character.[151] The following movie, *Avengers: Endgame*, spends a significant portion of time with the heroes rebuild-

---

151. This is reinforced (and foreshadowed) earlier, when Iron Man and his team nearly get Thanos' weapon away from him. However, Starlord is not able

ing their character. Thor's most significant moment in the final movie isn't in battle, but rather a conversation with his mother. He laments that he couldn't be the hero he was supposed to be. Frigga tells him:

> *Everyone fails at "who they're supposed to be," Thor. The measure of a person, of a hero, is how well they succeed at being who they are.*

This sets Thor on his path back to redemption.

~

I think audiences are attracted to Biblical character — maybe not religious character, even Jesus was wary of that.[152] Rather the values of self-sacrifice, perseverance, forgiveness, contrition, humility, peace, patience, self-control, fairness, honesty, compassion, wisdom, integrity, and responsibility[153], and love — including loving your enemies.

The MCU focused on such characters. And I believe they have proven such pursuits to be worthwhile.

---

to contain his anger, and spoils the hero's attempt. "If you are angry, you cannot do any of the good things that God wants done." James 1:19-20

152. Matthew 23:27-28, Luke 20:46-47, Matthew 7:21-23, Matthew 15:7-9, Matthew 6:5

153. Spider-Man's life verse is Luke 12:48, "When someone has been given much, much will be required in return; and when someone has been entrusted with much, even more will be required" (NLT). In the comics, it is paraphrased as, "With great power comes great responsibility."

CHAPTER FORTY

Forces of Antagonism

As we know, every Story has a hero, goal, and obstacle. The forces of antagonism are the people/things that prevent the forward progress of the Central Character toward their goal.

For most stories, there will be many obstacles. Antagonism comes from multiple sources — interior or the self, external in another person or individual, and the wider society or world.

Hamlet is up against Claudius, for sure. But he also must overcome his own doubts, at times his own inertia, his mother, Polonius, Laertes, Ophelia (he must at least get her off to the side), Rosencrantz and Guildenstern, as well as the societal conventions that frown on regicide — so the law of the land and the guards that maintain the law.

Before Dorothy can find her way home (*The Wizard of Oz*), she faces the wicked witch, the crab apple trees, the lion, the wizard, and those freaky flying monkeys. She also has an environment to overcome — poppies, terrain, and even a tornado. Plus, there are puzzles to solve along the way — how to get a scarecrow off a fence, how to get a rusted tin man moving, how to escape a castle.

Just as "hero" is a misleading term, as our Central Character need not be heroic (Walter White, Macbeth, Joker[154]), it follows equally that the forces of antagonism need not be "bad" or "evil." This is obvious in a story where the Central Character is a villain — Macduff is a heroic

---

154. *Breaking Bad, Macbeth, Joker*

antagonist to Macbeth; Fred Rogers borders on angelic as the antagonist to Lloyd Vogel.[155]

Some of the obstacles may even be on the side of the protagonist. Catherine in *Hidden Figures* is constantly up against opposition from her teammates, all working towards the same goal. Boromir provides many points of dissension throughout *The Fellowship of the Ring*. Malcolm in *The Sixth Sense* is opposed by Cole, the boy Malcolm is trying to help. *Friends* often pits friend against friend; *Modern Family* relative against relative; *Brooklyn Nine-Nine* fellow officer against fellow officer. Sometimes the friendly fire opposition is only for individual scenes and moments, yet still provides the obstacles to make the story dynamic.

Forces of antagonism may be neutral as far as intent. The river in *1917*, the barbed wire in *War Horse*, the storm in *Up*. These obstacles must be overcome even though they are just objects or parts of nature.

There is a direct relationship between the strength of the forces of antagonism and how interestingly the story plays out. A sporting event that is a blowout is only interesting to the die-hard fans of the winning side — and even then, mismatched sporting events are often the least attended.

The Harlem Globetrotters started out as a straightforward basketball team, an all-black group in the era before basketball was integrated. They were a bit too good — they regularly beat the best of the NBA teams, and with their game outcomes a foregone conclusion, attendance took a dive. They realized they needed to bring in more entertainment. Thus, they started implementing comic bits and showing off skills focused more on impressing the audience than scoring baskets.

Without a strong force against them, the Globetrotters were just not as interesting.[156]

So strong forces against the Central Character makes for good storytelling. Want even better stories? Provide forces of antagonism that are

---

155. *Macbeth, A Beautiful Day in the Neighborhood*

156. The modern Globetrotters no longer focus on the game at all, being a pure comedy and skills show.

stronger than the Central Character. This is a direct Biblical lesson —
the weaker Central Character against the stronger Antagonist.

David versus Goliath.

Gideon versus the Midianites.

Elijah versus the prophets of Baal.

Wrong person, seemingly dumb idea.[157]

John Yorke tells us, "...the more effective the forces of antagonism,
the greater the story." Michael Welles Schock (*Screenwriting Down to
the Atoms*) takes it from the other angle:

> *A character who merely causes trouble but does not oppose the
> Story Goal cannot be the antagonist. That character is only a
> PEST.*

Ryan George is a comedian and creator of "Screen Rant Pitch Meetings," a YouTube series that pokes fun at the movies. Ryan plays a
screenwriter in a meeting with a producer (also played by Ryan), imag-
ining the pitch session for existing movies. Along the way, he jokes
about all the plot holes, mistakes, and absurdities of those films.

A recurring gag found in every episode comes when the screenwriter mentions an obstacle and the producer replies that it must be hard

---

157. I am self-referencing the earlier section on Reluctant Hero (Ch. 6).

for the character to overcome that hurdle. The screenwriter replies, "It will be super easy. Barely an inconvenience."[158]

This joke is funny (every time) because we, the listeners, know that "super easy, barely an inconvenience" is bad writing and boring storytelling.

Luke is up against Darth Vader, a Death Star, and the force of the Empire. Hamlet stands alone against a king wielding the full power of the throne. Schofield and Blake are on their own against impossible terrain, booby-trapped tunnels, and the entire enemy army. The Doctor faces down armies of Daleks, Cybermen, Weeping Angels, and the Silence armed with little more than a sonic screwdriver.[159]

We yearn for such stories in part because (as previously discussed) greater opposition brings out the character within us. And, I think, because we know that we face battles that appear to be way out of our league.

For we are not fighting against flesh-and-blood enemies, but against evil rulers and authorities of the unseen world, against mighty powers in this dark world, and against evil spirits in the heavenly places.

—Ephesians 6:12, NLT

We know that we are Luke, Hamlet, Schofield, and the Doctor. We don't need story to help us understand our easy battles. We need stories to help us muddle through the battles that are hard — to encourage, educate, and elevate us in those confrontations. To help us get back up again ("I can do this all day")[160] when others tell us to stay down. To remind us that doing right is worthwhile, even when it is not easy.[161]

---

158. "Oh, really?!"

159. *A New Hope, Hamlet, 1917, Doctor Who*

160. Steve Rogers' catchphrase in the MCU

161. Yes, this Dumbledore quote is one of my favorites and thus gets repeated a lot. And it is worth repeating.

Antagonist and Contagonist

Antagonist

Also known as:
Opposition Character
Big Bad
Nemesis

Contagonist

Also known as:
Threshold Guardians

Sometimes the main force of antagonism is embodied in a main villain, the "big bad" that the Central Character must defeat if they are to win their goal. Usually, the Want of the antagonist is in direct conflict with the Want of the protagonist. Hogarth wants to protect the Iron Giant; Kent wants to expose the Iron Giant. Ted Lasso wants to have a winning season; Rebecca wants the team to lose. Hamlet wants to get revenge on his father's killer; Claudius wants to keep his life and his throne.[162]

As seen in the last section, a good antagonist must have the power and ability to block the efforts of the main character. If not, they aren't really an antagonist, just a pest.[163] Besides which, a great villain makes for a very memorable character. Disney is making hay these days by coming up with stories starring their villains, including *Maleficent* and *Cruella*.[164] Superhero stories have done the same with *Joker* and *Birds of Prey and the Fantabulous Emancipation of One Harley Quinn*.

---

162. *Iron Giant, Ted Lasso, Hamlet*
163. Michael Welles Schock, *Screenwriting Down to the Atoms*
164. At the same time, they are having trouble keeping those characters villainous.

With "antagonist" used to describe the big bad, we could use a term for all the obstacles between the protagonist and the final battle. And we do have such a term — contagonist. The contagonists can be directly allied to the antagonist, such as the henchmen in a Bond movie, or Thanos' cronies in *Infinity War*. Or they may be unattached to the main villain, like Blanc in *Knives Out* or the alien who loses his hand in the cantina in *Star Wars: A New Hope*. Or somewhere in between, like General Rogard in *The Iron Giant* or Polonius in *Hamlet*.

Contagonists are very useful, especially in stories where we want to delay the climactic confrontation. In fact, in many stories there is more juice to the interactions with the contagonists than with the big bad.

Anthony Hopkins won the Best Actor Oscar for playing Hannibal Lecter in *The Silence of the Lambs*, and one would be hard pressed to claim that the scenes with Hopkins and Foster aren't the standout moments in the film. Yet Lecter is not the antagonist of the story — Foster's FBI agent Starling is hunting the serial killer, Buffalo Bill. Lecter is a character that Starling must get through to get to Bill; Lecter is a contagonist.

Star Wars: A New Hope introduced us to one of the best villains in the sci-fi world: Darth Vader. Vader gets the best scenes, his own theme music, and one of the coolest voices on the planet (yes, Mr. Jones, I'm talking about you). And yet, Vader is not the main antagonist of the film. The power that must be stopped for Luke to win is the guy who Vader is ostensibly working for: General Tarkin. Vader must be defeated to make way for the destruction of Tarkin and his Death Star. (Vader becomes the big bad of *The Empire Strikes Back*, and returns as a contagonist to the Emperor's antagonist with *The Return of the Jedi*.)

To win Maria, Tony has to deal with Anita (*West Side Story*) although Chino is the real big bad. Bond, James Bond, must go through Nick Nack/Tee Hee/Onatopp/May Day/Jaws/Oddjob/Thumper & Bambi/Irma Bunt before he can face off with the pick-the-film's main baddie. All the suspects in the murder during an episode of your favorite detective show are contagonists — well, except for the one who is actually guilty.

Here is the thing that helps to make contagonists so interesting: it is good for the protagonist to defeat her enemies.

It is stronger when she turns her enemies into allies.

Typically, it is in the contagonists that we see this successfully done. Westley in *The Princess Bride* must face the swordsman, the giant, and the brain in order to rescue Buttercup from Humperdinck; he converts two of the contagonists to allies, and fights alongside them in the second half. (Or at least is carried by them during the second half.) Thor builds his team out of contagonists — Hulk, Valkerie, and Loki — in *Thor: Ragnorak*. *12 Angry Men* (play and film) is two hours' worth of converting contagonists to allies — and ends when the antagonist himself (Juror #3) is won over.

- *Jojo Rabbit*: the kid and the monster in the closet become allies
- *The Shawshank Redemption*: Red starts out rooting against Andy, then roots for Andy
- *Harriet*: Walter goes from tracking Harriet to being her right hand
- *Toy Story*: Woody and Buzz
- *I and You*: Caroline and Anthony
- *The Band's Visit*: Zakaria and Dina
- *Shrek*: Shrek and Donkey
- *The Mandalorian*: Mando and Cara Dune or Bo-Katan or Fennec Shand or Boba Fett or Ahsoka

Wow, it seems like the Mandalorian's main job is to turn contagonists into allies.

This of course is rooted in a Biblical principle. From Jesus' lips: "But I say, love your enemies! Pray for those who persecute you."[165]

Conversion rather than destruction: our call is to turn our enemies. We must resist the forces that get in the way of good; turning those forces to the light is better than destroying them.

Do not forget that there is an enemy to fight, and while it is best to win them over, not all can be won over. Sauron will not be won over;

---

165. Matthew 5:44, NLT

Sauraman and Gollum (*The Lord of the Rings*) have a shot all the way to the end. Voldemort will never work for the side of good; Snape has a shot at redemption (*Harry Potter*). *Spider-Man: No Way Home* is a brilliant study in this theory — Otto Octavius, Norman Osborn, Flint Marko, Curt Connors — some will become allies, some will not.

Satan will not be won over; but all the contagonists on his side can be. In the end, some will not (Judas); yet, shockingly, some will (Paul of Tarsus).

✠ CROSS FADE: Biblical Contagonists ✠

Christianity could be seen as a series of stories about a Central Character (God) converting contagonists (humanity) into allies. We all, at one point or another, are at odds with the creator.

Not a single person on earth is always good and never sins.

—Ecclesiastes 7:20, NLT

It is no surprise that the Bible itself is chockful of examples for us. Jesus puts many contagonists-turned-allies into his parables, including the Prodigal Son and the Good Samaritan.

Paul of Tarsus is a prime story of conversion. One of the nastiest contagonists the early church had to face, Paul oversaw the stoning of Stephen. He was on an unholy mission, zealous to rid the land of the followers of Christ, when he was knocked off his horse[166] by the voice of Jesus. His encounter with the living God turned him into one of the most zealous supporters of the cause.

Paul went on to witness the transformation of many contagonists himself. The Philippian jailor went from imprisoning Paul to hosting him for a meal after an earthquake opened up the cells. The island of Malta traces its Christian roots straight back to Paul and the miracles done there, including Paul healing the father of the leader, Publius.

---

166. The Bible doesn't say he was knocked off a horse — but the dramatist in me loves the image, so there you go.

Some conversions took very little time; some longer. Nathaniel started out mocking the enthusiasm of his friend Philip who wanted him to meet Jesus. "Can anything good come from Nazareth?" (John 1:46, NLT) is his reply. Within moments of meeting Jesus, he changes his tune, declaring: "Rabbi, you are the Son of God — the King of Israel!" (John 1:49, NLT).

Rahab was a part of Jericho's population, a prostitute, and a pagan. Yet she saw clear to help Joshua's spies, and in exchange united with the Israelite community. Not only did she join God's side, but she is also name-checked in Jesus' family tree (Matthew 1:5).

Naaman, a commander of the Syrian army, seeks out Elisha for healing. His country is so at odds with Israel that when he shows up at the palace asking for healing, King Joram assumes it is a ploy to give the Syrians an excuse to attack his country. After he is healed, the enemy commander swears that he would serve no other god than the God of Israel (2 Kings 5).

Nebuchadnezzar was a clear enemy of Judah, not only in conquering Jerusalem but by taking the best and brightest of the nation's youth back to Babylon with him. Through years of interactions with the captive Daniel and his companions, the king went from respecting God to defending God to praising God (Daniel 1-4).

We often forget that Moses did not start out as God's man on earth. In fact, he wasn't a practicing Jew for most of his life. Raised in the home of Pharaoh, he was brought up as an Egyptian. He then spent forty years as the son-in-law to a priest of Midian. He did not live with fellow Israelites until after his conversion experience at the burning bush (Exodus).

Joseph's story was almost cut short by his jealous brothers, who, on the verge of killing their sibling, opt to sell him into slavery instead. (Get rid of Joseph and make a quick buck — win-win!) After Joseph's rise to power, he masks his identity to his brothers and toys with them a bit before confirming that they are indeed now friends. Those brothers go on to become the twelve tribes of Israel (Genesis).

Many Biblical contagonists start out looking like allies. Jonah was working as a prophet of God quite swimmingly before he got the call to go preach to the residents of Nineveh. Jonah immediately became a force of antagonism to God, heading in the opposite direction. God used a big fish to turn Jonah back to his duties, although begrudgingly.

The ultimate irony of Jonah's turn away from God is the fact that he was motivated by an understanding that God liked to turn enemies into allies. While we often think that the prophet ran away because he was afraid to go to the city of his enemy, Jonah confesses his real motivation after the Ninevites repent:

> Didn't I say before I left home that you would do this, Lord? That is why I ran away to Tarshish! I knew that you are a merciful and compassionate God, slow to get angry and filled with unfailing love. You are eager to turn back from destroying people.[167]

Jonah hated his enemy and did not want to see them restored. He was hoping for God's sternness, and fearful of God's compassion and love. He praised God's work in his own life yet had a hard time rooting for his own contagonists.

> But I will offer sacrifices to you with songs of praise, and I will fulfill my vows. For my salvation comes from the Lord alone.[168]

---

167. Jonah 4:2, NLT
168. Jonah 2:9, NLT

CHAPTER FORTY-ONE

Fully Developed Supporting Characters

S upporting players are there to support the story and the Central Character. Of course — right? The trick for good supporting players is that they keep their function[169] in mind. It is too easy in storytelling to have characters who either are distracting or super-fluous to the story.

Upstaging is a trick used by actors to force attention on themselves. The literal use of upstaging (and the namesake) is quite simple: with multiple actors in a scene, one will surreptitiously move upstage — away from the audience. This forces the other characters to turn to converse with the wayward actor — and in the process turn their backs to the audience. Thus, all the actors on stage are turned away from the adoring public and focused on the upstage actor.

The term grew to apply to any actions that steal focus and is consid-ered a grievous sin in the world of the theater. Yet sometimes an actor doesn't have much choice but to upstage, especially if the writer and director do not keep their supporting players in their proper role.

An example for me personally (and I don't pretend that all will agree with my opinion) is the television show *Will & Grace*. I never became a regular viewer in part because I found the supporting characters of

---

169. For a list of possible functions for supporting characters, see Appendix E: Functions for Supporting Characters

Karen and Jack to be so much more interesting than the show's core — Will and Grace. Nothing against the actors (both lead actors won Emmys for this show); it's just that by comparison the supporting players made them less central to me.

Supporting players should, by function, be less dimensional than the Central Character. At the same time, to serve the story well they should be fully developed with backstories of their own. The closer the character is to center, the more fully developed they should be. (My actress wife will remind me that every character is the Central Character of their own story.)

Each character should have goals of their own as well. When their goals intersect with the Central Character, dramatic conflict arises — even among allies.

- In *Star Wars: A New Hope*, Han Solo wants a pay day. His worldview is a constant source of conflict between Han and Luke, and later with Han and Leia.

- Anita (*West Side Story*) wants to protect Maria. Her tactics alternate between preventing and helping Maria get together with Tony.

- Lady Macbeth wants her husband to seize power. She must convince and cajole him into action, and even step in herself to help clean up after the murder. Once he becomes king, his actions of pushing her aside and outgrowing her adds even more internal conflict.

Another way in which supporting characters distract is the idea of "throw away characters." These are supporting players who do not serve a function in the story.

Whatever in a work of art is not used is doing harm.

—C.S. Lewis, *"On Science Fiction"*

Characters will likely have many functions; the closer the character is to the Central Character, the more Story roles they are likely to fulfill. Giving multiple functions is also a good way to avoid a nearly useless character — one with only a small function.

WRITER'S
TIP

In the process of rewriting, listing characters by function is a quick way to see if one can double up a role.

Note that Story function or role is how the character serves the story — it is not a job they have in their lives inside the story. For example, waitress, bartender, police office, science teacher — these are NOT Story Functions. See Appendix E for a list of character functions.

PART TEN

Subtext and Dialogue

CHAPTER FORTY-TWO

Dialogue Function

Sharp words cut like a sword,
but words of wisdom heal.

—Proverbs 12:18, CEV

I n evaluating dialogue, my friend Beth Amsbary would ask, "Why break the silence of the universe?" The silence has value and power, so why are we dispelling that silence?

God hovered over the darkness, planning his words. He shattered the silence of the universe with, "Let there be light!" His dialogue had power and purpose; it was thought out, and it was good.

Dialogue must be there for a reason, otherwise it is getting in the way. The plot moves forward, conflict is engaged, character is revealed, the audience is entertained. David Trottier says dialogue must be organized and have direction.

Organized in that it should not be random — it is designed for effect, both by the character speaking and by the writer. Direction meaning the dialogue moves the story forward.

People speak to get what they want. If we find a character's motivation, we can find their dialogue — and not just in what they say, but how they say it.

Matthew 22 tells us that the Pharisees got together and plotted out how they could trap Jesus (intent). They sent their disciples to him, and first attempted to lull Jesus off his guard. "Teacher, we know how honest you are. You teach the way of God truthfully."[170]

Then they set him up, putting him in the corner. "You are impartial and don't play favorites." Now for the trap itself, "Now tell us what you think about this: Is it right to pay taxes to Caesar or not?"

Motivation is disclosed, conflict is engaged (all good drama is about conflict), and character is revealed. The text tells us that Jesus saw right through this, calling out their "evil motives." Jesus understood that people speak to get what they want, so he was able to fully understand the layers of their dialogue.

Dialogue is a window into how a character thinks; all dialogue is unique and distinct, as everyone thinks in their own way. Dialogue also reveals character background and interior life.

Good dialogue sounds right. It may not be right, but it sounds right. There is an odd notion that in writing dialogue a writer should write how people really talk — and that is laughable nonsense. The way people talk is often boring, crock-full of misunderstanding and miscommunication. Alfred Hitchcock said, "...drama is life with the dull bits cut out."

Good dialogue doesn't revel in keeping in the dull bits. Rather than being the way people talk, the scriptwriters need to convince the audience that this is the way these characters talk in this situation: it must sound right. No one speaks like Shakespeare's characters; they didn't speak that way even in Shakespeare's time. Yet ten minutes into a good production of *Richard III* and it all sounds correct. The high-falutin' folksy dialogue of *Firefly* is outrageous, and perfectly normal within the world of this space western.

To maintain this illusion of correctness, dialogue must be proper to the character. For example, it should represent the historical time and era — again, not what people actually sounded like, but what the audience assumes they sounded like. So, *Downton Abbey* will sound different from *Big Little Lies*.

---

170. Quotes taken from the NLT

My play *Moreau* is set in the 1890s. In a critical moment, I have one character (Kate) confessing that she doesn't know who she is supposed to be, feeling caught among expectations. Her scene partner (Edward) tells her to be herself — and she takes that advice, ultimately leading to a horrific end to the civilization set up on Moreau's island.

Here's the problem: Edward's line never came off sounding believable. "You be you" is such a hippy-dippy sentiment, the line — no matter how I worded it — always sounded like it came from the 1980s, not the 1890s. Through rehearsals, we reworked the line and never came closer to making it sound right. Yet I knew the sentiment was not a modern one, and we needed that moment for the drama to work.

Our company's manager overheard the director and I venting about this vexing line, and solved our problem with two words, "Quote Shakespeare." Duh. The line was changed to, "To thine own self be true." The audience recognized it as Shakespeare, and knowing Shakespeare came much earlier than HG Wells, never questioned the sentiment again.

We made it sound right, not according to historical accuracy, but to the ear of the audience.

Dialogue must also be proper to place and region (Birmingham, England will sound different from Birmingham, Alabama), class and education (lawyer Atticus Finch will have a more elevated vocabulary than the farmers he often represented).

Age plays into dialogue as well. The obvious examples are the difference between a kid speaking and an adult speaking. It also reflects when the character was a child; we pick up our slang, references, and speech construction from when we were teens. A character in her 80s would still use the lingo from 60 years earlier.

And dialogue needs to be proper to the personality of the character. How they speak reflects their inner life — introvert, extrovert, narcissist, person with low self-esteem. In *Knives Out*, Blanc speaks with a slow, assured pace, choosing his words. He is not reluctant to speak yet is also not afraid of silence. This reflects the confidence and intellect inside the man.

On the other hand, Marta chooses silence in defense — even when she might want to speak. Her dialogue is much more casual, often less thought out — and at the same time more guarded. These are the choices of a woman less sure of herself, feeling constantly under scrutiny, yet wanting to be relaxed.

In a well-written story, each character has their own voice, their own rhythm, their own care or carelessness with words. They have their own ticks, patterns, and style. People are unique, and so are their words.

CHAPTER FORTY-THREE

Dialogue as Action

The adage for good storytelling says, "Show, don't tell." I once heard a film professor say that this maxim applies to film — an image-driven medium — and not to theater; since theatre is mostly dialogue, it cannot help but be driven by "telling."

This is a major misunderstanding and leads to a lot of bad dialogue. Spoken words can also "show." Good dialogue is action and subtext; it shows by avoiding being literal, by "telling it slant."[171]

Rather than say, "I am mad at you for staying out late last night," the character could show their anger by saying, "How come you never cook my eggs right?"

Or imagine a character saying, "I'm sad. I've wasted my life." That is dialogue telling. Instead, imagine this exchange between two men:

"Hey, Fred, how's it going?"

"Same old, same old."

"Hey, that's funny."

"What is?"

"Same old, same old. You say that every time I say hi."

"Really? I hadn't noticed."

"Funny phrase, don't you think?"

---

171. "Tell all the truth but tell it slant," poem by Emily Dickinson

"Maybe. My uncle used to say it. I guess I got it from him."

"He still saying it?"

"Doubt it. He died years ago. In a home."

"Sorry."

"No, it was probably good for him. Alone, you know."

"Well, he's got something different now."

"I must have been saying that since I was ten. Forty years."

"Funny, the things we say without thinking about it."

"Yeah, funny. Unless it's true."

That is all dialogue — and all show.

The "show" factor of dialogue is what gives it power and true meaning. "Showing" requires interpretation — the audience has to take it in and give it meaning, thus such dialogue digs in deeper.

Take the exchange Jesus has with the people at the end of John 8. He has just told them that Abraham rejoiced looking forward to Jesus' coming. The people are naturally confused and demand an explanation. Jesus could easily say, "I am the Messiah, the Christ, the Son of God. I am one with the Father."

Instead, he uses dialogue that forces interpretation by his listeners and says, "Most assuredly, I say to you, before Abraham was, I AM."[172]

That line holds so much more power. We know it was effective because his audience immediately picked up stones to kill him.

The dialogue of *Knives Out* shows the distinction of character without the need of description. When interviewing Linda, Elliot asks if she and her husband work for a real estate company. The immediate succinct response:

It's my company.

---

172. John 8:58, NKJV

Setting the record straight of who is in charge. A little later in the scene, Elliot asks Walt if he runs Harlan's publishing company. The response,

> Yeah. It's my — it's our, it's the family's publishing company, Dad trusts me to run it.

He wants to claim the power, yet doesn't feel like he quite can without hedging, so fumbles through his response.

Screenwriter Rian Johnson also uses dialogue to show how each character humblebrags — and at the same time reveals what each character considers to be brag-worthy. When the identity of Blanc is revealed, Joni pops in with:

> Wait a minute — I read a tweet about a New Yorker article about you.

Joni is proudly in the know, on top of social media. Linda has also heard of the detective:

> Mr. Blanc, I know who you are. I read your New Yorker profile.

Linda is also well informed, but not as shallow as her sister-in-law. She doesn't read tweets about *The New Yorker*. She reads *The New Yorker*.

A few moments later, Richard gets his chance to brag. After quoting *Hamilton*, Trooper Wagner shows he knows the reference by repeating, "Oh, *Hamilton*!" Richard points out, "I saw it at the Public."

In other words, he saw it before the musical was famous. He is that cool.

Dialogue in theater is even more strictly held to the "show" standard, as clunky dialogue can't be masked by action or beautiful camera work.

In *A Streetcar Named Desire*, Tennessee Williams wants to tell us Blanche is vain, seeks after praise more than a lady should, and always wants to be compared favorably to others; all while wishing others thought of her as humble and gracious.

Instead of being literal, we get an exchange between Blanche and her sister:

Blanche: You haven't said a word about my appearance.

Stella: You look just fine.

Blanche: God love you for a liar! Daylight never exposed so total a ruin! But you — you've put on some weight, yes, you're just as plump as a little partridge! And it's so becoming to you!

In the back and forth, we are shown a complete picture of Blanche.

Fencing

Good dialogue, then, is image and action. In a scene with two characters each with a goal (and in good scenes, the characters have goals), the dialogue becomes a fencing match — action in words.

Let's return to the religious leaders trying to trap Jesus in Matthew 22. They have a plan for attack — start by flattery, get Jesus to let his guard down; then box him in — Jesus is not one to pick sides, is he?; and then the blow: Do you think we should pay money to Caesar or not?

A well-crafted thrust. If Jesus says they should not pay to Caesar, then Rome will brand him a rebel and take him out. If he says they should be paying money to their oppressors, the people will turn against him and his ministry withers to nothing.

Jesus fights back with his words. First, he destroys their first feint, their claim to be friendly. "You hypocrites!" he throws at them; no, we are not friends as you pretend. Then using jujitsu techniques, he puts the onus on them, demanding they show him their money.

Note that he doesn't tell them whose image is on the coin but asks them — putting them in the box. "Caesar's image is on the coin," they say; so, they themselves have admitted that this is Caesar's money.

He gives the final blow by both acknowledging what they already said — "give to Caesar what is Caesar's" — and by giving them an order, "give to God what is God's." Their response? They leave without an additional word. What could they say? "You are wrong, we shouldn't pay taxes!" Or "You are right, we should pay taxes."

Jesus put them in the same box they tried to put him in.

Moreover, Jesus recognized that this was a battle of words, and there would be a winner and loser to the battle. The religious men came as the authorities, attempting to defeat Jesus; they left with Jesus standing as the clear authority, ordering them to do their religious jobs.

CLOSE UP: Fencing
The Social Network

The opening scene of *The Social Network* by Aaron Sorkin is a masterpiece of verbal fisticuffs, often described as an intense action scene despite being just two people sitting at a table the whole time.

There is much to talk about with this dialogue-driven scene, including the weaving in and out of topics, the clear character reveals, the delicious rhythm, and the thematic power (the plot and goal are laid out in this opening repartee). For purposes of this section, I will focus on the duel — as each character tries to get the winning position. Let's track the thrusts and parries throughout this scene.

At the start, over darkness, Mark and his date Erica are in neutral positions as they discuss China and genius IQs. Mark establishes the first position of power, controlling the conversation with his question:

Mark: How do you distinguish yourself in a population of people who all got 1600 on their SATs?

Mark stays in control with the humblebrag of a perfect SAT score. Erica regains an upper hand by pointing out that to a woman, brains may not be everything. She mentions that singing a capella could be attractive, and:

Erica: On the other hand, I do like guys who row crew.

At this point, the couple is still bantering — this is a humorous response to his earlier joke. Mark still takes it as a dig, and reasserts himself by bringing her back to his point:

Mark: Yes, it means I got nothing wrong on the test.

A few lines later, Erica attempts to get the conversation back by pointing out that he can be difficult to speak with.

Erica: Maybe, but sometimes you say two things at once and I'm not sure which one I'm supposed to be aiming at.

Mark ignores her, continuing the conversation about how he doesn't row crew, until he gets a concession from her that her comment was not relevant.

Erica: I guess I just meant I liked the idea of it. The way a girl likes cowboys.

Mark "forgives" her with a simple "Okay." Erica attempts to change the topic — Mark ignores her attempt and brings the conversation back to his goal, discussing getting into a final club. He starts to win her over as she contributes a positive from her perspective:

Erica: Is it true that they send a bus around to pick up girls who want to party with the next Fed Chairman?

The conversation sours as Erica asks which club is easiest to get in — despite being her way to try and contribute, Mark takes this as an insult, and the tone becomes combative again.

Mark: I think you asked me that because you think the final club that's easiest to get into is the one where I'll have the best chance.

They argue over what she did or did not mean, until Erica attempts a blow.

Erica: You're obsessed with finals clubs. You have finals clubs OCD and you need to see someone about it who'll prescribe you some sort of medication.

Mark parries this attack with a simple correction — showing his superiority.

Mark: Final clubs. Not finals clubs and there's a difference between being obsessed and being motivated.

And Erica deflates his attempt by agreeing with him.

Erica: Yes, there is.

That simple line says, "You are right. And so am I. You are obsessed." Mark accuses her of being cryptic — which really is his attack on her saying how hard it is to talk with him — and moves back to his topic — final clubs.

He gets the upper hand again, pointing out that Teddy Roosevelt did get elected President by being in the right final club.

Erica attempts a little sarcasm:

Erica: Well, why don't you just concentrate on being the best you can be?

Which Mark immediately shoots down as trite (in comparison to him trying to do something important). He comes in with the killing blow — being Mark's girlfriend has such great benefits, she should be grateful.

Mark: If I get in, I'll be taking you...to the events, the gatherings...and you'll be meeting a lot of people you wouldn't normally get to meet.

Erica responds by setting him up, making him think he has won the conversation.

Erica: You would do that for me?

He replies with "of course," saying, "We're dating." And then she takes the power with:

Erica: Okay, well I want to try and be straightforward with you and let you know that we're not anymore.

From here on out, Mark's topic (final club) is off the table, and Erica's topic (their relationship) has the centerpiece. Mark confirms that she is breaking up with him, and she confirms he is being condescending:

Erica: You're going to introduce me to people I wouldn't normally have the chance to meet? What the fff— What is that supposed to mean?

Note that the lack of f-bomb here is not my edit, but in the script. Erica is at a boil but trying to hold it together; she is trying to be civil. Mark is not, going for a low blow:

Mark: Erica, the reason we're able to sit here and drink right now is cause you used to sleep with the door guy.

Erica slaps back by explaining that, unlike Mark, she is a decent human being who sees others as fellow human beings — and then twists the knife by pointing out how Mark himself is not a better class of people.

Erica: The door guy, his name is Bobby. I did not sleep with the door guy, the door guy is a friend of mine. He's a perfectly good class of people and what part of Long Island are you from — Wimbledon?

It could have ended here, but Mark insists on trying to get Erica to stay, despite her saying she has to study. He wants to talk; she says she can't.

Erica: Because it's exhausting. Dating you is like dating a stairmaster.

The conversation continues with Mark attempting to apologize and explain his comments. It crescendos to:

Erica: I have to go study.

Mark: You don't have to study.

Erica: Why do you keep saying I don't have to study?

Mark: Because you go to B.U.!

And there it is — Mark thinks that Erica is an inferior intellect at an inferior school. Of course, she should be honored to be with him, she is dating so far above her level. Completely unaware, Mark thinks his point has won the day, and suggests they order food.

Erica does not think Mark has won. She suggests that they should just be friends. Mark (summing up the one thing it turns out he wishes he could have) says:

Mark: I don't want friends.

Neither does Erica, she was just being polite. As he makes one more attempt to excuse his behavior, she closes the battle with the devastating final shot.

> *Erica: You are probably going to be a very successful computer person. But you're going to go through life thinking that girls don't like you because you are a nerd. And I want you to know, from the bottom of my heart, that that won't be true. It'll be because you're an a**h**l*.*

This time the edit of the swear word is mine. Sorkin uses the foul language to show that Erica is done; earlier she holds herself back from swearing, trying to maintain a civility that Mark doesn't seem to possess. Now she is over it, and not censoring herself at all.

The scene is indeed a contest, with two players actively trying to get what they want. Ultimately there is one victor; and the other player will spend the rest of the movie trying to re-win this losing conversation.

CHAPTER FORTY-FOUR

Character Subtext

Anyone with ears to hear should listen and understand!

—Matthew 11:15, NLT

Subtext is all about having ears to hear — in understanding what is being said without having to spell it out. Subtext is the meaning under the text, between the lines, the unspoken emotional content of the words.

Dialogue gives us words with literal meaning — yet as we've seen with the section on Character and Dialogue as well as our dialogue breakdowns, the real meaning of the words is rarely what is literally said. Good use of subtext in writing makes the drama feel more real, pulls the audience into the story more (as they must interpret the signs), and makes the whole experience all that much more delicious.

John Yorke tells us, "Explanation kills drama, as does the impulse to make everything everyone says immediately clear."

Producers and executives are notorious for fearing that audiences will not understand a story, and thus push for literalism in scripts. Subtext requires interpretation, and the producers are left to wonder, "What if we can't control the audience's interpretation?"

What they don't understand is that interpretation is the very value of the subtext. The audience becomes an active participant in the drama by having to evaluate what they hear and see and provide meaning. It draws them in.

I think of Ralphie in *A Christmas Story* leaning in as the radio announcer gives the clues he must then decode with his ring. Ralphie is deeply invested in the words from the announcer, crafting his (yes, his!) solution to the riddle through the work he puts in twisting the ring. Hopefully the stories we tell will be more satisfying than "Drink more Ovaltine," but the point here is how vested the listener was in the journey.

Jesus was very aware of this; his parables and teachings often drew the audience in as they worked out the subtext. "A sower went out to sow..." (Matthew 13) is a story with a very literal meaning about seeds and weeds and birds and such. The story also had a sub-meaning, a secondary and greater truth to tell. He closed out the story with his, "Anyone with ears to hear..." line quoted above.

His disciples ask why he uses parable and metaphor instead of just preaching it plain. Jesus' response:

> *To those who listen to my teaching, more understanding will be given, and they will have an abundance of knowledge. But for those who are not listening, even what little understanding they have will be taken away from them. That is why I use these parables, for they look, but they don't really see. They hear, but they don't really listen or understand.*

—Matthew 13:12-13, NLT

Jesus' parables were meant to be contemplated. Rushing just to a nutshell explanation would weaken the contemplation — making the meaning only that of an explaining Rabbi or pastor or priest — not the meaning of the listener.

Jesus also confounded his enemies when they attempted to trap him in literalism, and he instead gave subtext. The "Give unto Caesar..." story is an example. When Jesus completes the phrase with "...and give unto God what is God's," it has the additional message of, "give yourselves over to God instead of to your masters who send you to trick the Son of God."

Matthew 15 records a time when the Pharisees and teachers of the law confront Jesus about why his disciples break their tradition of ceremonial hand washing. Jesus does not offer a defense but turns the argument on them: "And why do you, by your traditions, violate the direct commandments of God?"[173]

He then proceeds to give a specific example of how their traditions do just that. He ends by quoting Isaiah:

> *"These people honor me with their lips, but their hearts are far from me. Their worship is a farce, for they teach man-made ideas as commands from God."*[174]

Jesus doesn't answer the original charge directly. Subtextual, he makes it clear — my disciples honor God with their hearts, and are not beholden to those who use God for their own power and position.

Throughout his teaching, Jesus is giving a warning to the literalists — if you are unable to see the meaning under the meaning, you will not be able to understand the full Gospel. Stopping at surface understanding is choosing to not have ears to hear.

When Jesus told the teachers of the law that the temple would be torn down and raised again in three days, they missed his message by taking him literally.[175] At another time, he chastised the people for being unable to read the signs of the times. They were able to look at the weather and interpret what those conditions said about the future; but when it came to their religion, they were stuck in surface meanings.[176]

And thus risked missing the way, the truth, and the life.

~

Understanding a line of dialogue falls into three categories: the surface intention of the line; the conscious secondary meaning by the character; and the unintentional (unconscious) reveal of the dialogue.

---

173. Matthew 15:3, NLT
174. Matthew 15:8-9, NLT
175. John 2
176. Matthew 16

Surface Meaning

The first, and most obvious, is surface intention. When you were a teen and came down for breakfast, and your dad greeted you with:

Good morning!

The surface meaning may have been: "I hope you have a good morning" or simply, "Hello to you!"

Conscious secondary meaning comes in when the character knows that the literal meaning is one thing, but they intend another.

It is three a.m., and you sneak into the house after missing curfew by four hours. You are halfway across the room when the lights snap on. Your dad sits in his armchair. He says:

Good morning.

The surface meaning hasn't changed, but your dad is communicating something very different from "I hope you are having a good morning." More like, "You're caught, and not only that but boy am I going to make you suffer."

Characters use subtext by design either to increase communication or to mask communication. The dad's "Good morning" is increasing communication: he is adding to the meaning being received by his hearer.

Sarcasm is another form of subtext where there is no intent at all to mask the secondary meaning. In the pilot of *Lost*, after the survivors on the beach hear a horrifying screech coming from the jungle, and watch the trees moving by the size of whatever made that noise, Charlie sums up the response of the terrified characters with: "Terrific."

He does not expect that anyone thinks he is pleased by this development; he just thought that going opposite was the best way to communicate his feelings.

Double entendre is another way of handling subtext — where both the literal meaning and the secondary meaning are in play. In *Casa-*

blanca, Renault greets the arrival of the Nazi Major Strasser with this warning: "You may find the climate of Casablanca a trifle warm, Major."

The major responds with assuring Renault that the Germans are good in all kinds of weather — but then he gets the secondary meaning. "But perhaps you were not referring to the weather."

Renault sidesteps this; he meant the weather and he meant much more than the weather, but he isn't going to clarify his point.

Characters intentionally using subtext have the added power of creating a story in the minds of the hearer (showing — yes?). The *Veronica Mars* pilot uses this technique in a devastating way. We've been getting to know Veronica, who is also our narrator, as she goes through her day. She is a girl with a very clear reputation for being loose. After one encounter, narrator Veronica addresses the audience:

> *Quite a reputation I've got, huh?*
>
> *(beat)*
>
> *You want to know how I lost my virginity?*
>
> *(another beat)*
>
> *So do I.*

Veronica doesn't answer her question, and she does answer the question. The subtext causes the listener to create a story, and that story is seismic in how it changes this world. Witty, devil-may-care, rebel Veronica is masking a deep pain; her casual jokes about sex belie a night in her past that likely involved the date-rape drug. She is not loose; she is violated.

The subtext gives that line shattering power.

Masked Conscious

The other use of conscious dialogue subtext is when the character is trying to mask their meaning. In *Hidden Figures*, Katherine, Dorothy, and Mary are speaking with a police officer, who just found out they work at NASA.

White Cop: NASA. That's somethin'. Had no idea they hired—

He stops himself from saying "coloreds." Or worse.

Dorothy: There are quite a few women working in the Space Program, sir.

She saves him the embarrassment.

Dorothy's line is ripe with subtext and designed to mask its own meaning. She is communicating, "Hey, we both know you aren't racist, so of course you were surprised by our gender and not our color." And yet the subtext says, "Hey, we both know you are racist, but it's better for all of us if we pretend it isn't so."

The literal text calms the situation; the subtext is really understood only by the women.

In this exchange from *A Streetcar Named Desire*, Stanley and Blanche both want to reprimand the other — Blanche upset that Stanley went through her belongings without her permission; Stanley ready to accuse Blanche of spending the family money on herself. The dictates of society and their situation prevents either one from saying what they really mean, so instead they mask their intent while trying to get the other party to confess.

Blanche: It looks like my trunk exploded.

Stanley: Me an' Stella were helping you unpack.

Blanche: Well, you certainly did a fast and thorough job of it!

Stanley: It looks like you raided some stylish shops in Paris.

Blanche: Ha ha! Yes — clothes are my passion.

Stanley: What does it cost for a string of fur-pieces like that?

Blanche: Why, those were a tribute from an admirer of mine!

Stanley: He must have had a lot of — admiration!

A mask of civility covering (barely in this case) true intentions. Writer Ted Talley reminds us that in writing dialogue, what's important isn't the emotion they're playing, but the emotion they're trying to conceal.[177]

This sometimes comes in projection — when a character talks about another character/situation and they really are talking about themselves. This is the very common, "I'm asking for a friend..." line when the person is asking for herself. In *Pushing Daisies*, waitress Olive chastises Ned for not petting his dog, claiming:

> *The dog needs to be touched. We all need to be touched.*

Olive is encouraging Ned to get physical with his dog, when really her hope is that someday he will get physical with her.

Storytellers can have fun with masked versus open subtext — as can the characters themselves. In *Hamlet*, Claudius asks his nephew/son why he is still so gloomy, even after the joyous occasion of Claudius marrying Hamlet's mother. "How is it that the clouds still hang on you?"

Hamlet pretends to take Claudius literally, and rejoins: "Not so, my lord; I am too much in the sun."

Hamlet is deflecting his uncle's question, pitting clouds against the sun. He is including a masked meaning, playing off the homonyms of "sun" and "son" — in essence saying he is gloomy because, "I am too much Claudius' son now."

The added fun of this exchange is how many ways it could be played — the actor in the role of Hamlet could be full on pretending he didn't understand the question; or could play it somewhat snide. He could choose to completely mask the "son" subtext or make it just clear enough that Claudius might get it — and dare his stepdad to name it.

Unintended Meaning

The third form of dialogue subtext is unconscious, when a character gives subtextual meaning without realizing what they are doing. Freudian slips are a form of unconscious subtext. In the "Noel" episode of *The West Wing*, Josh accidentally says the word "sirens" when he means to

---

177. Per John Yorke, *Into the Woods*

say "music." It is discovered that this slip was because Josh was subconsciously reliving the day he was shot.

Sometimes projection is also done subconsciously and will come out in the subtext. In the pilot for *Pushing Daisies*, Olive (the waitress with an unrequited love for pie shop owner Ned) explains to a customer her sales technique.

> *Every day I come in, I pick a pie and concentrate all my love on that pie. If I love it, then someone else will love it.*

She is masking her true, unspoken feelings by projecting on the pie the love she has for Ned, and the hope that if she concentrates all her love on him, he will love her back. Unlike her quote above about touching the dog, Olive doesn't realize that she is making this projection with her love of pie.

This is the character-revealing subtext we discussed in Character and Dialogue. The Pharisee praying in the temple means to show himself as righteous and superior; the unconscious subtext reveals he is proud, petty, and inferior.

Characters try to control their dialogue; and yet their subconscious constantly peeks through.

CHAPTER FORTY-FIVE

Story Subtext

There is another kind of subtext that isn't between two characters, but rather between the storyteller and the audience; lines, actions, or images that have a primary meaning for the story, and a secondary meaning intended just for the viewer. This is Story Subtext or Thematic Subtext.

The characters would never be aware of Story Subtext (unless they are fully aware they are in a work of fiction, like Deadpool). A sly example is found in *Knives Out*, in the first scene with Marta and her family. Her sister is listening to a detective show, which her mom makes her turn off. When Alice, the sister, sees how upset Marta is, she says, "No, I guessed who did it anyway. I'm sorry Marta."

To the characters, the line makes perfect sense. Alice dismissed the importance of watching the end of her murder mystery and is sorry that she was callous in watching a show about dead people when Marta has just experienced a loss.

For those watching the movie, however, there is a secondary meaning. "I guessed who did it, I'm sorry, Marta" can be read as "I guessed who killed Thrombey, and I'm sorry to say it is you, Marta." This is writer Rian Johnson being sneaky and giving away the plot. There is no way for the characters to know this secondary meaning.

Edgar Wright is notorious for playing sly with the audience in this manner. Before the zombie attacks in *Shaun of the Dead*, Ed suggests a list of bars to attend the next day, including phrases like, "Bloody Mary," "get a bite at," "stagger back," and "shots." Turns out that each phrase matches a location where they would fight for their lives. Clearly meant for audiences — and only on their second viewing.

Wright also uses subtext to speak to the audience above the heads of (or behind the backs of) the characters in a manner that the audience is meant to understand. Shaun hears about the zombie attacks — or rather doesn't hear about them as he flips through TV channels. The various stations put together an explanation of what is happening in a way hidden from Shaun and obvious to the audience. Imagine the channel change on each line:

> *Reporter: Religious groups are calling it Judgment Day. There's —*
>
> *MTV: The Smiths sing: Panic on the streets of London —*
>
> *Another reporter: — as an increasing number of —*
>
> *Soccer commentator (as one player tackles another): — serious attacks on —*
>
> *Yet another reporter: — people who are literally being —*
>
> *Wildlife show as lions attack a gazelle: — eaten alive —*

And on. A clever way to get the information to the audience at the expense of the clueless character.

In Action

Story Subtext is in no way limited to dialogue; action can also carry a secondary message to the audience. Early in the pilot for *Pushing Daisies*, as Young Ned watches Young Chuck leave, he has an interaction with his dog. At this point we know that if Chuck touches the dog, the dog will die. (It's a long story, and a lot sweeter than macabre.) The action line says:

> *After a moment, Young Ned's dog Digby returns and bounds right up to Ned. He reaches out to pet Digby and the dog pulls away. Despite this, Digby wags his tail and smiles, keeping a safe distance.*

The message to the audience: Digby understands the rules of this world — and learned them faster than Ned did. Also, there is hope for happiness for Ned; Digby doesn't judge the boy (in the moment of the boy's greatest guilt); nor does he leave Ned, despite the danger Ned poses to him. Digby continues to love and support his owner; so, there is hope that someday someone else will too.

In Images

Story Subtext often comes in visual metaphors. In the story of the Lost Son, the younger son at his lowest gets a job working among pigs. Inside the story, this shows how far he has sunk, to the point of being envious of the pigs' slop. For the Jewish audience Jesus was addressing, this image represents being unclean — another way of showing that the younger son was not only out of his father's graces, but he was also out of God's graces.

Casablanca gives the audience several messages through visual subtext. Near the opening, the Brandel's watch a plane landing. They see the plane as a sign of hope, wondering if they will be on it the next day. Yet the audience clearly sees the swastika prominently displayed on the craft; we know the plane actually represents hopelessness.

We will see many more examples of Story Subtext in the section on Visual Imagery.

CROSS FADE: Subtext of the Stoning of the Adulterous Woman

John 8 chronicles the meeting between Jesus and the adulterous woman. While he was teaching in the temple, the Pharisees, religious leaders, and a crowd dragged in a woman they caught in adultery. Hoping to trap Jesus, they pointed out that the law of Moses called for stoning as the punishment, and demanded Jesus weigh in on her judgment.

At first, Jesus seemed to ignore them, writing instead with his finger in the dirt. He then said okay — but let the person without sin throw the first stone. He resumed his drawing in the dust.

The accusers left one by one, starting with the oldest. When they were gone, Jesus asked the woman where her accusers were — did any of them condemn her? She said they didn't, and he followed up by saying he didn't condemn her either. And finished with, "Go and sin no more."

This little incident is chock-full of subtext — more said underneath than in the actual text, in fact.

Right away we see Character Subtext: while claiming to give Jesus authority in the law, the religious leaders were really trying to trap him.

There is also a bit of Story Subtext up front, in the form of a question that no one asks, and is never addressed: if the woman was caught in the act, then a man was also caught. Why wasn't the man brought to them for stoning? That is a question that becomes more significant to audiences over the centuries.

After asking Jesus for his opinion (calling him "teacher"), Jesus responds by saying nothing. There is a lot of silence in this story — and the good writer knows that silence *is* dialogue. There are several theories about what Jesus was drawing in the sand; my favorite theory comes from Earl Palmer who suggests that Jesus wasn't drawing anything. He was just doodling.

As if to say — "I don't exist for your time. I exist for mine." The doodling also gives a moment for the crowd to pause, maybe let some of the bloodlust die down.

Then Jesus speaks:

All right, but let the one who has never sinned throw the first stone.[178]

Straightforward for surface interpretation — the sinless guy gets to start the stoning. Underneath, a whole lot of subtext.

---

178. For direct quotes in this section, I'm using the NLT.

First off, Jesus is taking an authority beyond that given by the leaders. They asked him to weigh in on guilt and sentencing, in essence asking him to act as jury and judge. He goes one step further and also takes on executioner — in charge of how the punishment will be given.

Throughout the gospels, Jesus responds to the religious leaders in a way that makes this clear: they do not give him authority. His *is* the authority. In this case, he and he alone gets to decide the fate of this woman.

Another meaning of the line, which is borne out in action, is that there isn't anyone there without sin. Jesus doesn't say, "You all are as screwed up as she is. What gives you the right to judge?" Instead, he uses subtext for each person in the crowd to create their own story: deciding for themselves that they are screwed up and don't have a right to judge. They speak in action, by slipping away without a word — yet with a clear subtextual message.

Another meaning comes in the "all right." Jesus doesn't say, "Hey, you're wrong. She doesn't deserve to die." Instead, he says, "I am not here to counteract the law of Moses. I'm here to fulfill it — yet in a way you may find surprising." She is guilty, she deserves death, she won't die today.

But wait, there's more. This line also has an even deeper subtext, one that many miss. I know I missed it for years.

Jesus says the one without sin gets to throw the first stone. Two key points here. First, the punishment will happen, and the crowd gets to participate. They just can't start in until the first stone is thrown.

And second, as each accusers disappears, we assume the earlier subtext: there is no one there without sin, therefore no one to throw the first stone.

But there is someone there without sin, and Jesus knows it. When he says, "Let the one who has never sinned throw the first stone," he is saying, "I get to throw the first stone for this woman's punishment." Jesus was pointing to himself in calling out the crowd.

The crowd will later get to be active participants in delivering the punishment for this woman — as they yell out to Pilate, "Crucify him!

Crucify him!" They will see her punishment carried out as they watch Jesus carry his cross. They will get their stones cast in the form of nails in his hands and feet. They will get their death as punishment for sin, as Jesus dies on the tree.

Jesus takes on the authority to deliver punishment, and he puts that punishment on himself.

The text of this passage is about the saving of one woman.

The Story Subtext is the salvation of all people.

PART ELEVEN

Setups, Images, and Ideas

CHAPTER FORTY-SIX

Setups and Payoffs

Setup: Planting of information in a script

Payoff: When the information is shown for its full meaning or utilized

Setups & Payoffs is a very simple concept, and yet a very lush tool for writers. There is such a satisfaction to a good setup and payoff. An obvious use is Q in the James Bond movies. Near the beginning, Q explains a gadget to Bond (setup); later Bond will use that item (payoff). Q pleading with Bond to be careful and not damage his gadgets tends to be a setup for Bond completely destroying that gadget.

Setups & Payoffs fulfill several functions for the creators. Here are a few:

Foreshadowing

In foreshadowing, setups are used to prepare an audience (often unconsciously) for an event that will happen later. Dallas Jenkins uses this frequently in his series *The Chosen*. The Hook/Teaser will often be a scene that at first seems disjointed, separate from the show, then later ties in thematically with the rest of the episode.

For example, "I Am He" starts almost two thousand years before the events of Jesus and his followers with a scene of patriarch Jacob digging a well in Shechem; followed by a contemporary scene at that well of a

Samaritan woman drawing water. The main action of the story is taking place in Capernaum, completely unrelated to the well. Until the final scene, when Jesus meets the Samaritan woman and uses Jacob's well to explain that he is the Messiah.

In the opening scene of *Soul*, Joe describes to his band students his first experience with jazz, where the pianist gets lost in the music — floating off the stage. Later we use this as a measure for Joe's success (or lack thereof) in playing; when he goes into the zone during his audition, we know he's got it. Visually he leaves this world, lost in the world of the music.

And then towards the end, Joe plays his way into the zone as a method to get back to the astral plane in the afterlife. The surreal experience of music in act one gets us ready for the very real use of the surreal experience in act three.

New Response

Here we use the setup to show a response to a given action, giving insight into the state of mind of the character. Later, the payoff shows the action again with a different response, presenting the change in the story or character.

In the early part of *Knives Out*, Marta is with a dying person and chooses to not call 911 in order to save herself from looking guilty. Toward the end, she is with a dying person and chooses to call 911 despite knowing it will put her in prison. She has changed.

When we first meet Rick in *Casablanca*, he is callously sending Yvonne away, showing his lack of concern for others. At the end of the movie, Rick acts callous in sending Ilsa away; this time we know he is masking the new self, the Rick who cares more about others than himself.

"I'm not throwing away my shot" is Hamilton's life philosophy. He makes sure that he never misses an opportunity to win, to get ahead. We hear that line throughout the story, setting up the ending when he literally throws away his shot. The comparison of beginning to end is confirmation that he has changed, his arc is complete.

Justify Story Devices

Sometimes the gadgets in James Bond are impossibly over the top, like Batman happening to have Bat Shark Repellent in his tool belt. The Q setup scenes are designed to alleviate this feeling in the audience. If Q explains how a laser watch works in the early part of the film, we don't stop to go "nuh uh!" when Bond uses his watch to cut through some bars. The setup answers the credulity question before the audience can ask it.[179]

This can work for most any story device that might seem questionable. Marley's knocker turning into a ghost head sets us up for the arrival of the supernatural in *A Christmas Carol*. Seeing Sherlock be impossibly brilliant in the teaser lets us buy his smarts throughout the rest of the episode.[180] Watching Zoey (*Zoey's Extraordinary Playlist*) experience the singing of strangers on the street lets us accept her just happening to hear the inner thoughts of a key romantic interest later in the episode.

Knives Out has great setups and payoffs in just about every scene and plays out just about every function for the device. The most outrageous idea in the movie, which is critical to the plot, is Marta's inability to lie. If we don't believe that she can't lie, several key points of the movie simply do not work. When we first learn she can't lie, and she throws up while trying to fib, the setup is complete. We are now ready for later when Ransom forces her to tell the truth about what happened to Harlan; and we understand why she does it. Writer Rian Johnson doesn't stop there...

We have a second setup when Marta doesn't tell the whole truth in her official explanation of the events of Harlan's death to Blanc. When she finishes, she races to the bathroom to upchuck. This lets us know that she can hold the vomit in, at least for a little while. Then in the final confrontation, when she gets the confession from Ransom — well, I shan't describe it. Her actions are fully in line with the setup — she can

---

179. It doesn't always work. I never bought the invisible car.
180. *Sherlock, Elementary*

lie and not vomit immediately, so we shouldn't be surprised when she lies to Ransom. And yet we are.

Unity of Story

Inventive setups and payoffs create a sense of unity in the story, a feeling of completion — even if the audience isn't consciously aware of the setups and payoffs. The "this therefore that" gives the story an inevitability, an understanding that the storytellers have carefully constructed the tale they are telling.

There is an idiom in theater called "Chekhov's Gun." It comes from a quote by playwright Anton Chekhov. There are several versions, this one is from a letter to another writer:

> *One must never place a loaded rifle on the stage if it isn't going to go off. It's wrong to make promises you don't mean to keep.*[181]

The idea is that you do not want to have something that feels like a setup without a payoff. If the audience is wondering (perhaps just in the back of their minds) when the gun is going to come into play, and it does not, the conclusion is that the writer broke their promise.

A negative example can be found in the 2008 movie *Journey to the Center of the Earth*. Early in the film, Trevor is trying to find a way to bond with his nephew. He finds a yo-yo, which initially is a pretty lame thing for a 21st Century boy — until Trevor explains that the toy was originally conceived as a weapon; hunters would take down prey with the contraption.

Later in the movie, our heroes are attempting to cross a lake when they are attacked by flying piranha. They have no weapons to fight off these creatures — so what do they do? You guessed it — and you guessed poorly. They do not pull out the yo-yo and use it as a weapon, instead they make a run for it. Most viewers didn't consciously remember the setup; yet I guarantee they felt like something was missing.

---

181. Per Wikipedia, from an 1889 letter to Aleksandr Semenovich Lazarev. Apparently, Chekhov was referencing a monologue with no payoff later in the play.

Setups and payoffs help signal to the audience that the storyteller has the story under control.

Quality Setups

A good setup has multiple meanings. When the setup is first planted it has one meaning; then when the payoff hits, it takes on a second, more important meaning. There is a rush of insight that comes with good payoffs.

When Macbeth is told by the witches that he cannot be killed by one of woman born, Mackie takes that to mean he is immortal. It calms him enough to keep going. When MacDuff reveals that he was not born (rather, from his mother's womb untimely ripped) the first meaning changes. The witches were not conferring immortality on the man, rather they were dooming him, knowing he would open himself up to his own downfall.

Another quality of a good setup along these lines is that the setup works completely in the setup scene. A good setup disappears to the audience, because it works by itself without needing to foreshadow or justify a future moment. Otherwise, you have a setup that is too heavy-handed. The payoff works best when the audience isn't waiting for it; if the setup doesn't have a function in the scene where it is setup, the payoff is undercut.

Marta not being able to lie is used in the scene where we first encounter the information. Joe getting transported by music shows us his passion — to his students and in his audition. Hamilton refusing to throw away his shots in life is a great way to explain his drive to an audience. When a setup is used in its own scene, it makes the writing feel less obvious and formulaic.

More than that, it boosts the power of the payoff. As humans we naturally get a sense of satisfaction when a pattern is completed. When the payoff comes and we aren't expecting it (such as Marta's final showdown with Ransom), the satisfaction is intoxicating.

My favorite example of setup and payoff is Thor's hammer in *Avengers: Age of Ultron*. The concept that only "he who is worthy" can lift the hammer is set up in the first *Thor* movie. In *Ultron*, an early scene shows the team hanging out after a party, and the hammer is used as a character study. Each person reveals something about themselves as they try and prove themselves worthy.

Hawkeye (a non-super powered character) mocks the very idea of the hammer. Tony and Rhodey are both convinced that their mastery of science far outstrips the backwards nature of magic (faith). Banner plays it off as a joke, pretending to get mad enough to transform into the Hulk. Natasha makes clear her stance when she points out that she doesn't have to prove anything to this room full of men. Even Thor gets a character moment as he winces when it looks like Captain America might be able to lift the thing.

A marvelous use of the hammer and the concept of worthiness to establish character distinctions.

Then we meet the Vision, a creature created by Ultron, their enemy. He offers to fight alongside the Avengers — and they don't know whether they should kill him or trust him. He explains that while there is no way he can prove himself trustworthy, they don't have time for debate. As he says this, he lifts Thor's hammer and hands it to the Asgardian.

Proving that he can be trusted, that he is more worthy than the rest.

The first meaning of the hammer is a character study, showing the camaraderie of the group. The second meaning: The Vision is worthy — you can trust him.

The writers were not done with this setup — giving an even bigger payoff many, many movies later. In the final battle of *Avengers: Endgame*, Thor is about to be killed by Thanos when his hammer careens off the villain, knocking him back. The hammer then zooms back to its sender — Captain America. Thor says what we all hoped for, "I knew it!"

When I watched *Age of Ultron*, the audience cheered when Vision picked up the hammer. In *Endgame*, when Captain picked up the hammer the audience went absolutely nuts. We were in no way expecting this callback; yet it was perfectly set up.

An intoxicating satisfaction.

✝✝ CROSS FADE: Biblical Setups and Payoffs ✝✝

By this point it shouldn't surprise you to hear me say that God is *the* master of setups & payoffs. Setups prepare the hearer for a later payoff. The more complex setups have a full meaning at the time of the setup; the most satisfying payoffs come with a rush of insight, a way that is even more fulfilling than the original use of the setup.

Personal confession here: I used to be bothered by a lot of the Biblical prophecies, like Psalm 41:9: "Even my best friend, the one I trusted completely, the one who shared my food, has turned against me."[182]

We are told that this is a foretelling of the betrayal that Jesus will encounter. But isn't David just complaining about a friend who turned against him? So, I would wonder, which is it?

Then I started to understand the elements of story and recognized that this type of prophesy is using the setup & payoff device. In the setup, there is a meaning for David, a purpose within the setup. And in the context of the whole story, there is a greater fulfillment, a new and more satisfying insight, an even bigger payoff.

When taking the wide view, the Old Testament becomes one long series of setups to explain Jesus. The promise given to Eve; the belayed sacrifice of Isaac; the blood of the Passover lamb marking the doorposts in Egypt; the covenant of the king to come through the line of David; the temple sacrifices; the grace offered in Jonah; the prophecies of major and minor prophets; the fourth man in the fire; and the list goes on.

> *Then Jesus took them through the writings of Moses and all the prophets, explaining from all the Scriptures the things concerning himself.*

> —Luke 24:27, NLT

Let's look more closely at some of the Biblical setups & payoffs.

---

182. NLT

Joseph's Dream

The story of Joseph and his amazing technicolor dream coat (well, Tim Rice described it as amazing and technicolored) is found in Genesis 37-50. When Joseph is 16, God gives him a dream of stars and stalks bowing down to Joseph, indicating that his brothers are going to bow down to him.

Now Joseph is definitely spoiled (his brothers are off working when he is at home lounging) and a bit of a snotty brat. He doesn't hesitate to brag about his dream to his brothers, about how God clearly intends Joseph to inherit the ranch someday, and his brothers will work for him.

Joseph's bragging drives his brothers batty — so much so the beat him up, toss him in a well, and sell him to slave traders heading to Egypt. The dream has an important function in this part of the story and serves its purpose — it takes Joseph off the couch and on his journey.

The story, of course, is not over. Joseph becomes a slave, then a prisoner. Finally, he catches Pharaoh's eye, and gets promoted to second in command. At this point he has been in Egypt for two decades. By the time his brothers show up, the dream (the setup) has been forgotten.

After some shenanigans, Joseph reveals himself to his brothers. They bow down before Joseph — and wham! We have the payoff decades in the making. Instead of ranch boss, Joseph has control over most of the known world; not only his brothers, but an entire kingdom and beyond bow down to him.

Another aspect of wonderful payoffs: it is surprising in how they are fulfilled, and the good ones are more wonderful than we would have thought.

The Bronze Snake

While Moses and his merry band were wandering around the desert, the people started whining about God and being in the wilderness and how God isn't doing enough for them — you know, our usual complaints. God responded by sending poisonous snakes; all the biting made people focus on the issue at hand and realize that maybe it was a tad sinful to be so gripey (Numbers 21).

The people confessed, and Moses asked God if maybe he could accept their repentance.

> Then the Lord told him, "Make a replica of a poisonous snake and attach it to a pole. All who are bitten will live if they simply look at it!"[183]

Moses did just that; he made a snake out of bronze, put it on a stick, and held it up high. And those who chose to look up were healed.[184] People were sinning; because of their sin, people were dying; all people had to do to live was look up. It's a little bizarre, but the bronze snake works within the story; it has a function and fulfills it well.

Centuries later, Nicodemus is having a late-night chat with Jesus. The befuddled Pharisee asks Jesus how sinful people could possibly live. Jesus answers with this:

> And as Moses lifted up the bronze snake on a pole in the wilderness, so the Son of Man must be lifted up, so that everyone who believes in him will have eternal life.[185]

An old event acts as a setup to explain something new and a tad difficult to understand. Nicodemus was no slouch in the brains department, and even he needed a little help. So, the bizarre choice in the desert all those years ago? God taking the opportunity to create an object lesson that would make crystal clear what his Son was planning to do later.

Peter's Denial

I mentioned that payoffs are heightened when the audience has forgotten about the setup. The rush of remembrance adds to the power of the payoff. This can also apply to characters who are given obvi-

---

183. Numbers 21:8, NLT

184. Robert G. Lee wrote a short of Moses retelling this story. He called it "Snakes on a Plain." He is very proud of that title.

185. John 3:14-15, NLT

ous setups that they themselves forget or ignore. Julius Caesar being warned about the ides of March, for example.

Peter's denial is such an example (Luke 22). We all remember this story: it is the Last Supper (although only two participants know this will be the last one). Peter says he would never betray Jesus, and Jesus points out that he will. Three times and before dawn in fact.

We often forget in this story what Jesus says to Peter just before letting him know about the upcoming denials:

> *Simon, Simon, Satan has asked to sift each of you like wheat. But I have pleaded in prayer for you, Simon, that your faith should not fail. So, when you have repented and turned to me again, strengthen your brothers.*[186]

Peter is so thrown by the idea that he would fall away, he focuses on that aspect of Jesus' words. In fact, most of us focus on the denial, and not the full line. When Peter does deny Jesus three times and realizes he did so, the first and obvious payoff to the setup is complete.

Notice, though, how Jesus has already given the resolution to Peter's upcoming disaster before pointing out the hard times to come that night: "...so when you have repented and turned to me again..." It isn't until Peter is restored on the shores of Galilee that we remember this setup.

> *A third time he asked him, "Simon son of John, do you love me?"*
>
> *Peter was hurt that Jesus asked the question a third time. He said, "Lord, you know everything. You know that I love you."*
>
> *Jesus said, "Then feed my sheep."*[187]

The best payoffs are the surprising ones, where salvation overcomes troubles. The eucatastrophe of sudden, surprising — yet completely set up — joy.

---

186. Luke 22:31-32, NLT
187. John 21:17, NLT

CHAPTER FORTY-SEVEN

Images: Delivery and Motifs

Images convey that to which we can react emotionally as well as intellectually;
images evoke associations well beyond the factual or conceptual;
images provide for personal, individual communication
because we react, in most ways, uniquely.
Images are not frills; they are hefty building blocks.

—David Ball, *Backwards & Forwards*

Image is the language of film and drives storytelling in the movies. Images also drive television, either in support of the storytelling (for half-hour comedies) or as the main language for filmic one hours. And as the quote above makes clear (Ball's book is all about theater) images are also critical for plays — even though we tend to think of theater as being about dialogue.

In his book, Ball talks about two kinds of communication: the first is the direct, literal kind that describes a thing one element at a time, like a dictionary definition. The second gives a feeling for the combination of elements that together "express the fullness and totality." The first specifies and limits so we can understand the subject. The second expands and evokes, really concerning itself more with our reaction to the subject.

To make clear the two forms, Ball uses a definition of the moon, and then a Shakespearean quote about the moon. I offer a similar set of examples here, focusing instead on the rainbow. First the direct form:

Definition of rainbow: An arc or circle that exhibits in concentric bands the colors of the spectrum and that is formed opposite the sun by refraction of the sun's rays in raindrops, spray, or mist.

—Merriam-Webster

Now the second approach:

Triumphal arch, that fill'st the sky
When storms prepare to part,
I ask not proud philosophy
To teach me what thou art.
Still seem as to my childhood's sight,
A midway station given,
For happy spirits to alight
Betwixt the earth and heaven.
      —Thomas Campbell, *"To the Rainbow"* first two verses

The former describes rainbows as a literal object; the latter how one feels about rainbows. The second form is the realm of the artist and is what we call Images. Images, in a story sense, compress while giving a lot of information in small spaces. "She left her husband like a bat out of hell" paints a vivid picture with only a few words. It gives not just the facts of her departure but imbues emotion into the action.

Mark Twain marked a need for the poetic, image-driven approach to life when he quipped:

We have not the reverent feeling for the rainbow that the savage has, because we know how it is made. We have lost as much as gained by prying into the matter.[188]

Story Images have a power beyond explanation in part because they become symbols. The visuals given to us by the storytellers mean more than the literal; they carry a subtextual weight.

We instinctively sense that each object has been selected to mean more than itself and so we add a connotation to every denotation.

—Robert McKee, *Story*

For a story element to be an Image (with the capital "I"), it must have a deeper meaning. Visuals on a set are decoration; Images tell a story.

---

188. Mark Twain, *A Tramp Abroad*

Now I said "the visuals" — but we really mean more than just visuals when speaking of Story Images. David Ball reminds us that the artist is really drawing on what can be perceived by all five senses — visual, aural, scent, tactile, and taste. In our movies, television shows, and plays, sight and sound are the most obvious and direct tools.

There has been experimentation with direct Images using the other senses in theater. I attended a play where the actress baked bread from scratch throughout the course of the show. The smell of freshly baking bread permeated the theater. (And concessions sold a lot of bread post-play.) I heard of a production of the life of Christ that handed out food during the scene of the feeding of the 5,000 — adding taste to the experience.

Film experimented with Smell-O-Vision for a thankfully brief period. Although the Disney "Soaring over California" ride is very much enhanced when the smell of orange blossoms is misted in.

Images are not limited to direct, actual sights, sounds, and smells. The script can reference things that tingle the senses and achieve the effect of Images. Tim Keller[189] speaks of the sensory language of the Bible, that the book attempts to fully engage the reader by speaking to all five senses: drink of my goodness; taste and see that the Lord is good; hear o Israel; touched my mouth; the fragrance of Christ. It is one thing to take in the knowledge of God; it is another to experience it — even in the reading — to drink in God with all our senses.

The subtextual meaning given to Images can either come from an existing meaning, or one created by the script. Robert McKee refers to these as external and internal meanings.

When Juliet says, "A rose by any other name would smell as sweet," Shakespeare is counting on us not only knowing the literal way a rose smells, but to connect the flower as a symbol of love. This is the external meaning.

Arthur Miller's *All My Sons* creates a new meaning with his use of the tree in the Keller back yard. Typically, a tree is used as a symbol for

---

189. There is a great discussion of sensory Biblical language in "Lord of the Wine," Gospel in Life.

life — the external meaning. In the play, the tree becomes a symbol of hope — more specifically of false hope, of holding on to the past. The tree falls in the opening; lays on the ground as a reminder throughout act one; is cut off and removed in act two; and remains as a stump — a rooted reminder of the sins of the father, the denial of the mother, and the poisoned future of the son.

An Image that colors, enhances, and deepens the story through its subtext.

~

The complexity of Images (a delicious complexity) allows for a writer to deliver the imagery to the audience in multiple ways.

The first is in laying out what we see and hear: through the scenery, the costumes, the props, and the sound effects.

In *West Side Story*,[190] we know that Tony and Maria are falling in love at the dance by the visual/audio cues around them: the music changes from the contest rhythm to romantic swells; the lights shift; the cast slows down behind them as time stands still.

Action and movement become another way to create Image. How the characters move, what they choose to do, how the movement juxtaposes to the rest of the scene: all these things can add up to deeper meaning. For film and television, this includes how the camera moves around the subjects.

Willy Loman planting in *Death of a Salesman* reflects his inner state of hope against all circumstances.

Any gangster kissing another gangster in *The Godfather* series is fraught with internal meaning, and never bodes well for the kissee.

Natasha pushing Bruce into the hole in *Avengers: Age of Ultron* is not just blocking (stage movement); it is an action elevated to Image — telling us so much more about Natasha and her priorities than any line could.[191]

---

190. Here referencing the original Broadway production and the 1961 film. The 2021 film moves this scene off the dance floor.

191. Note this setup — in *Ultron*, Natasha shows she is willing to sacrifice personal love and happiness for the greater good. The payoff comes in *Endgame*

Speaking of lines, dialogue too can become an Image when the words are not literal or defining, but rather when they paint, when the line evokes and expands beyond its words. Here are some examples:

Memory, my dear Cecily, is the diary that we all carry about with us.

—The Importance of Being Earnest

I don't want to talk to you no more, you empty-headed animal food trough wiper! I fart in your general direction. Your mother was a hamster and your father smelt of elderberries.

—Monty Python and the Holy Grail

"Remember, this gun is pointed right at your heart."

"That's my least vulnerable spot."

—Casablanca

Each line evoking and expanding. Note this delicious exchange from *Justified*, "Decoy":

Nicky: I got to ask. Where'd you get all those teeth?

Boyd: Courtesy of the American taxpayer while serving our great nation in Desert Storm.

Nicky: Man, I love the way you talk...using forty words where four will do. I'm curious. What would you say if I was about to put forty bullets through that beautiful vest of yours?

Boyd: What're you waiting for?

Nicky: Oh, you're cool, huh?

Boyd: I tried keeping it to four words. You'll allow the contraction as one.

Where dialogue leaves words to become poetry; where the artists paint pictures rather than list descriptions. Beautiful.

---

when she makes the ultimate sacrifice.

Blatant or Implied

In a script, the imagery might be spelled out, or it might be left up to the imagination and interpretation of the reader. Sometimes a script is very direct. This is the opening of George Bernard Shaw's *Major Barbara*:

> *It is after dinner on a January night, in the library in Lady Britomart Undershaft's house in Wilton Crescent. A large and comfortable settee is in the middle of the room, upholstered in dark leather. A person sitting on it [it is vacant at present] would have, on his right, Lady Britomart's writing table, with the lady herself busy at it; a smaller writing table behind him on his left; the door behind him on Lady Britomart's side; and a window with a window seat directly on his left. Near the window is an armchair.*

Compare this to the following scene from *Hamlet*, where all the imagery is implied.

Elsinore. A platform before the castle.

FRANCISCO at his post. Enter to him BERNARDO

Bernardo: Who's there?

Francisco: Nay, answer me: stand, and unfold yourself.

Bernardo: Long live the king!

Francisco: Bernardo?

Bernardo: He.

Francisco: You come most carefully upon your hour.

Bernardo: 'Tis now struck twelve; get thee to bed, Francisco.

All we are given is a platform. However, in our mind's eye we see a battlement; we imagine them in armor, carrying weapons — spears, maybe swords. We also "see" that it is dark — they do not recognize each other; maybe there is even a fog. A clock is striking twelve.

All implied; all created in our minds eye.

Image Motifs

When Images build throughout a script, they create a motif or pattern that creates a deeper subtext. The tree in the Keller yard in *All My Sons* is powerful as an individual image, but by remaining (and altering form) throughout the play, it gains all that much more power.

Robert McKee calls this an Image System. He emphasizes that to become a System, the Image needs to repeat with persistence and variety. It also should be subtle as a message, communicating subliminally. The tree in the play is talked about, but the emotional meaning to the audience is never articulated; it is between the creators and the viewers.

I once saw a production of *The Glass Menagerie* by Tennessee Williams that did not understand the power of subtlety. Laura's collection of glass figurines is an obvious Motif; the stagers of this production didn't feel that Williams made it obvious enough. The menagerie case was positioned down center, nearly blocking the view of the action on the stage. And every time the figurines were mentioned in any way by the characters, all actors would freeze and then slowly turn and stare at the case as lights would shine down on the set piece, blinding the audience with its gaudiness. Then the actors would slowly turn back as the lights readjusted and the play would continue.

It was a dreadful experience. Image Motifs are meant to work on the emotions of the audience from inside out. David Ball puts it this way:

> As a play progresses, emotional responses and associations accumulate. Eventually the accumulation of reactions helps the audience to emotionally experience, not merely understand. The simultaneous communication of both understanding and emotional experience is the domain of art.

Below are some examples of Images and Image Motifs.

Star Wars

The original *Star Wars* trilogy had some fun with costume colors. Over the course of the three movies, Luke's outfit goes from white to black. The external meaning might suggest the colors in terms of good and evil; and may even play on Vader's constant attempts to turn Luke to the dark side.

However, the movies created an internal interpretation for the colors of the uniforms. White represents inexperience and low position; the faceless stormtroopers are in all white. Black represents mastery and power — Darth Vader and the Emperor wear black. Luke's costuming traces his progression from novice to master.

Fences

Like *Glass Menagerie*, this August Wilson play puts the main Image in the title. Troy spends the play trying to build a fence around his yard. He sees the fence as a way to protect his family; and his wall mirrors his attempts to keep his family together, to keep them from fracturing. He completes the fence only after his family has been blown apart.

The fence initially represents keeping within; and ultimately represents all the things that Troy does that drives his loved ones away. The fence theme is reinforced by Troy's brother, Gabe. After Troy's death, Gabe attempts to blow his trumpet to alert Peter that it is time to open the pearly gates for Troy. Gabe believes he is successful; the audience is left to wonder if God's fence is one of keeping in or keeping out.

The Shawshank Redemption

Frank Darabont's movie is based on Stephen King's novella, *Rita Hayworth and the Shawshank Redemption*. The title plays homage to the movie poster that is prominent in the plot; and Darabont picks up on this theme using movies/opera as a motif of escape. The movie screenings inside the prison provide the rare laughs for the inmates. The broadcasting of the opera over the speaker system transports the entire prison population to someplace well beyond their troubles. Note how an opera was chosen rather than an upbeat pop song. And of course, we have all the posters — Rita, Marilyn, and Raquel — that literally cover Andy's escape.

Oedipus Rex

The Sophocles play uses the concept of vision to create its system of Images. Sight is discussed often throughout, a constant reminder of the motif. The blind prophet is the one who sees clearly at the beginning, while Oedipus, a sighted man, is blind to what is happening in his own house. The Oracle's understanding is referred to as a vision. And when the king is finally forced to face the truth about himself and his wife/mother, he gouges out his own eyes.

Sight becomes associated with truth in an inverse way to the expectation. Emphasis on the physical "blinds" one to the truth — the distractions of temporal life are too much. Stripping away the "sights" of life is the only way to finally see through to the truth.

CROSS FADE: Biblical Image Motifs

Word and image find their ultimate expression and integration in Christ.

—Colin Harbinson, *"Narrative, Symbol, and Ritual"*

The Image is a critical expression of the Bible, a communication device used to fully explore God's Word to us. Remember that the idea of the Image is that it evokes and expands. The Image represents more than itself.

So to say, "The Kingdom of God is like a mustard seed," assumes we know that the mustard seed isn't the kingdom but holds an aspect of the kingdom. You have to look through and beyond the mustard seed to see the kingdom.

Colin Harbinson says that symbol "...connects the knowable to what we do not yet fully know. And connects the natural with the supernatural."

Saint Augustine pointed out in his *Sermons*, "If you think you understand it; it isn't God."

Not to say that God is not knowable, just that He is not fully knowable — not on this side of Heaven, at any rate. Which is why the Bible doesn't rely on direct and literal language.

Another wonderful aspect of the Image is that it grows with understanding; the more we get to know God, the richer and more varied the same Image systems become. I love "The Lost Son" for this reason — at different phases of my life the story has taken on different levels of meaning: me as prodigal, me as father, me as the older son.

In learning more about the culture in which the parable was first told, the Images grow even more for me. (I highly recommend Kenneth E. Bailey's *Jacob & the Prodigal*.) Men in long robes in that tradition did not run — to do so would be embarrassing. The father foregoes that cultural norm to run to his younger son when he returns home.

There was great shame associated with a son who lost his father's inheritance to the Gentiles — there even was a ceremony for the community to be able to punish such a person. And this is exactly what the younger son had done. The father running to his son now has an additional layer of purpose — to get to his child and reestablish him as an heir before the community can step in.

To take on the humiliation of running in public now becomes more than an act of joy — it is also an act of sacrifice for the safety and honor of the child — the very one who disgraced his father.

Living Images grow in meaning with time, retelling, and understanding. The first meanings do not go away; the joy of a good Image is that it expands to encompass all the layers of significance.

Danger

There is also a danger in the use of — and interpretation of — images. Go too far and we stray from understanding to idolatry.

Remember the bronze snake from our Biblical setups and payoffs? Moses made the bronze snake and lifted it up in the desert. This was a symbol designed by God. The Israelites kept that statue, and later began to worship the snake as an idol.

He removed the pagan shrines, smashed the sacred pillars, and cut down the Asherah poles. He broke up the bronze serpent that Moses had made, because the people of Israel had been offering sacrifices to it.

—2 Kings 18:4, NLT

A symbol is a symbol — not the thing. A sign points towards something; it is not the object itself. Jesus restored the bronze snake as a symbol when speaking with Nicodemus. Making a symbol concrete not only loses the power of the Image, but it also corrupts the image.

∽

In looking at Biblical Images, it might be helpful to remind ourselves of how Imagery is used. Madeleine L'Engle, when asked how her faith affected her art, replied that she felt it was the other way around — her art helped her understand her faith. I have the same reaction here — studying the art of storytelling helps me understand God the storyteller more.

We use Images to add to our understanding — while at the same time preventing that understanding from being stunted and boxed in. Evoke and expand. The kingdom is like a mustard seed, yeast, a banquet, a hidden treasure — each Image exploring a facet of a larger concept.

We also use Images to create a reaction — to move our audience. Jeremiah breaking jars outside the city walls; Isaiah preaching naked; Ezekiel building a model of Jerusalem under siege and lying next to it for over a year. Each action creates a symbol — all designed not to bring attention to the symbol, but to garner a reaction (a movement) from the observer.

We also use Image to help find our place in God's narrative. Kenneth E. Bailey (*Jacob & the Prodigal*) says this:

A biblical story is not simply a "delivery system" for an idea. Rather, the story first creates a world then invites the listener to live in that world, to take it on as part of who he or she is. Biblical stories invite the reader to accept them as his or her story.

The parables (like all good stories) draw us in and place us inside the story. We are the leaders who walk past the man beat up on the side of the road. We are the victim, lying helpless. What if we were the Samaritan?

We are the workers who were there all day and got paid the same as the guy who showed up late. We are the widow who wouldn't stop bugging that judge. We are the guy selling everything we own to get that one pearl. We are the man begging for Lazarus to come give us a taste of water.

We are in the narrative, and so can better understand our place in the greater story of our own lives.

Images also help us experience the fullness of life, faith, and God. To engage the intellect, the emotional, and the philosophical all together. Remember what David Ball says about Image systems, "The accumulation of reactions helps the audience to emotionally experience, not merely understand."

The repetition or persistence of an Image, becoming a system or motif, helps us enter that experience. Here are a few examples of Biblical Image Motifs.

Sheep

The Bible uses the idea of sheep repeatedly across the books from Genesis to Revelation. The Old Testament establishes the connection of God as the tender of the flock. From Psalm 23 (NKJV):

The Lord is my shepherd,
I shall not want.
He makes me to lie down in green pastures;
He leads me beside the still waters.
Yea, though I walk through the valley of the shadow of death,
I will fear no evil;
For you are with me;
Your rod and Your staff, they comfort me.

This system culminates in Jesus, who is both the lamb of God — the sacrifice — and the Good Shepherd — the powerful comforter.

I am the good shepherd. The good shepherd gives His life for the sheep.[192]

Water

The Image of water starts in creation, as the waters are separated.

And the Spirit of God was hovering over the face of the waters.[193]

Water goes from part of creation to the means of destruction.

Look! I am about to cover the earth with a flood that will destroy every living thing that breathes. Everything on earth will die.[194]

Then, akin to the bronze snake, Jesus redeems the symbol of water from one of supreme destruction to one of ultimate life.

Jesus replied, "Anyone who drinks this water will soon become thirsty again. But those who drink the water I give will never be thirsty again. It becomes a fresh, bubbling spring within them, giving them eternal life."[195]

Walking

Walking is a practical action in the Bible — as the major mode of transportation. As used in the Bible, though, walking develops into an Image, a symbol meaning closeness and teaching. Walking with the Good Shepherd; Enoch walking with God; Jesus walking on water — and calling Peter to join Him; the risen Jesus walking with the couple on the road to Emmaus.

Paul tells us to walk in the Spirit. Walking is no longer just a function of getting from here to there; walking is a sign of discipleship.

---

192. John 10:11, NKJV
193. Genesis 1:2, ESV
194. Genesis 6:17, NLT
195. John 4:13-14, NLT

He who says he abides in Him ought himself to walk just as He walked.[196]

Donkeys

I think my favorite Biblical Image Motif is the lowly donkey. To me, the word "donkey" translates to "with God." Let me explain.

Sampson wields the jawbone of a donkey, which I have to say sounds like a pretty useless weapon. But with God, Sampson uses that jawbone to destroy a thousand of the enemy (Judges 15:16).

Balaam, while trying to act against God, is instructed by a talking donkey. Balaam misuses the beast, and still the donkey knew more than Balaam and saved his life (Numbers 22). We don't think of a donkey as a symbol for intelligence; yet with God, the donkey is a source of great wisdom.

A donkey carried Jesus twice — first while He was inside His mother's womb in the days before his birth.[197] The second was for his "triumphal" entry into Jerusalem, days before his death (Luke 19).

A king rides a stallion, a mighty horse. Jesus announced his kingship atop a lowly beast of burden. Well, normally it is a lowly beast of burden, but with God it becomes worthy of carrying the King of Kings.

I am greatly encouraged by this Image Motif because quite frankly I am often confronted with the fact that I am no more than a donkey. Just a dumb, stubborn, beast of burden.

But with God...

---

196. 1 John 2:6, NKJV

197. According to tradition. The Bible doesn't mention that Mary rode (or didn't ride) for part of her journey to Bethlehem. Skye Jethani makes a nice connection with the donkey image in his devotional, "Advent & Agony."

CHAPTER FORTY-EIGHT

Theme

It turns out your philosophy is every bit as important as your craft.
Or let's put it this way: It doesn't really matter how cleverly
you say stuff if you really have nothing to say.

—John Vorhaus, *The Little Book of Sitcom*

Theme

Also known as:
Message
Premise
Moral
Meaning
Story Question
Controlling Idea
Universal Statement

There are many ways to talk about theme. The terms above aren't really synonyms; each carries a slightly different approach to what a story is trying to say. Which is a good thing. Theme is so complex and varied within stories that to try and box its meaning to one type is likely to be counterproductive. Even stories designed specifically to teach — fable, parable, allegory, illustration —

come with a wide variety of approaches. In thinking of theme, a broad approach may be best.

Theme defined: The subtextual idea that permeates a story

The theme (in well-crafted stories) tends not to be what the story is saying on the surface. Theme comes out in the action, in how the characters are shaped.[198] A character may voice a theme — but the theme itself is found under the action. Besides, you can't count on the characters getting the theme right. Macbeth never quite figures out the theme of his story; if he did, his story wouldn't have gone off the rails.

Television asks about story in two ways. First, "What's the story about?" Meaning, what's the plot? What happens?

Then, "What's the story really about?" What is the story saying? What ideas are being explored by the story? In other words, what is the theme — the real function of why we are telling this story.

One Theme Theory (Bogus)

There is a popular opinion out there that a good story has only one theme. There are two justifications for this idea. The first is from a utilitarian approach to story. The feeling is that since the only purpose of a story is to teach a concept, having more than one concept in a story would be akin to a math teacher giving examples of subtraction while teaching addition.

I was told by a pastor that some seminaries teach this theory when talking about parables; in that arena, a parable by definition has only one possible meaning. (I have since been told by other pastors that this is a sign of the poor quality of the seminary the first pastor attended.)

---

198. Craig Mazin has an absolutely delicious episode of the *Scriptnotes* podcast (ep 403) called "How to Write a Movie." In it, Craig outlines a way to both structure and give character arcs by having theme (or "thesis") drive the story. We have our grad students study this episode.

This justification starts from a faulty premise — that Story has only a utilitarian function.

The second justification claims that having only one theme for a story helps focus the story. From this angle, the One Theme Theory isn't claiming that stories only have one theme; rather it is a marker of quality. The better the story, the fewer things it has to say.

Either way, the One Theme Theory is bogus. It simply doesn't play out in real life and is more driven by wishful thinking from those who hope to contain Story in a tidy box.

I will give some credit to the second justification: there are stories that are sloppy in their handling of theme. The result is a mishmash of ideas that get in the way and undercut each other. Often stories that overflow with thematic ideas are a sign of a writer who never quite figured out what story they wanted to tell.

Yet there are other stories loaded with themes — each focused and smartly edited — that prove the theory woefully misguided. A well-crafted story will have multiple themes connected through common action and complimentary paths.

The Parable of the Lost Son is a prime example. What it's about is a younger son who takes and spends his father's inheritance, then attempts to return home. What it's really about is a whole host of things.

Forgiveness: if one repents, forgiveness is possible. Love: there is a love that will wait, no matter what. Piety: putting judgment over forgiveness causes you to lose sight of everything important.

Three major themes, and that is just in a short story. Longer works have plenty of room for plenty of themes. To ignore this is to miss out on much of what good stories have to offer.

Meaning

Of the many names and approaches to the idea of theme, there are three that I have found the most useful in writing and evaluating scripts — Meaning, Story Question(s), and Subject & Theme.

David Trottier takes on the Meaning approach. The focus is with the author's intent: what motivates the telling of this story? What do they want to say?

In looking at the writer's intent, it is important to remember that we are still looking for the subtext of the story, the accumulation of aspects. A good story will not be a sermon. Bobette Buster[199] says that a creator can tell a message or give the experience of redemption. The Meaning should be found in the experience.

Writers (and audiences) who seek didactic stories miss the impact of this point. If a script (or a viewer) focuses too much on meaning, then the story is lost. And if the story is lost, then the meaning is lost. I think we've all sat through movies/plays that are so on the nose that the viewer is either: 1) already in agreement and pre-sold on the ideas, or 2) in disagreement and is completely disengaged. Neither is truly moved by the story.

Writers for children's content and religious writers tend to fall easily into this trap. While such shows might be good for rote learning (getting down the ABCs or realizing that "Jesus" is the correct answer for most any question), such telling is a very weak way to explore ideas.

---

199. From her many seminars.

Good stories avoid preaching, revealing theme through the elements of story rather than telling. Images, juxtaposition of images, dialogue exchanges, subtext of scenes — all these elements contribute to create theme.

Captain Marvel attempts to play around with this very idea — preaching themes as a negative example — to some limited success.[200] The film gave out a fake theme — and sermonized the telling of it — near the start of the film. "You've got to let go of your past," and "There is nothing more dangerous to a warrior than emotion."

The lines are delivered from a mentor character using all the tropes and wrappings to make us believe that this is a standard B-movie wearing its message on its sleeve. This is part of the ploy of the film — to convince us that the bad guys are the good guys by steeping us in Carol's POV; and only later will we come to realize that the badly presented themes are indeed, well, bad. The true theme is hidden in the action.

Ultimately, the resolution of any story verifies the ideas and meanings of the tale. The execution of the ending will either convince the viewer of the truth of the theme or will fail. If the theme isn't revealed through the action, then no amount of dialogue will make it so.

Romeo and Juliet's theme is borne out of the ending, and is a bit masked by all the romance. Romeo will tell you that his story is about love — and yet the ending makes us wonder what the heck William is trying to say about love. Love is a secondary topic for the play — the real theme is more like: "Indoctrinated hatreds will destroy hope, and in the process destroy the future of those who hate." The attempt of young love (or young romanticism) to breach the boundaries of generational hatred fails; this is a story about the power of hatred, not the power of love.

For Meaning to be relevant, it needs to be universal, and not specific just to a character. Yes, the theme needs to apply to the character, but is also should apply to the audience. Thus *Romeo and Juliet* isn't, "If Romeo and Juliet try to get together, the hatred of their families will

---

200. I think the failure of the movie to fulfill its potential is not due to the mishandling of theme, but other story elements.

get in the way." The story will apply to more than those two specific individuals if it is to have depth.

In *Hidden Figures*, rather than, "For Katherine, she was able to use her brains to rise above her station," a more universal meaning would be, "In the long run, true giftedness outlasts the petty roadblocks of bigotry."

There are some who would argue that many stories do not have any Meaning. Certainly, many writers aren't setting out to say anything at all — they are just trying to entertain. Comedies and action movies would be two examples. And yet, just about every story says something; it will either reinforce or question a worldview at the very least. This is an issue with the Meaning approach — it relies too much on intent, and not enough on results.

Monty Python's sketch, "The Ministry of Silly Walks," is indeed silly and laugh-out-loud entertaining. At the same time, it is an incisive commentary on bureaucracy.

Many a shoot-em-up action flick hides behind the mantra of "we're just having fun here." And yet a view of what society is and should be is presented in those simple worlds. If the creators are unaware of what they are saying, much damage can be done. For example, Robert McKee labels *Death Wish* as a vile film with a damaging theme.[201]

Grease has an ending with a surprisingly twisted moral — and one that I'm guessing was not the intention of the creators. "Love can be attained when a woman agrees to become an object to satisfy her lover." Hardly a theme to be proud of.

When Disney opted to change the ending of *A Little Mermaid*, they also changed Hans Christian Anderson's intent; his darker ending was a warning. The animated musical tries to say the movie is about love, but the action is about the advantages of women giving up their voices in order to attract a man.[202]

---

201. I wonder if the filmmakers knew what they were saying, or were simply care-less?

202. Much of the thematic damage of the movie is corrected (or at least attempted to be corrected) in the stage musical version.

Mark Twain made light of the idea of assigning meaning to a story in his introduction to *Huckleberry Finn*:

> *Persons attempting to find a motive in this narrative will be prosecuted; persons attempting to find a moral in it will be banished; persons attempting to find a plot in it will be shot.*

Tongue firmly planted in cheek, and a crack to the scholars who overthink such things; and yet one would be hard pressed to conclude that *Huckleberry Finn* is anything but chockful of powerful Meaning.

So, while author's intent is a good starting point, the actual meaning of a story lies in, well, the story.

Story Questions

A much less strict yet still intelligent way of approaching theme is to avoid looking for the answers a story gives, and instead look at the questions the script explores.

Three Billboards Outside of Ebbing, Missouri asks this question: "What is the best way to deal with the inequities of life?" The movie does not answer that question; it explores the possibilities in the question. Some characters seek revenge, some characters seek forgiveness; neither side wins or loses — and the audience is left on their own.

Stories like *Three Billboards* are very comfortable allowing questions to be asked without taking sides. Exploring the question is more important than giving the answer to them — and in many cases is much more profound as a result. If a question is answered within the body of a story, there is no driving need to answer it outside of the story.

And if the question is not answered inside the story, the audience must take the question home with them and wrestle with it there. This is precisely why Jesus has so many stories that aren't explained during his sermons. Or have unsettling answers... We are forced to continue the discussion even after the storytelling.

The story of Sampson (Judges 13-16) is an example of this approach to theme. Sampson is held up as a hero of the Bible, yet he clearly does things that are not Sunday school approved. The Bible never tells us when his actions and traits are good, God-approved actions, and when they are not. (Except for cutting his hair — the breaking of a vow.) He was blessed after almost every act, including those that we would consider without-a-doubt sinful.

The teller of the tale leaves it for us to figure out — to wrestle with, argue about, contemplate. "This is what happened," the author says. "You judge what it means."

Which is probably why you hear so few sermons on Sampson. Best to avoid the stickiness.

WRITER'S TIP

A great advantage to writing your script with the Story Question approach is just how open it is. As the story progresses, you are free to bounce around ideas, to ebb and flow amid the action. *The Two Popes* is driven by a question, "What is the right way of leading God's church?" It is fun to watch two great actors dig into the ideas, as they volley back and forth — and each discovering their stances changed after each volley.

The script plays fair — neither side is overwhelmingly right or wrong. The sense is that common ground is critical — for the very reason that right and wrong in this debate is counterproductive. Listen, contribute, and grow is the call of the day.

Personally, as a moderate, I often feel that neither side in an issue has all the right answers; usually the best path lies somewhere in between. This approach fits well for such a thought process.

Subject & Theme

My go-to method of evaluating message is the Subject & Theme method. I first heard this technique from writer Sheryl J. Anderson.

Rather than focus on intent, this system looks at the work itself and asks, "What is the work saying?"

There are two parts to this approach, as the title suggests. The first is "Subject"— typically one word summing up the idea being explored in the story. We are in the realm of "ideas" and not plot — so "bank robbery" or "the Titanic" or "tornadoes" could never be the subject. "Love," "greed," "nationalism," "pride," "forgiveness" — the ideas are the Subject. The "Theme" then is a one sentence description of what is being said about the subject.

- *Othello*
  - Subject: Jealousy
  - Theme: Giving in to jealousy destroys even the strongest of virtues

Note that we can't just stop with a subject. "My script is about love!" Without knowing the Theme, the subject is meaningless. What about it? Love is a waste of time? Love doesn't exist? Love gives life meaning? Love conquers all? The Theme is that element that gives the story focus (just remember that the story will have more than one theme).

Here are a few Subject and Theme examples. The first comes from Ryan King.

- *Monster's Ball*
  - Subject: Love
  - Theme: True love transcends personal demons and long-taught hatred

A good companion piece for *Romeo and Juliet*, eh? Here's another example.

- *Spider-Man: No Way Home*
  - Subject: Mercy
  - Theme: Selfless mercy overpowers the strongest of selfish motives and is the only way to true justice

Note again that Theme is not about plot, not about the action of the story. Character names would never appear in a good Theme sentence.

〜

The plot is not the Theme, yet the two are related. The story must bear out the Theme. If in the story, giving in to jealousy does not destroy, then that is NOT the Theme. Even if someone says it is in a voiceover at the end.

Pixar Story Rules

#3. Trying for theme is important, but you won't see what the story is actually about til you're at the end of it.

Now rewrite.

Pixar's point here is that the plot will tell you the Theme. They discourage their writers from putting a name to Theme until the first draft is completed. Once the Theme has been identified, the writer than goes back and starts focusing the story on the given meaning.

In essence, plot is how the Theme is articulated. Think of a story as a test: If the character does this action, what happens? Theme will be the subtext of what happens. The action will play out the thesis.

Which is why a good Theme sentence is active. It is never a simple statement of opinion: "Jealousy is bad." Rather, theme is idea in motion: "Giving in to jealousy destroys..."

Good themes can be tested. In fact, the whole point is to test the theme. "Does giving in to jealousy destroy the strongest of virtues?" To answer that, let's give someone strong virtues, have them give in to jealousy, and see what happens.

Orders and commands cannot be Themes because they can't be tested. "Love God." "Be a good person." "Eat vegetables." These may be good sentiments, possible fodder for a poster involving a kitten some-how — but not Themes.

A theory is posited, an argument explored, and a conclusion reached. That, in a nutshell, is what theme is.

—John Yorke, *Into the Woods*

Theme is an argument, not a statement. The script is a laboratory. The bigger the test, the more powerful the theme. *Spider-Man: No Way Home* is a wonderful example of fully testing a theme. The Crisis — the moment of Peter's greatest loss — is directly related to Peter's idea and pursuit of mercy. This is not an easy theme; it has a cost; and only in the cost can we see the value of any idea.

A big mistake all too often made by writers is protecting their theme. They keep it safe from real testing, pitting their ideas against straw figures and blatantly weak opposition. In doing so, the writer is admitting that their theme isn't really true — at least not in their own hearts.

We certainly see this in the submarket of religious programming. The holy hero goes up against the ranting, idiot atheist. The hero is clever and has just the right answers; the villain sputters nonsense, holding extreme positions that don't exist in the real world. Everything the hero touches blossoms under his fingers; the villain smashes everything and, having no heart, doesn't care.

We harbor our ideas in the safety of one-sided contests, rigging the results to make sure that God/faith/the Bible — whatever we are presenting — doesn't falter in the fight.

Hear this: the job of the writer isn't to take sides and protect his beliefs. The job of the writer is to tell the truth.

God himself has never been afraid of being truly tested. When Elijah took on the prophets of Baal, God did the opposite of the storytellers who would protect Him: he gave the opposition all the advantages. More priests, first choice of sacrifice, the best materials, and all the time they could possibly wish for. His protector was alone, with a small pile of water-soaked wood.

Neither God nor Elijah seemed worried; neither felt that there was a good chance that with a real test, God would fail.

If you really believe (insert theme here), then prove it in a fair fight.

Opposing Themes

As Theme is an argument, at least two voices are needed: contradictory voices on each side of an issue. Idea and Counter Idea — argument in action until one wins. To do this effectively both sides need to be powerful. Andrew Stanton points out that theme is not a message — it is a truth.[203] The story is there to try and prove that truth wrong.

One way to insure this is to have a character holding the opposing viewpoint. This can be a character in direct conflict with the Central Character, or a parallel character testing the same ideas in a subplot.

Star Wars: A New Hope has our Central Character, Luke, believing that one should live for the greater good. Alongside him for the journey is Han Solo, who very much believes that the goal should always be to live for yourself. Both characters try out their ideals in action.

A Doll's House, the play by Henrik Ibsen, is very much about domestic roles. Nora, wife and mother of three, can't find contentment in those domestic positions; her husband, Torvald, tries to maintain a decent, respectable domicile. In the end, their marriage implodes, and Nora leaves her family.

A subplot involves Nora's friend, Kristine, a widow trying to find a job, and Nils, a single father struggling to make a home for his children. Kristine and Nils have been forced out of the standard gender roles, and each finds they are good in these nonstandard positions: Kristine as an earner, Nils as a homemaker. The two also find each other — and create a marriage partnership honoring each other's giftedness.

They find the happy ending where the leads of the story cannot; the Theme in counterpoint to that carried by Nora and Torvald.

~

Theme is not different from plot, character, or dialogue; it is inseparable from the other parts of the story. In exploring theme, then, one should look at plot and character.

What questions are asked at the Final Straw? When the Central Character goes on the quest, what is at stake? What is the Central Character's Need? At the Crisis — what thematically is the worst that can happen? What is the change a character must take in order to "win"?

---

203. "The Clues to a Great Story," TedTalk

Remember that the best themes emerge from the story. A tacked-on theme or one laid over the top of a story isn't really the meaning of that story.

The more a Theme is natural and less forced, the stronger the Theme. The more a Theme is carried in action, the stronger the Theme.

> *I will use stories to speak my message and to explain things that have been hidden since the creation of the world.*
>
> —Matthew 13:35, CEV

CLOSE UP: Theme
Soul

Soul by Pete Docter, Mike Jones, and Kemp Powers is like all Pixar movies in its deep dive into theme. I want to look at one scene and character: the barber shop scene with Theme Carrier Dez.

Joe and 22 go to the shop to have Dez fix his hair. Joe sees Dez as someone who always knew their destiny, being "born to be a barber." In the process of fixing Joe's hair, Dez also fixes Joe and 22 with some deep thematic ideas.

Let's pull out six lessons to learn in how the writers handled this scene.

First

The scene is not about theme, at least from a plot point of view. The plot focus is to fix Joe's hair (well, 22's hair, but on Joe's body). This is a bit of magician misdirect; by giving us something to do, the story can slip in a discussion of theme without feeling so preachy.

Second

Dez is a fully formed character with a complete background, rich personality, and entertainment value of his own. The character isn't just there to spout words from the mouths of the writers; he has a life. We are going to watch Dez because he is interesting; the wisdom he might share is secondary.

Note how well this approach worked in the introduction of Yoda in *Star Wars: The Empire Strikes Back*. The entertaining, fully formed Muppet was more than a source of knowledge — he was his own entertaining being.

Third

The scene is full of humor. This is clearly a scene that is a stop to the main plot; it is here because the characters need the information to apply to their Need. To mask the obviousness of the scene function, a plot point is given (as above, to fix Joe's hair) and the scene is made entertaining. Enjoying education is one way around making it seem preachy.

Fourth

Joe's worldview is undercut when the theme is introduced (as 22 asks how one finds the right thing, their passion). Joe believes Dez was born to be a barber, someone who always knew their spark. Instead, we learn that Dez wanted to be a veterinarian. He only became a barber because life threw him curveballs, preventing him from pursuing his dream.

Fifth

Joe is cut down a bit as a person. Having a clearly positive view of himself (and his music), he is shamed as 22, in her first meeting with Dez, has a conversation about the barber himself; Joe has only ever talked about his own interests. The action here helps make Joe even more open to hearing the potential wisdom.

And Sixth

Joe is left with food for thought. The assumption has been that life is all about finding your spark. Dez found his, not by plan but by circumstance. He is happy with what life served him — not dissatisfied by what he feels he deserved. And this accidental life helps him be more focused on others. As Dez says,

> *That's why I love this job. I get to meet interesting folks like you. Make them happy…*

Dez is offered up as the anti-Joe. He had a dream, life veered from his dream, and he embraced life instead. He makes a difference, and that is more than enough. Joe has a dream and is disappointed in the way life has veered him off course; he is making a difference, and that is not enough.

Joe does not know how to be content in all things,[204] and how to serve (and find joy in serving) where he is at. The theme challenged, renewed, and reinforced through a haircut.

---

204. Think of Paul and Philippians 4:11-13

PART TWELVE

Redemptive Storytelling

CHAPTER FORTY-NINE

Redemptive Storytelling

In everything that can be called art there is a quality of redemption.

—Raymond Chandler, *The Simple Art of Murder*

In discussions about redemptive art in Christian circles, we get caught up in trying to define just what we mean by redemptive. I think what we really are trying to figure out is what kind of stories we want to tell — especially as followers of Christ. "Redemptive" becomes a code word we use to try and describe the stories that reflect the Kingdom in some way. Other terms include:

Gospel Stories
Stories of Hope
Kingdom Stories
Truth & Beauty
Stories of Light

The trick with labels is that they tend to put things into a box, and we don't want to be in a box. We want to tell religious stories and secular stories. We want to tell stories that may be explicitly Christian, and stories in worlds where Christianity doesn't exist (like Middle Earth).

God used all kinds of stories in His book — using positive role models, negative role models, religious and secular content. As creators in His image, we should have the same freedom.

And yet we also want to make sure our stories are pleasing to God. The fact that God used secular stories is not an excuse to ignore the responsibility that comes with storytelling.

So, when I say "redemptive," know that I mean stories that build the Kingdom.

There are a few things to keep in mind in this discussion.

First:

Redemptive stories are redemptive for the audience, not necessarily the characters.

We too often get confused when talking about redemptive or Godly stories by focusing on the characters inside the story. We think a story is redemptive because at the end a character changed, or she got the guy, or she defeated the villain. Instead, we should focus on the story's effect on the audience. Is the story redemptive for the viewer?

Second:

Some will assume that a Christian story is automatically an evangelical story; a story that evokes the Gospel message. I wouldn't disagree — in principle; although I would say in execution Christian stories may not look evangelical at all.

In talking about evangelism, Paul said:

I planted the seeds in your hearts, and Apollos watered it, but it was God who made it grow.

—1 Corinthians 3:6, NLT

We need to remember that it is God who gives the increase, not us. There seems to be a burden on so many to "close the deal" when it comes to faith, that we must somehow save the world.

I have a friend who graduated from a Christian college. She was contacted by her alumni office, asking for the number of people she saved since graduating — part of a campaign: "Our alum saved this many people!" sort of thing. She replied, "I saved the same number of people you did. Zero." Hubris aside, the question was faulty because it misunderstands just who has the power to save.

We are not called to save the world; only Jesus can do that.

But we are called to do our part — to plant the seeds, to water and nurture those seeds.

What we do is meant to be part of a journey, not the whole journey. We are here to actively build up the Kingdom. Stories are often best when giving pieces to the puzzle, not the whole picture.

Another friend of mine wrote a short, three-minute video for a ministry that wanted to put out stories on social issues. My friend's commission was to address drunk driving; his script covered the issue, showing the dangers of driving under the influence. The ministry liked the short and passed it to their theology department for vetting.

The theology department asked for a rewrite: while the script did indeed address drinking, it did not include an explanation of our need for Christ and did not walk the viewer through the steps of conversion to give their lives over to Jesus. My friend, after getting past the shock, pointed out that this was a three-minute video about drinking and driving — not an hour-long video on the details of faith.

The critics responded with this argument (paraphrased): "What if some kid stumbles on this video on the internet, and it turns out that this is the only contact they ever have with a Christian organization, and because we don't include the full Gospel story in the video he is never exposed to Christ, and then when he dies, he goes to hell? What then?"

My friend didn't reply; there is no reasoning with the unreasonable.[205]

The proper response would be: "If the kid dies with my video being the only exposure he has to God, then the Holy Spirit isn't doing his job."

The hubris to think that God only works through me, or my one film, or my one organization, or my one denomination even, is insulting to God, to His Spirit, and to His Son. God is active and at work in our world — and at times we have the privilege to be a teeny-tiny part of that work.

---

205. "Don't make a fool of yourself by answering a fool." —Proverbs 26:4, CEV

The "closers" in the Bible, those who bring the fallen to the Lord and witness their conversion moments, were all building on something else.

The Ethiopian eunuch was reading scriptures before Philip got there. God did not say, "Philip, go talk to this guy who has never had any contact with me; I, as God, am so boxed out of the world that this is the only shot we have." God was already at work; Philip was just assisting the One in charge.

Paul in Athens noted the pagans there were already worshipping — they just didn't understand what they were worshipping. God was already at work in their culture, if they had eyes to see it.

Jesus would begin illustrations with, "You heard it said..." He was building on prior knowledge. His own sermons and stories understood faith as a journey and did not belittle the process of getting to know Him.

Our stories may be meant to introduce the concept of sin, or give just a sliver of hope — just the notion that there is someone out there who cares. Our stories may be intended to introduce the concept of the supernatural, or the concept of grace. We may be planting seeds, or we may be nurturing those seeds along.

Therefore, go and make disciples of all the nations, baptizing them in the name of the Father and the Son and the Holy Spirit.

—Matthew 28:19, NLT

This verse has been labeled "The Great Commission."[206] Note that Jesus calls us to make disciples (also translated as "teach"), not "make converts."

We are called to tell stories that don't just introduce Jesus but guide us into better living. To disciple, to develop, to grow. An oft heard complaint about some movies is that they preach to the choir; I suggest that the choir needs to be preached to. The problem isn't that stories are

---

206. It should be noted that Jesus did not call this the Great Commission. Don't get me wrong, it is a very good commission, but according to Jesus the "Great" commission is Matthew 22:37 — "Love the Lord your God with all your heart, all your soul, and all your mind."

The second greatest commandment is to love your neighbor. Without these two being primary, the later commission is pretty empty.

created for the choir, the problem is that we tend to make stories for the choir with themes they already know, themes that they are comfortable with. Stories that are milk.

Even (especially!) the choir needs stories that challenge, that have meat to them. A call to change the world that doesn't include a call to change the church is a misguided call.

We are also to be telling stories of the full life, not just one piece of that life.

> I have come that they may have life, and that they may have it more abundantly.
>
> —John 10:10, NKJV

Our stories can't stop at the concept of redemption; we need stories that tell us what happens after redemption.

We need stories that speak to life itself.

> In their own way, literature and art are very important in the life of the Church. They seek to give expression to man's nature, his problems, and his experiences in an effort to discover and perfect man himself and the world in which he lives; they try to discover his place in history and in the universe, to throw light on his suffering and his joy, his needs, and potentialities, and to outline a happier destiny in store for him.
>
> Hence, they can elevate human life, which they express under many forms according to various times and places.
>
> —Pastoral Constitution of the Church in the Modern World, 1965

This is the call of the artist of faith: not just an introduction to life, but an elevation of life.

What Kind of Stories Should We Tell?

Or better yet, what kind of stories do we need to hear?

There is a wide variety of stories that we need, which is why we don't want cookie cutter writers. Paul says we are a part of a body. We all bring different pieces to the table, and it is only when we put those pieces together that we see the whole picture.

So, again — what kinds of stories do we need?

Order from Chaos

We need stories that make sense of the world, that bring order to chaos. Madeleine L'Engle (in *Walking on Water*) sees this as a function of art:

> *But to serve any discipline of art...is to affirm meaning, despite all the ambiguities and tragedies and misunderstandings that surround us.*

Ultimately, Madeleine asserts: "Art is an affirmation of life, a rebuttal of death."

WandaVision is a perfect example. Wanda herself is beset by chaos — tragedy at every turn. The limited television series is all about how Wanda attempts to wrap her head around the hurts the world has thrown her way — first by diving into the stories she watched as a kid that made sense of the world (sitcoms, mostly). She uses the story structure of television itself to slowly work her way from escapism to engagement.[207]

Lars and the Real Girl is similar in some ways; Lars cannot make sense of his life, and so creates an imaginary world (through a doll) and through her works out how to survive the "real" world. *The Curious Incident of the Dog in the Night-Time* (the play), *To Kill a Mockingbird*, *Pieces of April*: these are all stories trying to make sense of the world.

---

207. We are going to ignore *Doctor Strange in the Multiverse of Madness* for now, just as the creators of that movie ignored Wanda's entire arc in the TV series. Here is a case where TV did it oh so much better. So, let's agree that the movie was an alternate universe Wanda, and rethink the canon.

To Help Us Remember!

We need stories that help us — as a society and a culture — to remember. Earl Palmer calls this phrase, repeated throughout the Old Testament, the "artistic mandate":

> *Remember that you were once slaves in the land of Egypt, and the Lord your God redeemed you!*
>
> —Deuteronomy 15:15, NLT

We, the artists, are the rememberers for our society. This is our part, our position. There are assigned roles in the church: priests, teachers, administrators — and us rememberers.

Remembering in this context is more than just a cognitive nod, a thinking. Skye Jethani discusses memory for the Biblical culture:

> *In the Israelite culture, remembrance was more than the mental recollection of past events. Rather, it was the recalling of an event so that all of the power of that event can be experienced in the present.*[208]

The call to remember is more than, "Oh, right. I remember that." Rather, it is providing an experience. "I remember that; I feel that; I am living that; I now get that." This kind of remembering is the realm of Story. A record provides a piece of knowledge; art provides an experience.

There are two parts to this command to remember — darkness and light: we are to remember we were slaves, and remember we were redeemed. This makes room for cautionary stories of what it is like to be a slave — to be drawn to the darkness. Stories like *Macbeth*, *Death of a Salesman*, *Breaking Bad*, *Parasite*, and *The Godfather*. All stories that remind us of the dangers of when we were slaves.

And we also have stories of what it is like to be redeemed — which includes the cost or consequence of redemption. Stories like *Les Misérables*, *The Shawshank Redemption*, *My Name is Earl*, and *A Beau-*

---

208. Skye Jethani, *With God Daily*, 12-9-22

tiful Day in the Neighborhood. To be complete rememberers, we need stories of light and darkness.

Testing

We also need stories that test the world. That test God even. In 1 Thessalonians 5:21 (NLT), Paul instructs us, "But test everything that is said."

Dorothy Sayers (*Mind of the Maker*) says that theater (and by extension film/television) is the best way to test something. Our stories are a lab to perform experiments. She says:

> *Conversely, there is no more searching test of a theology than to submit it to dramatic handling; nothing so glaringly exposes inconsistencies in a character, a story, or a philosophy as to put it upon the stage and allow it to speak for itself.*[209]

What would life look like if the Gospel were true? *Lars and the Real Girl*, *Blue Bloods*, *Year of Living Biblically* or my favorite in this category, *Ted Lasso*, are all tests with characters trying to act out the teachings of Jesus.

Remember, we want true tests of faith. Not easy answers that some try to pretend is the purpose of faith. Flannery O'Connor points out:

> *What people don't realize is how much religion costs. They think faith is a big electric blanket, when of course it is the cross.*[210]

We use story to test worldview as well. *Battlestar Galactica* was an examination of post 9/11 views, choices, and social politics. *Man of La Mancha* tests the practicality of romanticism played out in real life. *Harriet* asks if there is a way of God within the darkness of a slavery world. *Parasite*, among many other themes, asks if consumerism or "things" can save. *Mare of Easttown*'s final episode pits justice against friends and family, asking if we can live in a world of true justice.

---

209. Dorothy Sayers, *Mind of the Maker*

210. *The Habit of Being: Letters of Flannery O'Connor*, edited by Sally Fitzgerald

Drama is a testing ground, a chance to see the world from another's porch without having to leave our imaginations.

Truth and Beauty

We also need stories that let us experience beauty and truth. Not show it — experience it.

> ...what at its best a religious novel can be — that is to say a novel less about the religious experience than a novel the reading of which itself is a religious experience — of God both in his subterranean presence and in his appalling absence.

—Frederick Buechner, *The Clown in the Belfry*

Beauty is a theme of God's creativity — and not just by happenstance. Jesus praised the way His father adorned the lilies of the field (Matthew 6); Ecclesiastes tells us that God made everything beautiful in its time (3:11). When making trees, God made them first beautiful, then good for food (Genesis 2:9).

Beauty in and of itself is a theme, a message, from God. Not one we can understand with words, but one meant to nourish the soul. Poet Robinson Jeffers speaks of "Divinely Superfluous Beauty" — a phrase that I think nails it. "Divine" — from God; "superfluous" — beauty is the goal in and of itself.

Beauty is wonder and awe.

Certainly theater, film, and television have provided moments of pure beauty. The opening of *The Lion King* — sitting in the audience as Julie Taymor's characters majestically march through the aisles. Bill Irwin and David Shiner's *Fool Moon* surrounds the audience with joy. Cirque d'Soleil's shows often have that same effect.

When Dr. Stone makes it into the airlock in *Gravity*, and curls up into a ball, I wept in the theater over the moment of beauty. *Nomadland* has too many moments of beauty to count. I think of Abuela's death in *In the Heights* — the combined songs of "Paciencia Y Fe" (Patience and Faith) and "Alabanza" (Praise) are painfully beautiful. God is in these moments.

We also have stories of appalling absence: the *Fargo* television series, *No Country for Old Men*, *Waiting for Godot*, and *Joker* for example. Such stories bathe us in the harsh worldview where there is no God. Much of the world holds this view; and viewing these worlds should help us be more empathetic to our neighbor.

We do have to be careful with such films — they are useful in showing an appalling absence — but they also tell a lie. They claim there is no God — and we, perhaps, have a different view.

Let's make a distinction here: just because a movie is useful for understanding does not mean the movie is Redemptive. *Joker* does an excellent job of showing its worldview, giving insight into the pain that those walking in darkness feel. Yet such stories show a world where God is not an option — thus is not a redemptive story.

Redemptive dark stories like *The Godfather*, *Parasite* or *Macbeth* show what it is like to *choose* to live in a world without God. The former is informative; the latter is cautionary. Hence the former is useful; the latter is Redemptive.

Themes

> *The best art always shifts our perspective. It invites us to see what we might otherwise overlook. It inspires us to imagine what we hadn't previously considered. Or, it challenges us to reconsider the familiar from another point of view.*
>
> —Skye Jethani[211]

We need stories that explore the important ideas of life, that present questions, explore answers beyond the superficial. Stories that ask: Who are we? Where did we come from? Where are we going?

And not just stories that talk about themes — we need tales that explore the ideas through the action of the story. Preaching is best left for preachers; artists should create experiences. We do not need stories

---

211. Skye Jethani, "Psalm 2: What Makes God Laugh?", With God Daily, May 2, 2023

that tell us that good is good and bad is bad; we need stories that let us taste goodness and badness for ourselves.

> *The experience sufficiently illuminates the truth that free curiosity has greater power to stimulate learning than rigorous coercion.*
>
> —Augustine, *Confessions*

Not telling; experiencing.

Kingdom stories then are "more than" stories; more than just retelling an incident; more than providing a simple moral; more than affirming what we already know and believe. Stories that elevate, that caution, that speak Truth in love. Stories that get to the eternal; that point toward the big Truth.

> *Art is an affirmation of life, a rebuttal of death.*
>
> —Madeleine L'Engle, *Walking on Water*

Point of View and Genre

The more time one spends following Jesus, the more we realize that this Christianity thing isn't about following a set of rules or religious traditions. Following Christ is a change in point of view; it is seeing the world through a different set of lenses.

As Christian artists approach Story, it is fair to ask of ourselves — "Do we see things any differently?" To illustrate this point, I'll be suggesting some ways that the faith-filled writer might approach genre that may be a tad "different."

Before I dive in, I would like to make a disclaimer. I am about to talk a lot about story content. However, let me be clear: as Christians, the content of movies/plays/shows is not the most important issue at hand. Even though content may be the most talked about, it is at best the third most important issue.

The fact of the matter is that God cares more about the content of your character than the content of your stories. If you want to change the world, your first job is to develop your own walk with God. The Church is built on relationship; relationship is about individuals (not mass media); so, one's character in Christ becomes more important than a broadcast message.

I am put in mind of Brother Andrew who felt called to bring Bibles to the people behind the Iron Curtain. (Note how I slip in that term to establish setting and era...) He would hide a dozen Bibles in his Volkswagen bug, drive through the checkpoint into the Eastern Bloc, then distribute the books.

One story tells of how Andrew was asked why he uses such a limited method — he could only smuggle a dozen or so Bibles at a time in his car. His questioner suggested a more efficient system: load up a plane with hundreds of Bibles, fly over the restricted countries, and send the books out into the countryside on little parachutes. Why not do it that way?

Andrew answered:

Jesus says to go into all the world, not dump into all the world.[212]

Before relying on Godly content, work on being profoundly Christlike.

Non-Christian Genres

Are there any genres that inherently are anti-Gospel? That cannot be redemptive?

---

212. This story may be apocryphal, but it sounds like the kind of thing Brother Andrew might say — and the sentiment is valid.

I believe there is only one: pornography. The very form is designed to be destructive, and no amount of content changes can redeem the form.

Other than that, I think every other genre is fair game for the Christian writer. All stories should be under the umbrella of God's stories — whether seemingly secular or seemingly religious.

> Basically, there can be no categories such as "religious" art and "secular" art because all true art is incarnation, and therefore "religious."

> —Madeleine L'Engle, *Walking on Water*

It isn't so much where a Christian may go, as much as what they do when they get there. I think it should be hard for a writer of faith to tell stories, because to do so properly takes a lot of thought, searching, and prayer. A lazy Christian makes for a bad Christian writer. The issue here is that many Christian writers take the easy route without really asking the right questions.

The real question for the writer of faith (really this should be the question of every writer) is: Am I bringing all of me into this work? We claim to have a unique point of view — so what do we see? When we approach genres, what is the unique angle we bring to the fore?

Let's look at some specific genres.

Horror

> To me, this genre deals more overtly with the supernatural than any other genre, it tackles issues of good and evil more than any other genre, it distinguishes and articulates the essence of good and evil better than any other genre, and my feeling is that a lot of Christians are wary of this genre simply because it is unpleasant.

> —Scott Derrickson[213]

Audiences automatically accept the existence of supernatural evil in the horror genre. And none would argue in such movies the existence of a supernatural good. So of course, it becomes easy to look at the world beyond the veil in such stories.

---

213. Interview with *Christianity Today*, "Horror: The Perfect Christian Genre"

The television series *Supernatural*, a show about demon hunting brothers, very naturally introduced angels to the cast. If there are demons, why not angels? The stories arced over the battle between heaven and hell, with earth standing in between.

A good majority of horror movies are exploitative, and dwell only on the existence of supernatural evil. Such movies can easily slide into glorifying the gory, reveling in darkness and pain. Not only are such movies shortsighted in their world view, but they are also shortsighted in their storytelling, missing opportunities for richer plots and themes.

A child of God might choose to come at the genre with a broader view — one that explores where the supernatural good also resides. There is a rich history of these kind of stories, so the Christian writer would be joining good company.

Derrickson's *The Exorcism of Emily Rose* includes — as the title suggests — a priest calling upon God to battle the demons inside a young woman. Like its cinematic godfather, *The Exorcist*, the movie depicts real supernatural evil — and its only solution is real supernatural good.

This puts me in mind of a time in the comic books when the X-Men fought Dracula (*Uncanny X-Men* #159). The creature of the night takes on the entire team in his attempt to turn Storm into a vampire. At one point, Wolverine uses his claws to make a cross; rather than repelling Dracula, he laughs. The vampire points out that it isn't the symbol that scares him, but the faith behind the symbol; as Wolverine has no faith in God, he has no power.

Nightcrawler, a practicing Christian character, does have that faith, and is able to drive the vampire away with a cross.[214] A bold statement about the power of God and of faith — and an easily acceptable one within the genre of horror.

---

214. Kitty's Star of David pendant also repels Dracula — while a cross she brandishes does not. Her faith is Jewish, not in the Cross — and it is the faith that has the power.

Science Fiction

Sci-fi is similar to horror in that faith can be assumed as a normal part of a created world. Madeleine L'Engle points out in *Walking on Water*:

> *I often seek theological insights in reading science-fiction because this is a genre eminently suited to exploration of the nature of the Creator and creation. I'm never surprised when I discover that one of my favourite science-fiction writers is Christian because to think about worlds in other galaxies, other modes of beings, is a theological enterprise.*

World building is a natural part of the genre; whether to include religion — even supernatural religion — is simply part of that world building. Arthur Doweyko says that when creating worlds, sci-fi writers need to consider how their characters deal with the big questions of existence.[215] He goes on to say, "Without that view expressed either directly or cleverly insinuated through the story, the characters will lack the moral and ethical motivation for their actions."

Star Wars created religion embodied in the Force; *A New Hope* includes the theme of faith at its core. *Star Trek: Deep Space Nine* includes a major religion for the local aliens, the Bajorans. The faith element figures into many of the storylines — in terms of addressing religion, culture, and politics. *Battlestar Galactica* plays heavily into religion, pitting the monotheistic faith of the Cylons against the pagan worship of the humans.

The *Doctor Who* episode "Gridlock" explores the religion on a future earth, presented primarily as an opiate of the masses — the regular calls to worship calming a public that should be a whole lot less calm. Interestingly, it also ends with a moment that reinforces the power of faith — and the potential community it creates.

Star Trek (the Original Series) has an interesting episode called "Bread and Circuses." The Enterprise crew finds themselves on a planet that seems to parallel earth — except on this world the Roman Empire

---

215. As quoted in the article "Faith in Film: Why science-fiction movies abound with religious themes," by Kandra Polatis, published in *The Deseret News*

never fell. The government is cruel, holding televised gladiator contests to the death. The away team encounters a group of rebels who worship the sun; the rebels preach peace and are considered the number one threat to the Roman society. The crew can escape the planet, and obeying the prime directive, choose to not aid the rebels in overthrowing their dictatorship.

However, the show ends on a very hopeful note. As Kirk, Spock, and McCoy discuss the interesting yet primitive religion they seemed to witness, Uhura corrects their take:

> Spock: Sun worship is usually a primitive, superstition religion.
>
> Uhura: I'm afraid you have it all wrong Mr. Spock, all of you. I've been monitoring some of their old-style radio waves. The Empire spokesman trying to ridicule their religion. But he couldn't. Don't you understand? It's not the sun up in the sky. It's the Son of God.
>
> Kirk: Caesar. And Christ. They had them both. And the Word is spreading only now.
>
> McCoy: A philosophy of total love and total brotherhood.

Book of Eli takes place on a post-apocalyptic earth. The plot focuses on a fight for the last known Bible still in existence. The villain, Carnegie, wants the book because he believes that controlling religion is synonymous with power. The story has interesting subtext on the nature of religion and religious institutions — especially in the context of political and personal power.

Even deeper is another theme — a hint at the idea that religion may be more than the manmade ideas of Carnegie. Eli, the guardian of the book, claims that he was guided to find the book by a voice in his head. And a twist at the end reveals that the only way Eli could get the book to its final destination required a supernatural guide.

Romance

My pastor in Hollywood, Mark Brewer, once said, "It is considered a sin in Los Angeles to be ugly."

He got the proper laugh — one of recognition as well as wit — during the sermon. Alas, he isn't far off the mark.

The standard romantic drama or comedy often comes down to knowing that the two prettiest people in the show are meant to be together — because they are the prettiest. Love is skin deep in many of our movies, television shows, and plays.

Another view might look at love as having more value than the eye can take in. Love may become defined by patience, kindness, a lack of jealousy. Love as maybe something that is not arrogant, that rejoices with the truth, that hopes all things and endures all things.

What would a romance be like that sees beauty as something more than simply looks? That focuses less on the value of how the world sees someone's form, and concentrates more on how God sees us?

There is a type of romance that has the lead character looking for the obvious love — and finding a truer love along the way. *Pride and Prejudice* stands out — in many of the versions. When done right, the audience will dislike Mr. Darcy as much as Elizabeth does — at least at first. And again, if done right, the audience should be surprised to learn that they themselves have fallen in love with the guy, just as Elizabeth is so surprised.

Sabrina (the original with Hepburn and Bogart) has a similar journey — the movie caught me off guard when the two found each other rather than the more obvious romance[216] with the "prettier" man. *It Happened One Night* takes much longer than a night for the couple to find they don't hate each other as much as they thought.

Dogfight with Lili Taylor and River Phoenix turns the Hollywood trope of beauty on its head. The date for the two leads starts because the "hero" thinks his choice is specifically not pretty, and the conflict arises when he gets to know her well enough to realize she is beautiful.

Lars and the Real Girl has an unlikely romance — a fantasy love, and one that comes with true patience, kindness, and endurance. *About Time* is the rare romance that doesn't stop at the getting together stage

---

216. The movie does have the all-too-common trope of the older man with the much younger woman — which dulls the romance quite a bit.

but explores love over time. *Eternal Sunshine of the Spotless Mind* focuses on the pain and difficulty of romance — some might say the real work of romance — more than the butterflies of cute meets.

There is also a form of romance that is more about friendship — and less about hooking up. *Lost in Translation, Roman Holiday*, and *Together Together* come to mind. Love is more than romance — yes?

The romance genre is ripe with opportunities to see the world through a point of view that has a deeper grasp of love than we often settle for. And, as the song says, what the world needs now is love — a true love.

Comedy

Earl Palmer, in his book *The Humor of Jesus: Sources of Humor in the Bible*, points out that there is such a thing as bad comedy. There is a source of laughter that is destructive and negative, that wounds. Think of humor that diminishes the other (racist humor or mocking, for example); humor that separates (like humor of anger or dislike — "us against them" humor); and humor that feeds chaos (darkness or fear-based humor).

The Office (American version) has a powerful moment in its later seasons, as Jim realizes that his constant pranking of Dwight is really mean-spirited bullying. And Jim doesn't like this realization. Jim's growth from child to adult comes, in part, with a shift from jokes against Dwight to coming alongside Dwight.

On the flip side, there is good, Godly humor. Connective humor, nourishing humor, humor that brings order to chaos. Palmer says:

> But there is a good laughter, and it has an altogether different result. The laughter that nourishes has the opposite result because at its motivational center, the humorist recognizes a connectedness toward those who surround his or her story so that the goal is to connect us and not to disengage us from that human linkage. Nourishing humor intends to build up and not to tear apart the sense of well-being of the object of the humorous story.

Insult humor — tear-down humor — is easy. Nourishing humor takes more work.

Ted Lasso is a great example of mostly nourishing humor. The jokes that stick are those that come from Ted putting himself in a position of building others up, a lot at his own expense. Another aspect of good humor is that often the joke is on the teller. Again, from Palmer: "Healthy humor connects human beings and creates self-understanding."

We know more about ourselves through a healthy joke; we gain insight into our own foibles.

> *Humor is the prelude to faith, and laughter the beginning of prayer.*
>
> —Reinhold Niebuhr, *Discerning the Signs of the Times*

Mostly, we know that laughter is healthy when it brings joy. Joy is a gift from God, and when humor brings us closer to Him, we are on the right track.

Action

Let's dig a little bit deeper into the action genre to see more of the thought process in melding one's personal worldview with scriptwriting.

The typical American action movie ending goes something like this: the hero confronts the villain, gains the upper hand, tosses the villain out a window while saying, "Yippe-ki-yah." The audience cheers and all is right with the world.

Is all right with the world? Can we justify that ending, where the villain is killed by the hero while the crowd cheers? I mean, as Christians — can we justify that choice?

Short answer: sure, we can.

> *He has shown you, O man, what is good;*
>
> *And what does the Lord require of you*
>
> *But to do justly,*
>
> *To love mercy,*
>
> *And to walk humbly with your God?*
>
> —Micah 6:8, NKJV

"But to do justly." Justice is a key component of God's character. Amos calls for justice to roll down like a river;[217] Proverbs gives a warning to those who call the guilty innocent, and a blessing on those who convict the evil doer.[218] God tells us, through Isaiah, that He loves justice.[219]

The enemy being stopped and punished is the very definition of justice. We have justified our action movie ending with justice.

Yippee-ki-yah!

Fine and dandy if we stop there. But what about the rest of the verse? Where is mercy and humility before God in our ending?

I get it; sometimes you just have to throw a guy out a window. This ending isn't necessarily bad — it just isn't best. Rather than asking, "Can we justify this ending?" We should ask, "What would it look like to show the whole verse in our stories? Justice, mercy, *and* humility?"

It is not bad to avoid bringing shame to God; it is a good deal better to bring glory to God. Jesus doesn't say, "Get vengeance." On the contrary, He says:

> *But I say, love your enemies! Pray for those who persecute you?*[220]

The mistake the conservative makes is to be only about justice. This is Javert's mistake[221] — and when he encounters mercy his entire world crumbles from under him.

The liberal mistake is to be all about mercy. Remember the warning from Proverbs:

> *If you let the guilty go free, people of all nations will hate and curse you. But if you punish the guilty, things will go well for you, and you will prosper.*[222]

(Note that neither side seems to be all that concerned with humility.)

---

217. Amos 5:24
218. Proverbs 24:24-25
219. Isaiah 61:8
220. Matthew 5:44, NLT
221. *Les Misérables*
222. Proverbs 24:24-25, CEV

Both sides are right and both sides are wrong.

How much harder is it to write a satisfying ending that showcases all sides of this Micah calling to what is good?

This then is the Micah Standard for action films — a test of the Gospel-ness of a story: how do they treat the villains? Is there justice, mercy, and humility with God? Hard to do, but there are several examples of Christian films that achieve this balance.

- *X-Men*: The 2000 movie ends with the capture and incarceration of Magneto (justice). Xavier continues to visit Magneto in jail — one of the "least of my brothers" actions Jesus lists in the sheep and the goats parable.[223] Xavier cares about his enemy, persevering in hope that his foe will come around and be saved.

- *Les Misérables*: Jean Valjean saves his enemy, despite the risk of being captured. Note that he puts no demands on releasing Javert — only that he be allowed to save the life of Marius. Javert, as mentioned earlier, is centered on pure justice; confronting someone sold out to Christ (in Valjean's words: "My soul belongs to God, I know, I made that bargain long ago...") destroys Javert; he cannot handle the dichotomy of justice and mercy thriving side by side.

- *Harry Potter*: The entire series showcases the battle for justice and mercy. Voldemort gets his rightful punishment — not out of vengeance, but out of justice. Mercy is offered to all the villains — most prominently seen in Snape, who suffers through mercy and justice in his own way. Draco is also the recipient of mercy on several occasions, and by the end of the series can break free from the hold that evil has on him.

- Harry Potter also showcases humility — and the battle for its importance. Harry is constantly bolstered as the boy who lived, and constantly tries to downplay that reputation. When his ego does rear up, it is often to disastrous effect. In contrast to Voldemort and his minions (Lucious and Bellatrix leap to mind) who

---

223. Matthew 25

are driven by pride, Harry is often able to win because he relies on powers other than his own.

- *Lord of the Rings*: Another series beautifully blending justice, mercy, and humility. Justice is served — Sauron meets his end. Mercy is abundant, in the many times Gollum and Saruman are shown grace. Note that Gandalf continues to offer mercy to Saruman up to the very end of the twisted wizard's life. And Frodo holds humility up in abundance.

Remember from our discussion of contagonists: it is proper and necessary for the good guy to defeat the villain; it is better for the good guy to convert the villain.

✟ CROSS FADE: The Jesus Standard ✟

Doctor Who: The two-parter "Human Nature" and "The Family of Blood" is a marvelous case study for combining justice and mercy, as well as a fantastic parable to explain the Gospel of Jesus Christ.

In the story we find the Doctor in hiding. The Doctor is a Time Lord, an alien with powers who travels through space and time protecting those who need protecting. At this point, he is hunted by a group of aliens called The Family. These creatures absorb the energy of other beings; they plan on feasting on a Time Lord and have found a way to track him through space and time.

So, the Doctor goes into hiding. He gives up his powers and becomes fully human (also giving up his second heart and his memories). The hope is that The Family won't be able to find him if he no longer has the power they wish to feed on. The Family instead capture the village and school where the Doctor is hiding and threaten to kill them all if the Doctor doesn't reveal himself.

The Doctor is restored to his true self and gives himself up in trade for the lives of the villagers. He stumbles onto the alien ship, seemingly frightened out of his wits by his upcoming end.

Of course, his wits are fully in place, and the Doctor quickly turns the tables on The Family and captures them. He places each of the aliens separately into cages designed just for them — a place where they will endure punishment for all of eternity.

And here is where the Doctor's terrible secret is revealed: while we all thought the Time Lord was hiding out of fear for himself, he was really hiding out of pity for The Family. The Doctor knew that if the aliens confronted him, he would be forced to punish them for their transgressions. He wanted to save them — so gave them a chance to pass him by. Instead of taking this gift, The Family insisted on their ways, and will now be under punishment forever.

To recap: A powerful being (a Lord) sets aside his power and becomes fully human as a sacrifice so that others (who deserve punishment) may be saved from their sins; yet they turn down that offer and suffer for eternity.

Sound familiar?

Conclusion

Creation is God's bailiwick. It is the first thing about Himself that He reveals to us, the first action whereby we start to understand His character. God spoke the world into existence...

As His image-bearers, we follow Him in creation, building off His designs, His deep understanding of character and structure. We tell stories based on His Story, stories that reflect those tales He created in us.

Story then becomes a fulfillment of creation. To repeat:

We have been given a promise, and we wait for the fulfillment of that promise. We know that we are not worthy, but only with God's grace can we succeed. We look for characters with a goal, but we know the truth is that we have a Need greater than our goals.

And the story of how that Need is fulfilled, even though it requires death, is the only story that will ever satisfy.

Appendix A: The Only Screenwriting Book

The only scriptwriting book you'll ever need...

Does not exist. And it certainly isn't this one. The scripted arts — theater, television, movies — are collaborative arts, which is among their great strengths. As a writer, I can write the best that I can write. Which is good (in my humble opinion). However, once I turn over my writing to a good director, she just makes it better. Multiply that by a good cast, good designers, good technicians — each one builds on the possibilities of the others.

And what can come out of the process is a script that is so much better than my best. And hey, I'm more than happy to look good based on the talents of others.

So being in the performing arts has helped me understand that a variety of skills, talents, points of view, and gifts makes the world better. So it is with scriptwriting teachers, books, and pundits.

I'm not saying that there aren't charlatans out there, hawking methods that are not at all useful. Or books (lots and lots of books) on screenwriting that are just copies of other books — and thus not needed at all.

What I am saying is that there have been a goodly number of folks who have studied the art of storytelling and come away with fresh ideas, insights, and points of view — and we are all the better for it.

I have learned from a wide variety of such books; personally, I could never understand aligning with one guru and leaving the others out. There is so much richness to be discovered!

I assign three books as the foundational texts when I teach scriptwriting. Trottier's *The Screenwriter's Bible* comes from a depth of practical knowledge, laying out the movie writing process with clarity, simplicity, and utility. David Ball looks at playwriting from a director's point of view in *Backwards & Forwards*. The little book is brilliant at getting the writer to shake up their preconceived notions on play crafting. And *Into the Woods* by John Yorke (my favorite book on the craft of story) is a deep dive into the craft, combining views from multiple gurus into a clear understanding of the form itself. Three texts that are practical, philosophical, and hold varied viewpoints — not a one made obsolete by the other books.

That's just my big three — there are many variations that continue to add to the knowledge base (rather than just repeating themselves). Ellen Sandler's *The TV Writer's Workbook*, Linda Seger's *Adaptation* (or any other Seger book), Buzz McLaughlin's *The Playwrights Process*,[224] Robert McKee's *Story*, Linda J. Cowgill's *Writing Short Films* — all bringing out alternate ways of understanding and implementing writing. If one wants to stop pretending that scriptwriting is a new art form, there is no better place to dive into how myth informs the present than Christopher Vogler's *The Writer's Journey* and the granddaddy of scriptwriting books, Aristotle's *Poetics*.

The journey of writing itself can reflect greatly onto the work, so our personal library gets the addition of Stephen King's *On Writing*, Anne Lamont's *Bird by Bird*, and William Goldman's *Adventures in the Screen Trade.*

The key in picking up any book on writing is whether the book provides something new — updating insights, deepening knowledge, providing a fresh point of view.

---

224. McLaughlin's book is a study in this very point, as he collects the wisdom of sixteen playwrights, from Edward Albee to Lanford Wilson.

This book hopes to add in two elements — thoughts from experience and other teachers that have not yet been popularized in standard writing books; and the fusion of story with Christian faith.

I will not pretend to be the first or only book blending theology with the staged arts — and I am deeply grateful to my predecessors who have helped me shape my own thoughts in that area: Madeleine L'Engle, Dorothy Sayers, Earl Palmer, Jeffrey Overstreet, Mako Fujimura, Gil Elvgren, Dean Batali, Steve Turner, Tim Keller, and the teeming hordes of peers, colleagues, and teachers who have peppered my life.

I hope what you hold in your hands provides a fresh take on old ideas and adds to the collection of the scriptwriting books you need.

Appendix B: The Number Three

Storytellers have learned, or know in their bones, the magic of the number three — it is the number of completion.[225]

If in our stories we want the audience to know something, we tell them.

If we want to reinforce the point, we tell them twice.

If we want it to be taken as Gospel truth, we tell them three times. Holy, holy, holy is the Lord God Almighty!

The Bible uses this truism to great effect. The Trinity — God in all His completeness. The faith of Abraham, Isaac, and Jacob references the whole of the Jewish faith. Jesus was dead for three days — a complete death, not a near death.

This is the core of the humor technique of threes. Ever wonder why it is always three people who walk into a bar, or are on a plane, or are on a hunting trip, etc.? A point defines a location; two points create a line and a direction — from point A to and through point B. Two points and we know where we are heading.

Then a third point appears that is not along the directional line, which creates the surprise and therefore the humor. John Vorhaus (*The Little Book of Sitcom*) terms these points as Introduction, Validation, and Violation. Other terms include Setup, Reinforcement, and Turn;

---

225. The only greater number of completion that I have found is seven. God created in seven days; Naaman dipped in the Jordan seven times; we are called to forgive seventy times seven. With seven as a number of completion/perfection — six is seen as the number of incompletion/imperfection. Hence, 666 (or sixes extended out as far as you want) is a sign of weakness; the number of the beast is a number meant to comfort us. Let me repeat that, as so many see it as a number to fear: the number of the beast is meant to comfort us. By assigning that number, God is reminding us that the beast (six) will never be as strong as God (seven).

or Point, Direction, and Variation. Three is the number of completion; our expectation is that the third in any set will complete the set, and we are (potentially) humorously surprised when the expectation isn't met.

My favorite storytelling use of three comes from Charles Schulz' *A Charlie Brown Christmas*. This is the best Christmas special ever — and for many reasons, not the least of which is Charles' ability to go deep into storytelling while convincing his audience that it is all lighthearted children's fun. For our purposes, I will focus on just one aspect of the special.

To understand what the story is really about we must follow the blanket.[226] Linus' security blanket is featured in five scenes.

In the opening ice-skating sequence, Snoopy tries to steal the blanket. Linus will not let go, resulting in Charlie Brown getting wrapped in the blanket and sent skidding into a tree.

During the snowball throwing practice, Lucy tells Linus that he will have to let go of the blanket when he becomes an adult. Linus explains that he will simply make a suit out of the blanket.

And in rehearsal for the Christmas play, Lucy threatens Linus — he must get rid of the blanket to be a shepherd. Instead, Linus makes a costume out of the trusty cloth.

Three times an attempt is made to rid Linus of his blanket — through force, mockery, and threats of violence — yet Linus does not let go.

This is the principle of three at play: Schulz is giving us a message that we must understand clearly: under no circumstances will Linus give up his blanket.

This is critical — if we miss this, we miss the point of the story; so, Schulz tells us three times to make it complete: under no circumstances will Linus let go of his blanket.

And then he does.

---

226. The term "security blanket" comes from Linus and his beloved piece of cloth. The importance of the blanket to Linus struck a nerve that runs deep in humanity, and gave an illustration for a concept that most of us experience subconsciously.

First, when reciting the Christmas story. For a moment, and just a moment, Linus forgets about the blanket. To be specific, on the words of the angels, "Fear not," Linus lets go of his other security. He retrieves the blanket the moment the recitation is over.

And then at the end, Linus gives up his blanket completely to wrap around the base of the tree, saying:

> I never thought it was such a bad little tree. It's not bad at all, really. Maybe it just needs a little love.

A little sacrificial love.

Linus tells Charlie Brown earlier that he knows what Christmas means; then he shows that meaning in action.

Sacrificial love.

Appendix C: Improv Game: CROW

The improv rehearsal game CROW can help us in giving out exposition in a succinct and clear way.

In the game, a player steps forward and starts a scene with a line. Another player joins with a second line, and the first player responds. Then the exercise is done. The idea is that in a maximum of three sentences, the players must establish: Character (who are these people), Relationship (who are they to each other), Obstacle (what is the problem that is going to drive the sketch), and Where (what is the location of the sketch).

Extra kudos to the players who can fulfill CROW in less than three sentences. Example games:

Player One: Quick, grab the children, the volcano is about to blow!

Player Two: Oh Claudius, I couldn't possibly leave now. I've just waxed the kitchen floor.

Player One: Great Zeus, Andromeda! Now's not the time to think about floors!

The game relies on inference, and the audience filling in the blanks based on the clues: children, volcano, Claudius, Andromeda, Zeus. We have a husband and wife (Character, Relationship) facing a volcano eruption (Obstacle) in Pompeii (Where).[227] Here's another example:

---

227. "Uhm, actually," says the history nerd, "Pompeii was a Roman city, so it should be 'Jupiter' and not the Greek god, Zeus." To which I say, "Hey, it's an improv game. They just came up with this off the top of their heads, which is pretty impressive, so relax and just enjoy the show!" Besides, clearly the Roman Claudius married a Greek woman, Andromeda, so maybe he is just giving a little religious pluralism a shot...

Player One: Jim, the boss is coming back!

Player Two: Oh no! What is he going to do when he sees that we knocked over two shelves of wine when playing pallet truck chicken?

Player One: Quick, get some straws!

The audience gets the clues for Character/Relationship (coworkers) and Obstacle (knocked over shelves) and Where (wine warehouse).

This is what we look for in our Balances — can we establish all the pertinent information with the least amount of page space. And the more we rely on the audience, the more interesting the telling.

Jesus used this technique constantly in his parables. Notice how quickly he gets us into the conflict of the stories:

If a man has a hundred sheep and one of them wanders away, what will he do?[228]

Or this one:

A Jewish man was traveling from Jerusalem down to Jericho, and he was attacked by bandits.[229]

Jesus' audiences instantly know the core of the story — character/relationship, obstacle, where. He relies on the hearer to take his clues and fill in the blanks. His audiences are active and drawn into the story. I imagine we've all sat through sermons that could have used this tactic to get us into the meat of the topic!

---

228. Matthew 18:12, NLT
229. Luke 10:30, NLT

Appendix D: Other Structures

I've focused this book in talking through the classic model of story structure. There are many models out there that look at story in other ways. Such alternate points of view on structure tend to fall into three general categories: the ones that are classic structure with different terminology; the ones that are a different approach to how to tell story, yet work with the classic structure; and then the one that is truly a different structure.

The first category includes most of the writing teachers/gurus out there — like Trottier, Snyder, Truby, McKee, Field, and last/least, Gaffney. These have value in that they tend to know what they are talking about (I did say Trottier, right?), and sometimes the new ways of approaching the age-old ideas resonates better in one voice than another.

I am not a proponent of *Save the Cat!*, but I know of many writers who didn't have their lightbulb breakthroughs in their craft until they embraced the cat saving book. The way story was presented by Snyder just rang clearer to them.

The second category — those that are a different technique but overlay with classic structure — can be very helpful to broaden a writer's scope and prevent falling into a rut of formula. Let's take a brief look at a few of them.

The Hero's Journey

This is a look at story through the myths of the ages. Articulated by Joseph Campbell, this method was embraced by George Lucas in the creation of *Star Wars*. Christopher Vogler has refined the ideas in *The Writer's Journey*, looking at mythic structure specifically for the storyteller.

I have found pieces helpful in my own approach and understanding of the craft (especially regarding character functions). This approach emphasizes "Refusal of the Call" — which is an interesting take on character, aligning with the reluctant hero concept. The Journey requires "Resurrection" — which as you know I find to be a critical way of thinking about character.

Here is how Hero's Journey matches up with classic structure.

Classic	Hero's Journey
Balance	The Ordinary World
Catalyst	The Call to Adventure
Response to Catalyst	Refusal of the Call Meeting with the Mentor
Final Straw	Crossing the First Threshold
Quest Part 1	Tests, Allies, Enemies Approach the Inmost Cave
Midpoint	The Supreme Ordeal
Quest Part 2	Reward The Road Back
Crisis / Wafer	(No specific point; can align with The Supreme Ordeal)
Climax	The Resurrection
New Balance	Return with the Elixir

The Hero's Journey expects the events to happen somewhat in order without dictating a specific flow. You can see where Lucas had to bend this form in *Star Wars: A New Hope* — including two Supreme Ordeals — Luke's near death in the trash compactor (closer in timing to the Journey model) and the death of Obi Wan (an Ordeal with lasting impact, and more closely aligned with Crisis).

Five Act / Multi-Act

The term "act" in storytelling has a couple definitions, as I ranted about earlier in discussing Three-Act Structure. Multi-Act structures are not in opposition to classic or Three-Act Structure; rather they are a way of both breaking up the story for the audience, and for sharpening the individual pieces of the story. Events such as Final Straw, Midpoint, and Crisis/Climax are strong tentpoles with Multi-Act storytelling, adding as many varieties of twists and turns as the story wishes to sustain.

Network television and theater are the most obvious uses of Multi-Act form. For television, each act is marked by a commercial break. In theater, acts are marked for the audience by an intermission — or multiple intermissions. Both media evolved their forms based more on business or technical needs rather than artistic draws; for broadcast TV, money is only made if commercial breaks take place. For theater, time was needed to trim the candle wicks (five act plays); and when electricity made candles obsolete, time was needed for a stretch and pee break.

Currently, writers can focus more on how the rhythm of acts helps their stories. Network television still requires a strict act structure; streaming isn't as strict. Interestingly, many streaming shows hold loosely to a commercial break structure, in part because of the way that thinking of such breaks helps keep a story moving.

TV act structure acknowledges that the easiest time for an audience to change the channel is during a commercial. So, it is important to give the audience a reason to stick around. Act breaks (blows, outs) tend to be entertaining peaks (action, comedy, character reveals); while slow/boring parts of the story are cut. The writing needs to move.

So, a show that isn't required to break for commercials might find a Multi-Act structure a useful tool, even without this being dictated by the networks.

The Five Act Structure is the most enduring of the Multi-Act models. Freytag's Pyramid aligns with the Five Act, and Shakespeare wrote in this mode. Shakespeare apparently knew his stuff — or so I'm told. I am again indebted to John Yorke's work in *Into the Woods* for fully articulating the Five Act Structure.

Five Act and Events Structure align so well, they are really both the classic structure. Here is how the two align:

FIVE ACT	EVENTS
Act One	Balance Catalyst Final Straw
Act Two	Quest Part One
Act Three	Quest Part One (cont'd) Midpoint Quest Part Two
Act Four	Quest Part Two (cont'd) Crisis
Act Five	Climax New Balance

Miniplot/Interior Story/Character Piece

Miniplot isn't a departure of classical structure as much as an internalization of that structure. The plot is secondary to character work, so tends to be flattened. The Event Points are not as dramatic; and in some cases, it may be harder to even identify plot points.

Character-driven plays by Horton Foote fit this mode; as well as interior-driven films like Jim Jarmusch's *Paterson*. We do see more of this in theater than in film or television — as the latter media are driven by the image, an external factor. Theatre is driven by relationship — which is naturally more internal.

These stories still have classic structure — but are not seen at all through the eyes of structure. Which works well with the next model.

Roadmap of Change

As articulated by John Yorke (*Into the Woods*), the Roadmap focuses on the steps that the characters go through in their interior changes, rather than the physical circumstances (events). The events are still there, but the point of view is always from how the events effect the characters.

The structure puts emphasis on the growth (or failure) of character, looking at the "knowledge" that a character needs to change. The Central Character starts in a state of No Knowledge, and progresses through stages such as Awakening, Acceptance, Experimenting, up to Total Mastery.

In stories of three-dimensional characters with a complete arc, the "knowledge" term applies directly to character change. Yorke also points to the fair number of stories that do not rely on character arcs, being centered on a two-dimensional character who does not change; in which case the "knowledge" is more literally information. An example would be the standard television cop show; the Roadmap would mark the movement of clues and information about the case.

This technique is much appreciated by writers who approach stories "character first." In my mind, it is even more helpful for writers who are "plot first"; paying attention to this model helps widen a narrow-mindedness of approach, and when taken alongside classic structure deepens the material.

Again, Roadmap of Change isn't in opposition to classic structure; rather the two work quite well together. Here is how Yorke aligns Roadmap with the Five Act structure — with me tossing in the Classic structure for comparison:

FIVE ACT	EVENTS	ROADMAP OF CHANGE
Act One	Balance Catalyst Final Straw	No Knowledge Growing Knowledge Awakening
Act Two	Quest Part One	Doubt Overcoming Reluctance Acceptance
Act Three	Quest Part One (cont'd) Midpoint Quest Part Two	Experimenting with Knowledge MIDPOINT – KEY KNOWLEDGE Experimenting Post Knowledge
Act Four	Quest Part Two (cont'd) Crisis	Doubt Growing Reluctance Regression
Act Five	 Climax New Balance	Reawakening Re-acceptance Total Mastery

Reversal Structure

A very simple format used by many playwrights comes from the basic idea that drama is about reversal. The characters go on a journey and come out changed.

The structure runs off the formula: "A, then not A".

At the start of the story, the situation is "A." At the end of the story, the situation is "not A." *Hamlet* starts with Hamlet as a moody college student, his uncle is king and married to his mother. The play ends with Claudius, Gertrude, and Hamlet dead, and Fortinbras is now king. A, not A.

Further, the acts are all marked with A, not A; each segment of the story providing reversal. Act Three of *Hamlet* begins with Hamlet being spied on by Rosencrantz and Guilderstern; Hamlet is in a relationship with Ophelia; Hamlet does not know for sure that Claudius is guilty of murder; and Hamlet is free to continue his investigation. At the end of Act Three, Hamlet has revealed to the spies that he knows about them, has broken off relations with Ophelia, has proven his uncle is a murderer, and is under house arrest for killing Polonius. A, not A.

Moreover, every scene also follows the A, not A structure, reversing things on a smaller level. Act Three, Scene 1 of Hamlet starts with Claudius and Polonius believing that Hamlet is moody because he is sick with love for Ophelia, who is very much in love with Hamlet. By the end of the scene, Ophelia is now disillusioned with Hamlet, and Claudius and Polonius believe Hamlet is not in love at all. A, not A.

Building stories using reversals keeps the drama moving and prevents sections (or entire stories) from bogging down into stagnation. If every scene must include change, then every scene is in motion; if the play as a whole requires change, then the journey guarantees a "New" in the New Balance. Every script can benefit from this structure no matter how they choose to organize their plot.

A classic *News Radio* episode ("Xmas Story") plays on reversals by doing a 180 on the plot and audience expectation multiple times throughout. Mr. James, after being accused of being cheap, buys everyone a car, except for Matthew who gets a set of tapes for the old-time radio show, *Fibber McGee and Molly*. The first act sees the cast worried about Matthew, who surely is disappointed that he got such a lame gift when they all got — well, cars. He isn't upset at all; in fact, he is very happy. Turns out he assumes that they all were given rentals, while he gets to keep his tapes. The joke is on them!

The second act reverses this completely, as Matthew discovers that they get to keep their cars, and he is angry at getting such a lame gift. He plots his vengeance for this slight.

And then act three completely reverses again, as Matthew learns that he wasn't given just tapes of *Fibber McGee and Molly*, James gave him *Fibber McGee and Molly*. As in ownership of the show, all rights in future republishing, etc. A gift worth far more than the cost of an automobile.

Each part of the episode is built on reversing the direction of the show. *Knives Out* also plays on reversals — starting as a movie about solving a crime, changing to a movie about getting away with the crime, to going back to being a movie about solving a crime. Reversals are a great enhancing tool when looking to pump up any script.

Rashomon Effect

Rashomon, the classic Akira Kurosawa movie, has given a name to another way of telling stories: by repeating the same story, only shifting points of view. Each retelling comes out different, as the characters put their own take on the story. *Hoodwinked*, directed by Cory Edwards, Todd Edwards, and Tony Leech, employs this technique. Most often, scripts using this style are structured as a series of shorter stories juxtaposed against each other.

Circular Stories

Circular storytelling ends where it begins. The play *La Ronde* by Arthur Schnitzler is a classic example. The play is ten scenes, each scene with two characters. A character from the first scene plays the second scene with a new character; that new character goes on to the next scene with another new character, and on until the last new character plays a scene with the character from the first scene. Schnitzler's circle shows the lack of values across all strati of society.

Stories often end where they began to make a point of lack of growth/change in the characters. *Inside Llewyn Davis* does this very thing, as it ends with the titular character facing circumstances nearly identical to his start.

Anti-Plot Structure

In this list, Anti-Plot Structure is really the only one in opposition to Events, designed to be a subversion of classic structure. Plot points are scrambled, the rules of the world are inconsistent and changeable, and actions do not necessarily lead to reaction. Events may happen randomly, and chaos reigns.

Monty Python and the Holy Grail is an Anti-Plot movie that works. The disjointed sketches are meant to feel movie-like with the running story of the grail search; yet the scenes come with random weight and the rules are extremely inconsistent — including the police raiding the movie and arresting our medieval knights at the end.

The Marx Brothers also lean towards Anti-Plot, where the story is just an excuse for the routines and bits they want to drop in. *All Dirt Roads Taste of Salt* is a dramatic example of Anti-Plot; as opposed to chaos, the movie simply ignores the idea of plot, instead becoming a poem of nearly pure cinematography.

For Anti-Plot to be effective, there needs to be aspects of the telling that replace expectation with entertainment or graspable meaning. Unless the creator's goal is just to push audiences away — which may well be the goal of some artists.

Choose Your Own Structure

While all story shares basic form, how a writer approaches the plot is in no way restrictive; creators can find whatever works for them. Most writers are unaware that they are following standard structure — which is a good thing. Being too aware in the creative process of such details easily veers into formulaic writing. That said, there are many unconventional approaches to Story that dovetail easily with classic story form.

For example, Harold Ramis in writing *Groundhog Day* based the plot on the five stages of grief. Phil faces his time-loop circumstance by going through each step in order: denial, anger, bargaining, depression, and acceptance. Once he hits acceptance, he can start to change his character, which leads to his release.

Wanda Vision's show runner, Jac Schaeffer, confirms that her show follows the same trajectory of grief stages over the nine-episode season. The writers met with a grief counselor to get it right.

I wrote a play that covers the lifetime of a couple; I used the seven stages of man from *As You Like It* to give a seven-act structure. I have known writers to base a script off the progressive lines of a poem, or with each act representing a season, or a series of stories based off a single location (like *The Dining Room* by A.R. Gurney).

Clybourne Park takes Lorraine Hansberry's play *A Raisin in the Sun* and tells the same events from the point of view of the white family selling the home. Act Two then jumps ahead in time to when the neighborhood is predominantly African American and tells the story of a black family selling the same house. The mirror stories of Act One and Act Two give deeper commentary to the issues.

There is no limit to inspirational structure ideas.

Appendix E: Functions for Supporting Characters

Here are some of the possible roles/functions that supporting players can fulfill. I'm including variants under the main role; and giving short descriptions if not self-evident. This list is by no means exhaustive — a character's role will be whatever is needed by the creators.

Let me repeat this note from our section on characters: Story function or role is how the character serves the story — it is not a job they have in their lives inside the story. For example, waitress, bartender, police office, science teacher — these are NOT Story Functions.

Here are some actual story functions:

- Confidant (an ear for a main character)
  - Sidekick (often but not always the Comic Relief)
  - Straight Man/Woman (for a comedy with a whacky protagonist)
    - Examples: Aaron for Moses; Riff in *West Side Story*; Willie's brother Ben in *Death of a Salesman*; Bruce Banner for Tony Stark in *Avengers: Age of Ultron*
- Comic Relief (helps balance the tone)
  - Jester / Fool (more than comedic, gives insight)
  - Harlequin (a professional fool; often a servant)
    - Examples: The persistent Widow (Jesus' parable); Nurse in *Romeo and Juliet*; Abby in *NCIS*; C3PO in *Star Wars*; Spider-Man in *Captain America: Civil War*
- Love Interest
  - Attractor / Romantic Interest
  - Romantic Runner Up (the one left behind in a love triangle)

- Examples: Boaz for Ruth; Marion in *Raiders of the Lost Ark*; Ophelia for *Hamlet*; The Other Woman in *Death of a Salesman* (a dark love interest)
- Theme Carrier (speaks to the positive or negative aspects of theme)
  - Examples: The Widow donating the mite; Uncle Ben in any movie about Spider-Man; Banquo in *Macbeth* (opposition to ambition); Olive in *Pushing Daisies* (Ned can't make connections due to his gift; Olive can't make connections due to being unseen)
- Shapeshifter (changes roles or appearance of role within a story)
  - Imposter / Pretender (masked by design)
  - Turncoat / Backstabber / Judas (actively switches sides)
  - Double Agent (actively works both/all sides)
    - Examples: Judas (naturally) or Nicodemus (not all shapeshifters are bad); Captain Smith in *L.A. Confidential*; Loretta in *The Sting* (we are led to believe she is a romantic interest — she is an imposter); Earnest (pick one) in *The Importance of Being Earnest*
- Mirror (reflecting the Central Character; on a parallel journey)
  - Foil (contrasting a quality of the Central Character)
    - In a romance, often the B plot romance; typically to show an alternate version or a variant.
      - Examples: The Older Brother in the Parable of the Lost Son; Laertes in *Hamlet* (seeking revenge for the murder of his father); Nathan Detroit in *Guys and Dolls* (mirroring the romance of Sky); Dorothy in *Hidden Figures*
- Mentor (teacher, trainer, gift giver)
  - Father Figure
  - Mother Figure
  - Source of Wisdom / Sage

- Caregiver
- The Spock (the logical advisor)
- The McCoy (the emotional advisor)
- Conscience / Jiminy Cricket (moral guide)
- Magician / Mage (marked by mystical powers)
- Absent Minded Professor (typically a comic relief as well)
- Wise Fool (appears to be a fool, but gives true insight/wisdom)
    - Examples: Samuel to Saul and then David; Jiminy Cricket in *Pinocchio* (gets a type named after him!); the Weird Sisters in *Macbeth* (can be dark mentors); Charlie in *Death of a Salesman* (can be ignored); Mo in *Zoey's Extraordinary Playlist*
- Threshold Guardian (blocks/tests along specific steps in the journey)
    - Theme Tester (challenges the Central Character on a thematic level)
    - Contagonist
    - Muscle / Henchman (serves the antagonist)
        - Examples: The guards in Jericho who confront Rahab while hunting for the spies; Big Julie in *Guys & Dolls*; Dean in *The Iron Giant* (one of his many roles); Captain Phasma in *Star Wars: The Force Awakens*
- Herald (messenger, bearer of information)
    - Scene Catalyst (their action or appearance kick-starts a scene)
    - Informant (provides explanation/exposition)
    - Storyteller (narrator — often outside the plot)
    - The Herald character often issues a challenge or provides the call for change; typically, their information is a catalyst for action.
        - Examples: John the Baptist; Hagrid in *Harry Potter and the Sorcerer's Stone* (announcing Harry is going

to Hogwarts); Hermione in all the Potter movies — as an Informant; Gandalf to Frodo (*The Hobbit*) and Bilbo (*The Fellowship of the Ring*) at the start of the adventure; Effie in *The Hunger Games*; Anita becomes a late Herald in *West Side Story*, announcing Maria's death; The Grandfather in *The Princess Bride* (Storyteller); Carson, the lisping announcer of all events in *Schmigadoon!*

- Shadow (energy of darkness)
  - Villain, Antagonist (at times)
  - Femme Fatale (beautiful but treacherous)
  - Tempter
    - Examples: Satan in the Job story and the temptations in the desert; Judge Turpin in *Sweeney Todd*; Ransom in *Knives Out*; the Weird Sisters in *Macbeth* (along with their mentor and herald roles); Potts in *Mare of Easttown*

- Trickster (intends to create trouble/chaos)
  - Misdirect (a character whose function is to lead the viewer in the wrong direction)
    - Examples: Young Jacob with his bowls of stew and fake-hair sleeves; the serpent in the Garden of Eden; Loki is a trickster shadow (in the movies); Bugs Bunny is a trickster protagonist; Gollum in *Lord of the Rings*; the Mandarin in *Iron Man 3* (Misdirect)

- MacGuffin (character who is the object or goal to drive the plot)
  - Damsel / Dude in Distress (focus of whole story is saving this character)
  - The Innocent (pure character, typically a child, the motivator for the protagonist)
    - Examples: The baby Jesus for the Magi and for Herod; the sure thing in *The Sure Thing*; Grogu (Baby Yoda)

in *The Mandalorian* (Innocent); the Jewel of the Nile in *The Jewel of the Nile*; Buttercup in *The Princess Bride* (Damsel in Distress)

- Audience Surrogate (stand-in for the audience)
  - Typically has additional functions.
    - Examples: Theophilus in the Book of Acts; Phillipe Gaston in *Ladyhawke*; The Grandson in *The Princess Bride*
- Tertiary (a character there mostly for atmosphere)
  - Redshirt (there to be expendable)
    - Periphery characters there to fill out the world; often extras or supernumeraries with clever names like Man 1 or Woman 3. The best writing acknowledges that people are people no matter how small[230] and will give a Tertiary who has lines a hint of personality. Sometimes that hint grows into a full-blown character, like Gunther the barista in *Friends*.
      - Examples: From the script to the *Veronica Mars* "Pilot," the high school crowd: Cat-in-the-Hat Raver, Band Dork, Pep Squadder, Pencil-Necked Geek, Clown

〜

Every character has a function, a role to play. The creator who ignores this does so at the cost of the story. Stanislavski is credited with the phrase, "There are no small parts, only small actors." This starts with the writing — if a part has a function, it has value; if it has value, it is not a throw-away part.

The human body has many parts, but the many parts make up one whole body. So, it is with the body of Christ...

In fact, some parts of the body that seem weakest and least important are actually the most necessary...

---

230. I learned this like you did from *Horton Hears a Who* by Dr. Suess

So we carefully protect those parts that should not be seen, while the more honorable parts do not require this special care.

If one part suffers, all the parts suffer with it, and if one part is honored, all the parts are glad.

—1 Corinthians 12:12, 22, 23, 26, NLT

References

I am deeply indebted to the works I perused, the movies/plays/shows I absorbed, and the minds I attempted to meld with. Here are the media I referenced throughout this book.

Non-Fiction Books

Astericks *(Ball, Trottier, and Yorke) indicate my most referenced books.

Aristotle. *Poetics*. Translated by S. H. Butcher. Introduction by Francis Fergusson. New York: Farrar, Straus and Giroux, 1961.

Bailey, Kenneth E. *Jacob & the Prodigal*. Downers Grove, IL: InterVarsity Press, 2003.

*Ball, David. *Backwards & Forwards: A Technical Manual for Reading Plays*. Carbondale: Southern Illinois University Press, 1983.

Barron, Robert. *Light from Light: A Theological Reflection on the Nicene Creed*. Garden City, NY: Doubleday, 1998.

Buechner, Frederick. *The Clown in the Belfry: Writings on Faith and Fiction*. New York: Harper & Row, 1977.

Bull, Sheldon. *Elephant Bucks*. Studio City, CA: Michael Wiese Productions, 2007.

Cowgill, Linda J. *Writing Short Films: Structure and Content for Maximum Impact*. Studio City, CA: Michael Wiese Productions, 2007.

Cron, Lisa. *Wired for Story: The Writer's Guide to Using Brain Science to Hook Readers From the Very First Sentence*. Berkeley, CA: Ten Speed Press, 2012.

Fitzgerald, Sally, ed. *The Habit of Being: Letters of Flannery O'Connor*. New York: Farrar, Straus and Giroux, 1979.

Frankel, Aaron. *Writing the Broadway Musical*. New York: Grand Central Publishing, 2009.

Goldman, William. *Adventures in the Screen Trade: A Personal View of Hollywood and Screenwriting.* New York: Warner Books, 1983.

Harbinson, Colin. "Narrative, Symbol, and Ritual." *Literature and Theology* 12, no. 1 (1998): 1-17.

King, Stephen. *On Writing: A Memoir of the Craft.* New York: Scribner, 2000.

L'Engle, Madeleine. *Walking on Water: Reflections on Faith and Art.* Wheaton, IL: Harold Shaw Publishers, 1980.

Lamott, Anne. *Bird by Bird: Some Instructions on Writing and Life.* New York: Pantheon Books, 1994.

Lewis, C. S. "On Science Fiction." In *Of Other Worlds: Essays and Stories.* New York: Harcourt, Brace & World, 1966.

Mamet, David. *Three Uses of the Knife: On the Nature and Purpose of Drama.* New York: Free Press, 1998.

McKee, Robert. *Story: Substance, Structure, Style, and the Principles of Screenwriting.* New York: ReganBooks, 1997.

McLaughlin, Buzz. *The Playwright's Process: Learning the Craft from the Masters.* New York: Back Stage Books, 2002.

Mernit, Billy. "Deepening Characters and Defining Their Arcs." In *Cut to the Chase: Writing Feature Films with the Pros at Naked Angels,* edited by Lou Venis, 119–38. New York: Perennial, 2002.

Niebuhr, Reinhold. *Moral Man and Immoral Society: A Study in Ethics and Politics.* New York: Charles Scribner's Sons, 1932.

Palmer, Earl. *The Humor of Jesus: Sources of Humor in the Bible.* Nashville: Upper Room Books, 1993.

Partow, Donna. *Becoming a Vessel God Can Use.* Eugene, OR: Harvest House Publishers, 2002.

Price, Reynolds. *Three Gospels.* New York: Scribner, 1996.

Pritner, Cal, and Scott E. Walters. *Introduction to Play Analysis.* Dubuque, IA: Kendall/Hunt Publishing Company, 1995.

Riley, Christopher. *The Hollywood Standard.* Studio City, CA: Michael Wiese Productions, 2003.

Sandler, Ellen. *The TV Writer's Workbook: A Step-by-Step Guide to Creating and Selling Television Scripts*. New York: Dell Publishing, 1999.

Sayers, Dorothy L. *Mind of the Maker*. New York: Harcourt, Brace and Company, 1941.

Schock, Michael Welles. *Screenwriting Down to the Atoms*. Studio City, CA: Michael Wiese Productions, 2006.

Seger, Linda. *Adaptations: From Narrative to Script*. New York: Henry Holt and Co., 1992.

Snyder, Blake. *Save the Cat! The Last Book on Screenwriting You'll Ever Need*. Studio City, CA: Michael Wiese Productions, 2005.

*Trottier, David. *The Screenwriter's Bible: A Complete Guide to Writing, Formatting, and Selling Your Script*. 6th ed. Studio City, CA: Silman-James Press, 2015.

Vogler, Christopher. *The Writer's Journey: Mythic Structure for Writers*. Studio City, CA: Michael Wiese Productions, 1992.

Vorhaus, John. *The Little Book of Sitcom*. Studio City, CA: Michael Wiese Productions, 2003.

*Yorke, John. *Into the Woods: How Stories Work and Why We Tell Them*. New York: Overlook Press, 2013.

Articles, Websites, Talks

Arndt, Michael. "On Endings…" Pandemonium Inc. http://www.pandemoniuminc.com/endings-video.

August, John, and Craig Mazin. *Scriptnotes*. Podcast. https://johnaugust.com/podcast.

Barth, John. "The Remobilization of Jacob Horner." *Esquire* (1958).

Bible Gateway. https://www.biblegateway.com/.

Box Office Mojo. https://www.boxofficemojo.com/.

Buster, Bobette. https://www.bobettebuster.com/.

Columbia University School of the Arts "Alumni Newsletter, May 2020". https://arts.columbia.edu/sites/default/files/content/PDFs/Alumni%20Newsletters/may_2020_alumni_newsletter.pdf

George, Ryan. "Screen Rant Pitch Meetings." YouTube series, https://www.youtube.com/@RyanGeorge.

Gunderson, Lauren. "How to Write a Play (Facebook Classes)." Facebook, March-April 2020. https://www.facebook.com/watch/LaurenGundersonPlaywright/1422875847897677/.

"Horror: The Perfect Christian Genre," interview with Scott Derrickson, *ChristianityToday.com*, August 1, 2005. https://www.christianitytoday.com/2005/08/scottderrickson/.

Keller, Timothy, "Lord of the Wine," *Gospel in Life,* November 17, 1996, https://gospelinlife.com/sermon/lord-of-the-wine/.

"Laughter is the Best Medicine," *Reader's Digest*, October 2018

Palmer, Earl. https://www.earlpalmer.org/.

Polatis, Kandra. "Faith in Film: Why Science Fiction Movies Abound with Religious Themes." *Deseret News*, April 6, 2014. https://www.deseret.com/2014/4/6/20538713/faith-in-film-why-science-fiction-movies-abound-with-religious-themes/.

Rotten Tomatoes. https://www.rottentomatoes.com/.

"Screenwriter Todd Komarnicki." *Act One Podcast*, episode 2, July 1, 2020. https://actoneprogram.com/episode-2-screenwriter-todd-komarnicki/.

Smith, Josh. "'We come in peace': What the writers of 'The Chosen' want you to know about the show." *Deseret News*, September 7, 2022. https://www.deseret.com/faith/2022/9/7/23321683/the-chosen-writers-jesus-texas-dallas-jenkins/.

Stanton, Andrew. "The Clues to a Great Story." TED Talk, July 2012. https://www.ted.com/talks/andrew_stanton_the_clues_to_a_great_story.

Tennant, David, and Georgia Tennant. "Everyone." *David Tennant Does a Podcast With...*, season 2, episode 8, November 19, 2019. https://podcasts.apple.com/gb/podcast/everyone-from-season-2/id1450005207?i=1000496172361.

With God Daily, Skye Jethani, "Remembering Christmases Long Long Ago," December 9, 2022; "Advent & Agony," December 21, 2022.

Wolf, Allen. "Timothy Keller, NY Times Bestselling Author & Speaker: Why Do We Need Artists?" *Navigating Hollywood*, episode 20, July 11, 2023. https://navigatinghollywood.org/timkeller/.

Movies

1917

About Time

Addams Family, The

All Dirt Roads Taste of Salt

Apartment, The

Aquaman

Argo

Arrival

Artist, The

Avengers, The

Avengers: Age of Ultron

Avengers: Endgame

Avengers: Infinity War

Ballad of Buster Scruggs, The

Batman Begins

Batman v Superman

Beautiful Day in the
   Neighborhood, A

Best in Show

Big Chill, The

Big Fish

Bird Box

Birds of Prey

Black Panther

Black Widow

Blue Jasmine

Blues Brothers, The

Book of Eli

Bridesmaids

Brittany Runs a Marathon

Bruce Almighty

Butch Cassidy and the Sundance Kid

Cabin in the Woods

Captain America: Civil War

Captain Phillips

Carrie

Casablanca

Casino Royale

Christmas Story, A

Citizen Kane

Cruella

Dark Knight, The

Dave

Dawn of the Planet of the Apes

Deadpool

Death on the Nile

Death Wish

Die Hard

Dirty Dozen, The

Doctor Strange

Dogfight

Dunkirk

Eternal Sunshine of the
   Spotless Mind

Executive Decision

Exorcism of Emily Rose, The

Exorcist, The

Favourite, The

Ferris Beuller's Day Off

Final Destination

Finding Nemo

Forrest Gump

Fried Green Tomatoes

Frozen

Get Out

Ghost

Glass

Godfather Part II, The

Godfather, The

Gravity

Grease

Greatest Showman, The

Greenbook

Groundhog Day

Guardians of the Galaxy

Harder They Fall, The

Harriet

Harry Potter and the Deathly
    Hallows: Parts 1 and 2

Hidden Figures

Hobbit, The

Hoodwinked

Hunger Games, The

If Beale Street Could Talk

Imitation Game, The

In the Heights

Independence Day

Inside Llewyn Davis

Inside Out

Iron Giant

Iron Man

Iron Man 3

It Happened One Night

It's a Wonderful Life

Jesus Christ Superstar

Jewel of the Nile, The

Jojo Rabbit

Joker

Journey to the Center of the Earth

Jurassic Park

Just Mercy

Justice League

King's Speech, The

Knives Out

L.A. Confidential

La La Land

Ladyhawke

Ladykillers, The (1955 & 2004)

Lars and the Real Girl

Little Miss Sunshine

Little Monsters

Lord of the Rings: Fellowship of
    the Ring, The

Lord of the Rings: Return of
    the King, The

Lord of the Rings: The Two
    Towers, The

Lost in Translation

Love, Actually

Mad Max: Beyond Thunderdome

Mad Max: Fury Road

Mad Max: The Road Warrior

Magnificent Seven, The

Maleficent

Man of Steel

Martian, The

Memento

Mighty Wind, A

Moneyball

Monty Python and the Holy Grail

Mr. Holland's Opus

Mr. Smith Goes to Washington

Muppet Christmas Carol, The

My Fair Lady

No Country for Old Men

No Time to Die

Nomadland

North by Northwest

Olympus Has Fallen

On Her Majesty's Secret Service

Once Upon a Time in Hollywood

Parasite

Paris Je T'Aime

Passion of the Christ, The

Paterson

Pieces of April

Pinocchio

Pride and Prejudice

Princess Bride, The

Proposal, The

Pulp Fiction

Pyscho

Queen of Katwe

Quiet Place, A

Raiders of the Lost Ark

Rashomon

Rocky

Roman Holiday

Sabrina

Saving Mr. Banks

Saving Private Ryan

Serenity

Seven Samurai, The

Shape of Water, The

Shaun of the Dead

Shawshank Redemption, The

Shazam

Shrek

Signs

Silence of the Lambs

Sin City

Sixth Sense, The

Skyfall

Slumdog Millionaire

Snowpiercer

Social Network, The

Some Like it Hot

Soul

Spaceballs

Spider-Man: Far from Home

Spider-Man: Homecoming

Spider-Man: Into the Spiderverse

Spider-Man: No Way Home

Star Trek

Star Trek II: The Wrath of Khan

Star Wars: A New Hope

Star Wars: Return of the Jedi

Star Wars: Rogue One

Star Wars: The Empire Strikes Back

Star Wars: The Force Awakens

Steve Jobs

Sting, The

Suicide Squad, The

Sunset Boulevard

Sure Thing, The
Taken
Thelma & Louise
This Is Spinal Tap
Thor
Thor: Ragnorak
Three Billboards Outside Ebbing, Missouri
Thunderball
Titanic, The
To Kill a Mockingbird
Together Together
Top Gun: Maverick
Tower Heist
Toy Story
Troop Zero
Two Popes, The
Up
Usual Suspects, The
Valentine's Day
Waiting for Guffman
Walk the Line
War for the Planet of the Apes
War Horse
Way, The
West Side Story
While You Were Sleeping
White House Down
Wizard of Oz, The
Wonder Woman
X-Men
Young Sherlock Holmes

Plays & Musicals

12 Angry Men by Reginald Rose

42nd Street by Michael Stewart and Mark Bramble (book), Al Dubin (lyrics), Harry Warren (music)

All in the Timing by David Ives

All My Sons by Arthur Miller

As You Like It by William Shakespeare

Band's Visit, The by Itamar Moses (book), David Yazbek (music and lyrics)

Betrayal by Harold Pinter

Brownie Points by Janece Shaffer

Christians, The by Lucas Hnath

Christmas Carol, A by Charles Dickens (various adaptations, but especially the one-man version adapted by Patrick Stewart)

Clybourne Park by Bruce Norris

Come From Away by Irene Sankoff and David Hein

Curious Incident of the Dog in the Night-Time, The by Simon Stephens
(based on the novel by Mark Haddon)

Death of a Salesman by Arthur Miller

Dining Room, The by A.R. Gurney

Doll's House, A by Henrik Ibsen

Doll's House, Part 2, A by Lucas Hnath

Doubt by John Patrick Shanley

Dybbuk, The by S. An-sky

Fences by August Wilson

Fiddler on the Roof by Joseph Stein (book), Jerry Bock (music), Sheldon
Harnick (lyrics)

Fool Moon by Bill Irwin and David Shiner

Frankenstein by Nick Dear (based on the novel by Mary Shelley)

Glass Menagerie, The by Tennessee Williams

Godspell by John-Michael Tebelak (book), Stephen Schwartz (music
and lyrics)

Guys and Dolls by Jo Swerling and Abe Burrows (book), Frank Loesser
(music and lyrics)

Hamilton by Lin-Manuel Miranda

Hamlet by William Shakespeare

I and You by Lauren Gunderson

In & Of Itself by Derek DelGaudio

Importance of Being Earnest, The by Oscar Wilde

Into the Woods by James Lapine (book), Stephen Sondheim
(music and lyrics)

Jane Eyre devised by National Theatre Company (based on the novel by
Charlotte Brontë)

Jesus Christ Superstar by Tim Rice (lyrics), Andrew Lloyd
Webber (music)

Johnny Pye and the Foolkiller by Mark St. Germain (book and lyrics),
Randy Courts (music and lyrics)

La Ronde by Arthur Schnitzler

Les Misérables by Alain Boublil and Claude-Michel Schönberg (book),
Herbert Kretzmer (lyrics), Claude-Michel Schönberg (music)

Lion King, The by Roger Allers and Irene Mecchi (book), Elton John (music), Tim Rice (lyrics)

Macbeth by William Shakespeare

Major Barbara by George Bernard Shaw

Man of La Mancha by Dale Wasserman (book), Mitch Leigh (music), Joe Darion (lyrics)

Moreau by Sean Gaffney (based on "The Island of Doctor Moreau" by H.G. Wells)

My Fair Lady by Alan Jay Lerner (book and lyrics), Frederick Loewe (music)

One Man, Two Guvnors by Richard Bean (based on "The Servant of Two Masters" by Carlo Goldoni)

Our Town by Thornton Wilder

Peter and the Starcatcher by Rick Elice (based on the novel by Dave Barry and Ridley Pearson)

Phantom of the Opera, The by Andrew Lloyd Webber (music and libretto), Charles Hart (lyrics), Richard Stilgoe (additional lyrics and libretto)

Raisin in the Sun, A by Lorraine Hansberry

Richard III by William Shakespeare

Romeo and Juliet by William Shakespeare

Shrek the Musical by David Lindsay-Abaire (book and lyrics), Jeanine Tesori (music)

Silent Sky by Lauren Gunderson

Smoke on the Mountain by Connie Ray (conceived by Alan Bailey)

Streetcar Named Desire, A by Tennessee Williams

Sweeney Todd: The Demon Barber of Fleet Street by Hugh Wheeler (book), Stephen Sondheim (music and lyrics)

Twelfth Night by William Shakespeare

Wait Until Dark by Frederick Knott

Waiting for Godot by Samuel Beckett

Waiting for Lefty by Clifford Odets

War Horse by Nick Stafford (based on the novel by Michael Morpurgo)

West Side Story by Arthur Laurents (book), Leonard Bernstein (music),
Stephen Sondheim (lyrics)

Wicked by Winnie Holzman (book), Stephen Schwartz (music
and lyrics)

Wizard of Oz, The by L. Frank Baum (novel), various stage adaptations

Television

24

Addams Family, The

Alias

Battle Star Galactica

Bernie Mac Show, The

Big Little Lies

black-ish

Blue Bloods

Brady Bunch, The,
   "Law and Disorder"

Breaking Bad

Broadchurch

Brooklyn 99

Buffy the Vampire Slayer,
   "Once More with Feeling"

Castle

Charlie Brown Christmas, A

Chosen, The, "I Am He"

Criminal Minds

Daredevil

Dead to Me

Doctor Who,
   "Gridlock,"
   "Human Nature,"
   "The Family of Blood"

Downton Abbey

Elementary

Extraordinary Attorney Woo, The

Fargo

Firefly

Flight Attendant, The

Fresh Off the Boat

Friends

Game of Thrones

Goldbergs, The

Good Girls

Justified, "Decoy"

Law & Order

Law & Order: SVU

Loki

Looney Tunes,
   "Rabbit of Seville,"
   "Long-Haired Hare"

Lost, "Pilot," "Walkabout"

Mad Men

Mandalorian, The, "The Jedi"

Mare of Easttown

Modern Family

Monty Python's Flying Circus,
   "Ministry of Silly Walks"

Morning Show, The

Ms. Marvel

My Name is Earl

NCIS

News Radio, "Xmas Story"
Office, The
Parks and Recreation
Picard
Pride and Prejudice (miniseries)
Pushing Daisies, "Pielette"
Reservation Dogs
Schmigadoon!
Sherlock
Simpsons, The
Star Trek, "Bread and Circuses"
Star Trek: Deep Space Nine
Star Trek: Discovery

Supernatural
Sweet Magnolias
Ted Lasso
This Is Us
Twilight Zone, "Occurrence at Owl Creek Bridge"
Veronica Mars
WandaVision
West Wing, The, "Noel"
Will & Grace
Year of Living Biblically, The
Zoey's Extraordinary Playlist

Short Films

"For the Birds"
"Hair Love"

"The Present"
"Snakes on a Plain"

Books of Fiction

Adventures of Huckleberry Finn, The by Mark Twain
Alice in Wonderland by Lewis Carroll
Amazing Fantasy #15 by Stan Lee and Steve Ditko
"Divinely Superfluous Beauty" by Robinson Jeffers
Green Eggs and Ham by Dr. Seuss
Harry Potter series by J.K. Rowling
Horton Hears a Who by Dr. Seuss
Lord of the Rings, The by J.R.R. Tolkien
"Medieval Romance, A" by Mark Twain
Rita Hayworth and the Shawshank Redemption by Stephen King
Simple Art of Murder, The by Raymond Chandler
Tevye the Dairyman by Sholem Aleichem
Ulysses by James Joyce
Uncanny X-Men, The #159 by Chris Claremont

Acknowledgments

One of the things that the MCU has taught us is that while the individual heroes may make for great movies, the team-ups are fantastic! The Bible agrees (Ecclesiastes 4:9-12, Hebrew 10:24-25, Proverbs 27:17, Matthew 18:20, Ephesians 4:16 and on and on...)

This book isn't only *better* because of all the people that helped on it; the book only *exists* because of all the people who worked on it. In no particular order, here are some of the folk that came alongside:

The early and consistent encouragers, Bob Lee and Jennifer Schuchmann. You never let me forget that I had a book to write; and never stopped believing that it was worthwhile.

Our editor and coach, Kitty Bucholtz. Illustrator and helper with cover and all things design, Bryan Ballinger. Cover designer and graphic sounding board, Sarah Hogencamp.

Dean Batali and David Gyertson – who not only read early drafts and gave feedback but graciously wrote the foreword and preface. I owe you dinner at Ramsey's.

The other early readers, whose opinions and feedback guided the books development: Cory and Vicki Edwards, Matt Webb, Leilani Squires, Seth Conley.

Those whose ideas and insights I took to add to my understanding of Story: Christopher Riley, Han Zhao, Bryan Coley, Andrea Nasfell, Gil Elvgren, Jack Gilbert, Bill Marsilii, Kris Young, Janet Batchler, Sheryl Anderson, and all the gang at Act One.

Asbury University and Jim Owens, for the grace and encouragement needed from an employer to pull something like this off.

Those who helped me shift into being a professional writer – I'm looking at you, Taproot Theatre, Scott Nolte, and Karen Lund.

I've had significant pastoral influences whose fingerprints are all over my theological insights: Earl Palmer, Tim Keller, and Mark Brewer. And the teachers that encouraged me to think outside the box – including Stephen Barry, Thea Albert, and this guy:

Howard Stein, who really launched all of this by suggesting I combine my faith and my art in the first place. His mentorship and our independent study on what makes a script good became the blueprint for this tome.

And my partner in all things, all steps, and all decisions, Catherine Gaffney. When God said, "It is not good for Sean to be alone," He gifted me with an introduction to Catherine. If there is any good coming out of me, it can be sourced back to her.

Bryan Ballinger

Bryan "Breadwig" Ballinger does illustration for children's books, websites, games, videos, ads, etc. He also does large- and small-scale murals, 3D toy design, and fine art. Bryan is the author and illustrator of *Animal Gas, A Pig Named Joe and His Quest to Be Fancy, The Big Wig Parade,* and *Counting Cows.* Bryan is a muralist, toy designer, and children's book author and illustrator. He was lead illustrator at Microsoft and 3D Design Lead for Big Idea Productions, the producers of the *VeggieTales* children's videos. Bryan was also a professor of Digital Media Arts at Huntington University in Indiana for 16 years.

He graduated from the Columbus College of Art and Design with a degree in Illustration. He also has a master's degree in Writing for Children from Lesley University in Cambridge, Massachusetts.

www.breadwig.com

Sean Gaffney

Sean Gaffney has authored thirty produced plays, three feature films, four commissioned television pilots, two published chapter books, as well as over two hundred produced videos, animation projects, YouTube series episodes, and short films (including for Big Idea and SuperBook).

Other publications include contributing to *Bigger on the Inside: Christianity and Doctor Who, It Was Good: Performing Arts to the Glory of God,* and *The Routledge Handbook of the Bible and Film.*

He was the Story Administrator for Warner Bros. Features, editor of Drama Ministry Magazine, the Managing Director of Taproot Theatre (Seattle), and General Manager of Lamb's Theatre Company (New York).

Gaffney currently is a Professor of Screenwriting and Media at Asbury University as well as Associate Dean of the School of Communication Arts. He received his BFA from Drake University, his MFA from Columbia University, and studied with Act One: Writing for Hollywood.

You can reach Sean Gaffney through his website:
www.gaffneyinkwell.com.

Other works by Sean Gaffney

Children's Books
LarryBoy and the Sinister Snowday
LarryBoy and the Emperor of Envy
LarryBoy and the Hideous Horde

Contributor To
Routledge Handbook of the Bible and Film
It Was Good: Performing Arts to the Glory of God
Bigger on the Inside: Christianity and Doctor Who
Scripts of Hope & Restoration
Scriptwriting: Building a Writing Ministry for the Church & Beyond

Feature Films
Not Your Romeo & Juliet
In-Lawfully Yours
Mary for Mayor

Videos
VeggieTales: King George and the Ducky (story by)
Larry Boy The Cartoon Adventures: Leggo My Ego
The VeggieTales Show: A ShakeSparagus Play
The VeggieTales Show: The Good Shepherd
The VeggieTales Show: Larryboy and the Angry Eyebrows Trouble
The VeggieTales Show: Larryboy and the Emperor of Envy
Wondermore: Baby Fanta and the Egg
Superbook (various episodes)
The Superbook Show (created by)
Gabriel and the Guardians (writing team)

www.ingramcontent.com/pod-product-compliance
Lightning Source LLC
Chambersburg PA
CBHW061547120626
46550CB00004B/1392